D0702403

In Wolf Country

In Wolf Country

The Power and Politics of Reintroduction

Jim Yuskavitch

Guilford, Connecticut

An imprint of Rowman & Littlefield
Distributed by NATIONAL BOOK NETWORK

Copyright © 2015 by Jim Yuskavitch

All rights reserved. No part of this book may be reproduced in any form or by any electronic or mechanical means, including information storage and retrieval systems, without written permission from the publisher, except by a reviewer who may quote passages in a review.

British Library Cataloguing in Publication Information Available

Library of Congress Cataloging-in-Publication Data
Yuskavitch, James.
In wolf country : the power and politics of reintroduction / Jim Yuskavitch.
pages cm
Includes bibliographical references and index.
ISBN 978-0-7627-9753-0 (paperback) — 978-1-4930-1390-6 (electronic)
1. Gray wolf—Reintroduction—Rocky Mountains Region. 2. Gray wolf—Reintroduction—Political aspects—Rocky Mountains Region. I. Title.
QL737.C22Y87 2015
599.7730978—dc23
2014037561

∞ ™ The paper used in this publication meets the minimum requirements of American National Standard for Information Sciences Permanence of Paper for Printed Library Materials, ANSI/NISO Z39.48-1992.

Contents

Acknowledgments

In researching and writing this book, I drew on a wide range of sources including news accounts, scientific papers, government reports and documents, as well as interviews with wildlife biologists, wolf researchers, wolf advocates, and many others. While everyone's kind assistance was of great value, there are a number of people who merit special mention. First and foremost, I would like to thank Curt Mack and Jim Holyan of the Nez Perce tribe's Wolf Recovery Project, who generously invited me to their offices to sit through interviews, and especially to Jim, who put up with my company on two lengthy expeditions into the Idaho backcountry in search of wolves. Also, my thanks to US Fish and Wildlife Service wildlife biologist John Stephenson and Oregon Department of Fish and Wildlife wolf coordinator Russ Morgan, who let me tag along on wolf search field outings and gave me the latest wolf updates.

I am also greatly appreciative to Tara Wertz of the U.S. Fish and Wildlife Service, Roy Heberger, former USFWS Idaho wolf recovery coordinator, Oregon Department of Fish and Wildlife biologist Craig Foster, past ODFW and US Forest Service biologist Mark Henjum, and Carter Niemeyer, formerly with Wildlife Services and USFWS, for relating to me their experiences with wolf B-45.

Other people who took the time to talk with me about wolves included Montana wolf biologist Kent Laudon; Montana wolf researcher and former Fish, Wildlife and Parks commissioner Bob Ream; Mike Phillips, Director of the Turner Endangered Species Fund; Utah State University wolf researcher Dan MacNulty; and advocates for wolf recovery Lynne Stone of the Boulder-White Clouds Council, Tim Preso of Earthjustice, Noah Greenwald of the Center for Biological Diversity, and Judy Calman of the New Mexico Wilderness Alliance.

My thanks also to a number of wolf researchers who sent me scientific papers and answered any questions I had, including Jessica Bell of Michigan State University, Mark Hebblewhite of the University of Montana, John Vucetich of Michigan Technological University, Robert Wayne of the University of California, and Dan Stahler, a wolf biologist with the National Park Service at Yellowstone National Park. Thanks also to the International Wolf Center, which sponsored the 2013 International Wolf Symposium and was a tremendous source of wolf information and contacts.

A special thanks also goes to Rob Klavins of Oregon Wild, who kept me on his mailing list to receive all the current wolf news from throughout the country and to Ralph Maughan and his blog, The Wildlife News, which I found to be an invaluable source of wolf information, leads, and contacts. Finally, my sincere thanks to all the journalists who have covered the wolf reintroduction from the beginning and whose news reports I relied upon extensively; they are credited in the reference section of this book.

Introduction

My first encounter with wolves was in Alaska in late summer of 1977. I was working on a research project to fulfill the requirements for my degree in Forestry and Wildlife from Oregon State University, spending part of my time in the Alaska Range within Denali National Park (still called Mount McKinley National Park back then) and the rest in the small town of Talkeetna where the Susitna River flows into the Chulitna. The gateway for mountaineers on their way to climb Mount McKinley, the highest peak in North America at 20,320 feet, Talkeetna was a busy place that summer, where expeditions, along with their copious amounts of gear, were being shuttled by local bush pilots from the town's small landing strip to the climbers' staging area on the Kahiltna Glacier, dubbed Kahiltna International because the base camp there was populated by climbers from all over the world.

There were two National Park Service climbing rangers assigned to Talkeetna that summer who checked in arriving climbers and gave them a look-over to make sure they had adequate gear and experience to attempt the climb. They were billeted in what was then the town's brand-new fire station and let me pitch my tent in the willows out back, where I lived for a good part of that summer, occasionally allowing me inside to take a shower.

At the end of the season, before I flew home to write my paper, one of the rangers and I decided to make a trans-Alaska Range backpacking trip through the park. Arranging for friends to drop us off outside Cantwell on the park's south boundary, we threaded our way through mountain valleys and upstream drainages, coming out at the headwaters of the Savage River, then hiked down that stream to the park road, where we would flag down a shuttle bus to take us out. On our last night, we camped beside the river a few miles from the road.

The next morning I awoke early, climbed out of the tent, and stood alone along the river, watching the water flow by. Suddenly two gray wolves appeared, loping along the gravel bar heading downstream. They were big and long-legged, but also a little gaunt and scruffy looking. Summers can be hard times for wolves. Prey is harder to catch, and although there may be an abundance of fawns and calves around, there is not a lot of meat on them; wolves often lose weight during that time of year. Passing me no more than twenty-five yards away, they were unalarmed by my presence but wary, each one continually looking back over its shoulder as if to say it knew I was a human and couldn't be trusted. I stood watching them, mesmerized, until they moved unhurried out of sight.

Fifteen years later, I experienced another wolf encounter, but of a different sort, while hunting woodland caribou on the Ungava Peninsula in Nouveau Quebec. It was September, time of the caribou migration, and the taiga and tundra country was beginning to show off its autumn colors.

The migrating caribou were a little more spread out that year, making them difficult to find, but Barnabe, our Montagnais First Nations guide, had an uncanny ability to divine where and when they would appear, allowing my hunting partner and me to kill our allowed two animals each. One morning Barnabe let us out of his freight canoe along the shore of the Delay River. Throwing my legs over the gunnels and dropping onto the sandy beach, there before me was a set of lone wolf tracks following the shoreline and looking relatively fresh. At that moment, it occurred to me that I was part of a scene that had played out uncountable times across that Ice Age landscape, humans hunting caribou alongside wolves hunting caribou. It was, of wolves and all other wildlife, as Henry Beston wrote in *The Outermost House*, that wild animals "are other nations, caught with ourselves in the net of life and time, fellow prisoners of the splendor and travail of the earth."

I have had other experiences with wolves between and after those encounters, but those two particularly stick in my mind—one in awe of the animals themselves, the other the realization that I could include them in my world and I in theirs, if I so chose.

Over the years, I didn't give much thought to wolves; the field guides I consulted on my various outdoor trips noting that in North America wolves were now relegated to Alaska, Canada, and a small area in the Upper Midwest. That changed in the mid-1990s when gray wolves were reintroduced into Yellowstone National Park and central Idaho. And when in 1999 a wolf from Idaho briefly dispersed into my home state of Oregon, I realized the wolves really were on their way back.

At that point I began to research the wolves' return to the West, attending meetings, reading scientific papers, and interviewing a variety of people involved with wolves and wolf reintroduction, as well as spending time in the field with wolf biologists, amazed at the complexity and difficulties involved in bringing this extremely symbolic animal back to a landscape it was deliberately extirpated from not all that long ago.

Virtually every wildlife biologist involved with wolves I talked to eventually volunteered that wolf management has nothing to do with wolf biology—it is all about dealing with people's perceptions of wolves and what wolves mean to them. I was especially taken aback by the intensity of those who don't like wolves, at the vitriol and even hatred they sometimes levied against the animals. Delving deeper into why they felt that way offered fascinating insights into the differing worldviews people have of nature and our place in it and how wolves represent those views. The high level of politicization wolf reintroduction triggered was also an eye-opener for me; from beginning to end it took several literal acts of Congress to bring them back and declare them recovered. As my research into wolf reintroduction deepened, it turned into a book research project and, ultimately, this book.

During one of my research trips, I traveled to Ketchum, Idaho, to meet with Lynne Stone, director of the Boulder-White Clouds Council and an outspoken wolf advocate. Over lunch in a small restaurant, Lynne told me about her work advocating for wolves in Idaho—how she would go out into the Sawtooth Valley shooting blank shells from a shotgun to scare away any wolves she saw, hoping to make them more wary of people and so less likely to be killed by hunters. She talked of packs shot up by government wildlife agents and of wolves lost that she had come to know as individuals. Before we parted company she told me that a serious impediment to wolf recovery was a public wolf narrative fixated on how many elk and cattle wolves kill. No one was saying good things about wolves, and it was up to the wolf advocacy groups to change that conversation.

In writing this book, I wanted to tell the story of the gray wolf's return to the northern Rocky Mountains and what a long, complex, and difficult endeavor it has been—an endeavor that is still ongoing as wolves continue to disperse beyond their original recovery area—and somewhere within these pages, hopefully, some good things about wolves as well.

ONE

B-45

Wolf B-45-F left the Jureano Mountain pack, into which she had been born eighteen months earlier, sometime after November 11, 1998. That was the last time the signal from her radio collar, which was being monitored by wildlife biologists from the Nez Perce tribe, placed her with the pack. There's nothing unusual about a wolf that age, heading into her second winter, going off on her own. Known as dispersal, it is how wolves find mates, start new packs, and colonize, or recolonize, territories. What made B-45 a wolf of note was not the fact that she dispersed from her natal pack but where she went and the future she foretold when she got there.

B-45 was born sometime in mid-April 1997 in the first litter of the Jureano Mountain wolf pack, whose territory ranged through the rugged central Idaho mountain country between the city of Salmon and the Frank Church River of No Return Wilderness. Her parents, the alpha male B-32 and alpha female B-25, were among the twenty wolves snared by trappers in British Columbia near Pink Mountain, just west of the Alaska Highway, the year before and released by the US Fish and Wildlife Service near Dagger Creek on the edge of the Frank Church River of No Return Wilderness. Those wolves were the second wave of releases by the USFWS as part of a bold and—to put it mildly—controversial plan, decades in the making: to restore gray wolf populations to the northern Rocky Mountains some sixty years after they had been deliberately extirpated from the West. The first gray wolf release was in 1995, with fifteen wolves captured in Alberta, Canada, set loose in central Idaho while fourteen were reintroduced into Yellowstone National Park. The following year, seventeen more were turned loose in Yellowstone and another twenty in central Idaho. The area including northwestern Montana, central Idaho, and the greater Yellowstone region was desig-

1

nated the Northern Rocky Mountain Recovery Region, and the newly reintroduced wolves were protected as threatened under the federal Endangered Species Act. The eventual recovery goal was set for thirty breeding pairs of wolves distributed relatively evenly across the three-state recovery region for three years in a row.

The formation of the Jureano Mountain pack and the birth of a litter just a year after B-25 and B-32's release was good news because it showed that, despite considerable hostility by many rural residents and the state government, the restoration was "taking" in central Idaho. In 1996, when B-25 and B-32 were set loose, there were three known wolf packs in central Idaho originating from the 1995 release and an estimated population of forty-two gray wolves. By 1997 there were seven wolf packs in the region and a population of seventy-one animals. The Jureano Mountain pack was one of six central Idaho packs that produced pups in the spring of 1997, and of the twenty-nine pups born (two of which died), one was B-45.[1]

Idaho wolves were being monitored by the USFWS and USDA Wildlife Services, along with biologists from the Nez Perce tribe, which had a contract with the federal government to help with the wolf reintroduc-

Wolf B-45's arrival in Oregon was a wake-up call that wolves would eventually establish packs in the state, like this young member of the Walla Walla pack born in 2011. Photo by the Oregon Department of Fish and Wildlife

tion after the Idaho state legislature, angry over the plan to restore wolves to Idaho, forbade the Idaho Department of Fish and Game from participating in the recovery program.

A critical tool for monitoring wolves are radio collars that emit a very high frequency, or VHF, line-of-sight signal that a biologist can pick up on a receiver to determine where and estimate how far away a wolf wearing a radio collar is, the direction it is moving, and even if it is dead. And because each collar emits a signal on a unique frequency, biologists can also identify individual wolves by their signals. Each wolf captured, usually by steel trap with offset teeth to prevent permanent damage to the foot or leg, and collared is given a letter and number designation. The "B" indicates the wolf is part of the central Idaho wolf population; the number identifies the individual wolf. An "F" or "M" means female or male, respectively. While un-collared wolves might be extremely difficult or impossible to find, a pack with a radio-collared wolf among its members betrays its location and allows biologists to find packs and pups, estimate how many wolves die each year, and determine the number of packs, how many wolves are in each pack, and the overall wolf population—all required information to help determine when wolves could be declared biologically recovered in central Idaho and removed from the Endangered Species List. For that reason, especially during the early days of wolf recovery, biologists tried to capture and collar as many wolves as they could.

Carter Niemeyer, who eventually became the USFWS's wolf recovery coordinator in Idaho but at the time worked for Wildlife Services, was the trapper who caught and collared B-45. Niemeyer was conducting a training session for a half-dozen or so biologists and technicians from the Nez Perce Gray Wolf Recovery Project who were in the process of taking over the task of wolf monitoring in Idaho, trapping wolves along Pine Creek near Shoup, Idaho, in the North Fork Salmon River region. Over the course of four days, Niemeyer caught four wolves—B-45 and two of her siblings, which he also collared and designated B-44 and B-46, along with their mother, B-25. Niemeyer caught and collared B-45 on June 6, 1998, and he remembers her well. The thirteen-month-old subadult wolf weighed sixty-five pounds and he thought she was "a scrawny little wolf, the runt of the litter."[2]

When B-45's radio signal went missing in mid-November 1998, biologists from the Nez Perce Wolf Recovery Program went looking for her, searching for her signal from an airplane, which allowed them to cover more ground and pick up her signal from a greater distance. On February 3, 1999, they found her just outside Halfway, Oregon, in the northeast corner of the state. B-45 had done something that, while not entirely unanticipated, happened far sooner than anyone had expected—she had dispersed out of the official northern Rockies wolf recovery area, looking to find a mate and start a pack of her own in a neighboring state that was completely unprepared to have wolves. And she was on the move. Three days later they found her again just east of Interstate 84 and south of Baker City. On February 12 she was between the towns of Unity and Sumpter, about sixty miles from where she was first located and heading relentlessly southwest through the Blue Mountains.[3] Carter Niemeyer's "scrawny little wolf" was about to become a very big deal.

While it can't be known for certain, the best guess is that B-45 dispersed from her natal pack's territory by heading up the South Fork Salmon River, a known wolf travel corridor, then crossing the Snake River into Oregon, perhaps even traversing unseen over Brownlee Dam, which would have put her about a dozen miles from Halfway, where she was first located in Oregon by Nez Perce Wolf Recovery Program biologists.

B-45 was a typical dispersing wolf, leaving her pack when she was about a year and a half old in search of a mate because her reproductive potential wasn't very promising if she stayed put, where breeding is usually confined to a pack's alpha pair. Wolves are long-distance dispersers, and their search for a mate can take them hundreds of miles—more than five hundred in some cases—from their point of origin. Although young wolves may disperse in pairs or even trios, most, as with B-45, go it alone, moving quickly and intently through unfamiliar country, pushing on until they find a place they like and, ideally, a mate as well. If you were to follow the tracks of a wolf on the move for a couple of miles down a forest road—big dog tracks making a straight beeline without any course deviations to mark a bush or sniff about—there is no question you are following an animal intent on getting somewhere, and nothing is going to distract from its destination.

* * *

Once B-45 left the Idaho wilderness and entered Oregon, she was traveling in more dangerous terrain. After leaving the Snake River, which forms Oregon's eastern border with Idaho, she likely moved through a geography that included public and private lands, forest and mountains, grasslands, farms, and near cities and towns, as well as the hazardous crossing of Interstate 84 and numerous rural highways. Whatever B-45's exact route in Oregon may have been, it was fraught with danger, and she was constantly at risk of being mistaken for a coyote and shot or being hit by a motor vehicle. But a wolf traveling alone can be like a ghost, moving surprisingly close to human settlements and activity while remaining unseen. It wasn't until late February that someone other than one of the biologists tracking B-45 spotted her—an Oregon Department of Transportation snowplow driver reported a wolf wearing a radio collar on the Sumpter Highway. But at the time B-45's presence in Oregon wasn't widely known among the general public, and his encounter was met with skepticism.

The Oregon Department of Fish and Wildlife and USFWS officials knew she was there, though; something needed to be done about her, but exactly what wasn't immediately clear. Mark Henjum, acting assistant supervisor for ODFW's Northeast Region in La Grande, didn't think that Oregon was prepared to deal with the eventuality of wolves dispersing into and recolonizing former habitat and thought the USFWS hadn't really thought much about how to respond to wolves dispersing out of the original release area in Idaho. While the higher-ups decided how to handle the situation, the obvious thing to do, since B-45 was wearing a radio collar and could be tracked, was to keep an eye on her and see where she went.[4]

* * *

Now the refuge manager for the Merced National Wildlife Refuge in California, in early 1999 Tara Wertz was an ODFW regional habitat biologist, also working out of the agency's office in La Grande. She, along with Oregon State Police pilot Ken West, had been doing a lot of flying—up to thirty hours a week—tracking radio-collared elk for an ongoing elk study. Since they were up in the air for a good part of each week, the job of finding and tracking B-45 fell to them—an assignment to which Wertz's response was "Cool!"

Because ODFW didn't have radio telemetry equipment that could pick up the frequency B-45's radio collar emitted, Curt Mack, gray wolf recovery project leader for the Nez Perce tribe, came over from McCall, Idaho, with the necessary gear. On February 26, 1999, Wertz, Mack, and West took off from the La Grande airport in West's Cessna 180 to try to find B-45.

"We did my flight first, found my elk, and then went off to look for the wolf," Wertz told me. "We were flying farther and farther west and were getting discouraged because it didn't look like we were going to find her."

They flew on, over the Malheur National Forest, down Long Creek and into the John Day River basin, their radio receiver set to B-45's frequency, waiting for the telltale beeps that would indicate she was nearby.

"Suddenly our ears pricked up when he heard her signal, and we all cheered," recalled Wertz. They had found her. She was in the headwaters of Clear and Hog Creeks, tributaries of the East Fork Beech Creek, which is a tributary of the North Fork John Day River in Grant County. She was hiding in heavy timber, and at first they couldn't see her. West dropped the Cessna in closer, and Wertz dug in her pack for the video camera she had decided to take along on the chance she might get some shots. Just as

Wertz got her video camera out, B-45 strolled into the open and she recorded a short clip of the wandering wolf.

* * *

By then the word was out that there was a real live wolf on the loose in Oregon, and the ODFW office in La Grande was inundated with calls from Portland television news stations pressing for information about B-45 and looking for Wertz's video clip, which she ended up having duplicated into B-roll for the media to use. "All the newspaper guys were calling too," she recalled. "I wasn't prepared for the onslaught."

Craig Foster, district wildlife biologist at the ODFW John Day office, wasn't prepared for the onslaught either. B-45 had apparently decided that the upper North Fork John Day River country, about three hundred miles from where she began her journey in Idaho, was to her liking, and she was now his problem—at least for the foreseeable future.

We can't know exactly why B-45 chose to stop where she did. Dispersing wolves are actively looking for a mate, and if they don't find one after a while, they may decide to settle down, establish a territory that might be as large as three or four hundred square miles, and wait for a potential partner to come to them. Perhaps that was what B-45 had in mind. The place she picked had plenty of prey species, especially elk, and a Nez Perce biologist tracking her on the ground one day found an elk she had killed. B-45 was being a "good" wolf, doing what wolves do and staying out of trouble with humans.

It was a little more complicated for Foster. He needed to know where that wolf was and what it was doing, so either he, Wertz, or assistant district wildlife biologist Ken Rutherford were out tracking her signal at least every other day, preferably every day, by air when the weather was good in Ken West's Cessna 180 and on the ground on bad weather days.

"She bopped around between Highway 395, Phipps Meadow, and the mainstem John Day," Foster told me. "She also got up to Dixon and up around Camp Creek and Grave Creek." She also ranged along the Middle and South Forks of the John Day River and was regularly covering twenty miles each night.

Despite staying out of trouble, B-45 covered so much ground while she was in Grant County that she couldn't remain completely invisible to people. One day a man living at the top of the grade north of Mount Vernon gave Foster a call to say he had wolf tracks in the snow on his driveway. Foster told him to put a coffee can over one of the tracks and he'd be out to have a look. Sure enough, B-45 had loped across the man's driveway sometime during the night.

One day Foster was flying with West and they got a signal from her collar up the North Fork John Day River. As they flew upriver over the Boulder Creek area, they spied a small timber operation below them and could see the skidder operator at work. And hunkered down in a willow thicket just eighty yards behind him was B-45. Foster knew that loggers who saw a coyote while they were on their way to work would stop and shoot it for the hide. The last thing he needed was someone mistaking B-45 for a coyote and killing her, bringing the Feds in to investigate the illegal shooting of an endangered species and a lot of very bad publicity. Hightailing it back to the John Day airport, Foster called the logging company owner and asked him to gather his crew at the jobsite so he could fill them in on the situation with B-45, and the importance of leaving her alone. The loggers listened politely to Foster's lecture, then told him they had been seeing B-45 around the jobsite for days and could easily have shot her if they'd wanted to, but no one had. Both Foster and Mark Henjum had a number of people tell them they had had B-45 in their rifle sights at one time or another but refrained from pulling the trigger. Whether those boasts were true or not, the fact is B-45 managed not to get herself shot—an all too common fate for dispersing wolves.

B-45 was now getting national publicity, and stories about her appeared across the country in newspapers and on television. The Hells Canyon Preservation Council and Nez Perce were sponsoring a contest to name her (eventually won by Cave Junction middle school student Cedar Hursh, whose essay proposed she should be named Freedom).[5] Both the La Grande and John Day ODFW offices were overwhelmed with calls about B-45. Henjum spent thirty straight days on the phone talking with the media and agency higher-ups, trying to figure out what to do with her. It was just as bad for Foster, who would start answering or returning calls at 7:30 in the morning when he got into work and would still be at it at 6:30 in the evening. A lot of people who called were just interested in finding out about B-45, where she was, and what she was up to. But wolves are polarizing animals, and B-45 was no different. Callers lobbied him with their views and opinions about wolves—some calling her an integral part of the ecosystem that should be allowed to stay in Oregon and others fearing she would drag children out of school buses and eat them. Foster shook his head over all the commotion. B-45 was just one wolf, not having much impact on the ecosystem and certainly no threat to humans.

One call Foster remembers in particular: A woman from nearby Canyon City who could "swear like a sailor" and wanted to know if he was going to kill "that wolf." "No, ma'am," he replied. "We know where she is, but we don't know what we are going to do with her." The lady told him, in a not very nice way, Foster recalled, that if he didn't kill "that wolf," the blood of Grant County children would be on his hands. "I just broke out laughing," Foster told me. "I said, 'Ma'am, I'm willing to take that risk.'" And with that, she hung up on him. After that conversation, Foster thought to himself, *"Little Red Riding Hood" is true. People really believe that the wolf is going to come inside and eat Grandma.*

But the question of what to do with B-45 still needed to be answered. For Oregon environmental organizations, the answer was easy. She had dispersed naturally into the state from Idaho. Let her stay. On the other hand, ranchers and hunters, both politically influential groups, weren't interested in seeing Oregon develop a wolf population. And the fact was that the state had no wolf management plan or even any basic protocols or policies for dealing with wolves.

Roy Heberger, USFWS Idaho wolf recovery coordinator at the time and based in Boise, provided regular briefing statements about wolf recovery activities in the northern Rockies to the USFWS Pacific Region office in Portland and during routine conference calls, but in his opinion the Oregon agencies viewed wolf recovery as "something going on next door."

"When the ODFW director called the USFWS regional director, neither agency was prepared to deal with wolves in Oregon," Heberger explained to me. "What was an everyday thing in Idaho and the two other recovery states became an emergency in Oregon. Wolf B-45 had not done anything in terms of livestock depredations or been hanging around ranches and people. She was just in the woods doing stuff—just there."

The consensus that B-45 had to go back to Idaho was beginning to grow, and the *Portland Oregonian*, Oregon's paper of record, was editorializing that the she had to go home and the state of Oregon needed to draw up its own wolf recovery plan in anticipation of future arrivals.[6] Finally, after discussions between Heberger, USFWS Pacific Region director Anne Badgley, ODFW director Jim Greer, and other agency staff, the USFWS agreed to capture B-45 and release her back in Idaho. But the agency did not want to become responsible for every wolf that dispersed out of the recovery region and made it clear this was a one-time deal. Any future wolves that wandered into Oregon, or any other state surrounding the northern Rockies recovery area, would not be their problem.

In late March 1999 a helicopter and crew from Hawkins and Powers Aviation, a Greybull, Wyoming, based company specializing in wildlife research and management support work, were on a Columbian whitetail deer project on the lower Columbia River, then on to another job in the Southwest. But, yes, they had time to detour to John Day to catch a wolf.

At that time B-45 was hanging around private lands on the southwest edge of the North Fork John Day Wilderness, near Huckleberry Creek. It's grassy, hilly country; and because it is also south facing, the area greens up early and by late March draws in thousands of elk, making it a very good place to be for a hungry wolf. Because it is open country, it's also a good place to catch a wolf with a net fired out of a helicopter. On March 26 the Hawkins and Powers crew lifted off from Ritter Butte Summit, heading east. Foster had asked the landowner on whose property B-

45 was for permission to enter his land and catch her, asking him to keep the operation to himself, which he did, not even telling his wife. (Another ranch owner in the area, sympathetic to B-45's presence, wouldn't allow ODFW access for a capture operation, but the wolf ended up never going onto his land.) Meanwhile, Wertz and West, who were going to fly the spotter plane to help find B-45, were at the Baker City airport, where it was snowing too hard to fly, and lamenting that after all their efforts monitoring the wolf they might miss the grand finale of her capture. But the weather cleared, and they were soon winging their way west to meet the helicopter.

* * *

West and Wertz in the Cessna flew high, searching for her signal, while the helicopter crew flew low, ready to swoop down and net her using a net gun—a net fired by a nonlethal gun propelled by CO_2 cartridges and commonly used by biologists to capture elusive or fast-moving wildlife.

But B-45 wasn't going to give in easily, and with aircraft buzzing overhead, she kept to the timber where the net gun couldn't reach her, not venturing out into the open until late morning. The helicopter crew's first netting attempt missed; they took off after her again as the wolf ran frantically across the rolling hills and vanished for a time. West and Wertz relocated her again off the end of a ridge above Bully Creek, a few miles northwest of Putney Mountain.

"All of a sudden she came out into the meadow, the helicopter swooped in, and we had a wolf on the ground," Wertz remembered. "Ken and I were waving and howling." Once B-45 was sedated for the trip to John Day, the Hawkins and Powers crew put her in the helicopter and took off. The news media hadn't gotten wind of the capture operation, so when the chopper set down at the John Day airport, only wildlife agency people were there to meet them, including Foster and Heberger.

Her Idaho release location had been decided—on Fish Creek, a tributary of the Lochsa River. The plan was for West and Wertz to fly B-45 to the Lewiston, Idaho, airport, where Curt Mack would be waiting to take her to the release site. Still a little groggy from the sedative she was given after she was netted, B-45 was put into a deer transportation crate—a tall, narrow box with a small opening near the top designed to transport animals while stressing them as little as possible.

* * *

By the time West and Wertz landed in Lewiston, the press had found out about the capture and a crowd of television and newspaper reporters, along with seven or eight bigwigs from the USFWS, were waiting. Wertz remembered it as "kind of a zoo" as they loaded B-45 onto the pickup truck. Then she, West, Mack, and Marcie Carter, also with the Nez Perce, piled in and headed for Fish Creek.

When Mack first took a look at B-45, he was worried. "She wasn't in very good shape when they caught her," he told me. "They chased her too far with the helicopter, and I thought to myself, *This wolf isn't going to make it.*" Burning daylight, they raced to Fish Creek, arriving in late afternoon as it was getting dark. To complicate matters, when they opened the crate to turn her loose, she wouldn't go. It took a catchpole and some crate shaking to finally get her out. For a moment she just stood there; then she bolted down the bank and into Fish Creek. They heard frantic splashing as the wolf hit the water and started swimming, then silence. Mack climbed down to the water's edge to check on her and, because Fish Creek is a rather large stream, expected to find her drowned. But he saw no sign of B-45. They drove back in the dark, greatly concerned about her fate, and Mack promised to return the next morning and look for her. "It was an awful feeling," Wertz recalled.

Wertz and West flew home to Oregon the next day, March 27. An hour and a half after she got home, Mack called. He had gone back out to Fish Creek with radio telemetry gear and picked up B-45's signal. She had survived.

Two weeks after B-45 was turned loose at the end of Fish Creek Road, she was located about ninety-five miles away, southwest of Fitsum Creek, a tributary of the South Fork Salmon River. By the following month, May, she may have mated and had pups. It was never confirmed, although she was spotted traveling with another wolf north of McCall seven times between late November 1999 and mid-August 2002. The last time her radio signal was detected was on August 29, 2002, near Josephine Lake, northeast of McCall. Then the signal went dead. Although Wildlife Services agents trapped her two years later while after wolves that were killing livestock, they inexplicably released her without replacing her collar, and B-45 vanished into the Idaho wilds.[7]

Despite all the trouble B-45 endured on her jaunt to Oregon, it was probably just as well that she left the Jureano Mountain pack, which fell on hard times. Back in Idaho, B-45's mother, B-25, wandered onto private property and was illegally shot and killed by the landowner. The pack had also taken to killing livestock, and her mate, B-32, was euthanized. That job went to Carter Niemeyer. "He was a beautiful blue-gray wolf, and I hated to do it," Niemeyer related to me. "But he had used up all his strikes." Wildlife Services shot two other pack members, which were implicated in a livestock killing, from a helicopter. Niemeyer caught and collared the pack's two pups of the year at the same time, designating them B-80 and B-81. But those remaining members of the Jureano Mountain pack took to hanging around a dairy farm, and although they never attacked any of the cows, they made everyone nervous enough that Niemeyer went in, caught them, and turned the young wolves over to the

Nez Perce biologists, who relocated the animals to a more remote area where they were less likely to get in trouble.

On October 18, 2006, a Wildlife Services agent out hunting came upon the carcass of a wolf wearing a radio collar in Squaw Meadows in the Payette National Forest northeast of McCall, Idaho. Judging by the condition of the carcass and the grass growing through the skeleton, the wolf had been dead for about a year. A little more than a week later the carcass and collar were retrieved, with the former going to the USFWS Forensics Laboratory in Ashland, Oregon, and the collar to the manufacturer to identify the serial number and radio frequency.

* * *

The results came back from the radio collar manufacturer. It was B-45's. The forensics laboratory wasn't able to determine the cause of her death but found ". . . radio dense fragments on the right front foot pad and toe nail." Radio dense materials are substances that X-rays cannot penetrate—lead, for example. As for B-45's old pack, her sister, B-46, eventually returned to the area, found a mate, and had pups; the Jureano Mountain pack has lived on.

By the end of 2006, the year B-45's remains were discovered, there were about 1,300 wolves in the Northern Rocky Mountain Recovery Region—673 in Idaho, 311 in Wyoming, and 316 in Montana. The great experiment in recovering gray wolves in part of the West was working. Once thought to be sensitive animals requiring remote wilderness areas to survive, gray wolves were proving to be resilient, adaptable, and resourceful animals. To thrive they mainly required protection from the small number of people who disliked wolves so much they were willing to kill them merely for being wolves.

B-45's seven-week excursion into Oregon was proof of that success. Wolves could not only recover in the northern Rockies, where they had been reintroduced by the government, but were also perfectly capable, given the chance, of recolonizing more of their former range throughout the West on their own. That was the message B-45 brought, not just to Oregon but to all the states surrounding the Northern Rocky Mountain Recovery Region, and every government wildlife agency administrator, biologist, wolf hater, and wolf lover alike understood it perfectly. Sooner or later the wolves would come. Be ready.

TWO

Return to the Rockies

Wolves have been around for a very long time and appear to have originally arisen in North America. About six million years ago, during the Miocene epoch, small woodland foxes in southern North America were evolving into larger, faster, and smarter predators; before the close of the Miocene they would become the common ancestor of all future wolves, coyotes, and domestic dogs within the genus Canis. While small canids had spread to other parts of the earth, the earliest wolflike ancestor is believed to be an animal known from the fossil records as *Canis lepophagus*. The animal identified in North America as the first true wolf species is *Canis priscolatrans*, also known as *Canis edwardii*, whose fossils have been found in the Southwest, West Coast, Midwest, Middle Atlantic states, and Mexico. By six hundred thousand to seven hundred thousand years ago, the modern wolves had risen. It is thought that wolves from North America crossed into Eurasia using the Bering Land Bridge, developed into a wolf more like today's *Canis lupus*, and then reinvaded North America in three waves. Also beginning several hundred thousand years ago was the relatively sudden development of the dire wolf, *Canis diris*, in North America—a large, robust wolf species that died out around eight thousand years ago. The demise of the dire wolf left *Canis lupus*, the gray wolf, along with the red wolf, *Canis rufus*—whose evolutionary origins are still being debated—as the remaining North American wolf species.[1]

It is difficult to say what the historical wolf population was in the American West, but some estimates put it as high as 850,000.[2] Bruce Hampton, in his 1997 book *The Great American Wolf*, guessed there might have been up to two hundred thousand in the Great Plains alone, supported by the immense bison herds that possibly numbered as many as sixty million (although other estimates put the historical bison population at ten to fifteen million, kept below their carrying capacity by Native American hunters, which would also mean the wolf population would have been much lower). A recent study by researchers Jennifer Leonard, Carles Vila, and Robert Wayne, published in the paper "Legacy lost: genetic viability and population size of extirpated US grey wolves (*Canis lupus*)," examined the genetic diversity of mitochondrial DNA in "pre-extermination" wolves, which suggested the historical population in the western United States and Mexico may have been about 380,000 animals. The presence of wolves is so prominently mentioned in the journals and reports of early travelers and explorers in the West that they were certainly common and visible animals. When the first European-Americans arrived in the New World, gray wolves ranged throughout the North American continent except for the Southeast, which was occupied by the red wolf, and the extreme Southwest in what is now Southern California and the Baja Peninsula. But by the middle of the twentieth century, North American gray wolf range was mainly limited to Canada and Alaska. In the lower forty-eight states, only a small remnant wolf population in the Minnesota north woods remained, and the red wolf was nearly extinct.

Settlers from Europe began killing wolves as soon as they arrived on the eastern shore of North America. The first wolf bounty was established in 1630 in the Massachusetts Bay Colony. The Jamestown Colony in Virginia followed suit in 1632, and it wasn't long before other colonies joined in. As European-American settlers moved west across the continent, so did the bounty system. By the mid-1880s, bounties were being paid for wolves in most states and territories. Between 1850 and the 1880s, "wolfers," professional wolf hunters and trappers, were killing wolves for their pelts and bounties throughout the Great Plains region. Their preferred method for catching wolves used traps baited with poisoned meat, and they killed large numbers of bison, elk, and deer for their bait supply. Some estimates put the annual wolf kill in the Great Plains between 1870 and 1877 by wolfers at one hundred thousand animals.[3] By 1900 gray wolf range had been pushed back to west of the Mississippi River, along with small numbers in the Upper Midwest and a few holding out in the Appalachian Mountains, although they were still abundant in Canada and Alaska.[4]

By the early twentieth century, the federal government became directly involved in the wolf killing business, even though the bounty system, along with the commercial value of wolf hides, had resulted in the virtual extirpation of wolves in the Great Plains, made them rare-to-extirpated in most regions in the East, and had been effective in substantially reducing wolf numbers in the West. Stockmen's associations were putting up money for bounties that were often higher than those offered by local governments to stimulate interest in wolf killing. In the 1890s the state of Wyoming was paying three to four dollars per wolf killed. In contrast, the Green River Valley stockmen's association was paying "$10 on each wolf pup, $20 on each grown wolf dog, and $40 on each bitch with pup." These bounties were in addition to the state payment of three dollars, along with another three dollars thrown in by the Fremont County government.[5]

In 1905 the Bureau of Biological Survey, precursor to the USFWS, began to locate wolves for the newly minted federal USDA Forest Service to kill. The Forest Reserve Act of 1891 designated large tracts of formerly public domain lands in the West as forest reserves (eventually to become national forests) under the control of the federal government. The forest service, now manager and overseer of these lands, was leasing grazing allotments, for a fee, where stockmen formerly ran their cattle and sheep for free. Ranchers had bitterly opposed the government's new involvement in Western cattle grazing—and especially being charged good money to graze their stock in "wolf infested" country. The forest service, looking to mend relationships with the stockmen after its "takeover" of public domain lands, found killing wolves a good start.[6]

By 1915 the federal government had become more directly involved in an organized predator control program in the West, driven by a livestock industry that reviled wolves, mountain lions, bears, coyotes, and other predators that attacked and killed their stock as it roamed the open range. And there was little doubt that wolves and other predators caused losses to the stockmen. Overhunting by people rapidly depleted native prey species such as bison, elk, deer, and pronghorn that wolves and other predators had relied on for food and were being replaced with cattle and sheep, which were much easier to kill; and by this time there were millions of beef cattle and domestic sheep grazing on public lands throughout the West. The biological survey estimated that each wolf and mountain lion cost stockmen one thousand dollars annually, bears five hundred dollars each, and coyotes and bobcats fifty dollars, although years later the agency admitted those figures were not based on any particular data.[7] One of the stockmen's major gripes was that the former public domain lands where they once grazed their herds at will for free had been turned into federally controlled forest reserves where they now were required to keep their animals on established allotments and pay rent. These lands, they claimed, were "breeding grounds" for wolves and other predators, and they wanted those animals exterminated. The Oregon state legislature emphasized that sentiment, common in the West, when it passed a 1915 resolution requesting that the federal government appropriate $300,000 to kill "carnivorous wild animals in the western public land states." To that end, in 1915 the Bureau of Biological Survey asked for $110,000 from the US Congress to fund animal killing demonstrations and experiments for the following year. In 1914 the bureau's total budget was nearly $170,990. Three years later its budget just for killing predators was $250,000.[8]

Vernon Bailey was a prominent biologist working for the Bureau of Biological Survey and an enthusiastic promoter of predator eradication in the West. Bailey wrote an instructional circular (Circular No. 55) and published by the Bureau of Biological Survey in 1907. Its title, *Directions for the Destruction of Wolves and Coyotes*, gave no ambiguity about where Bailey or his agency stood on the subject. With . . . "losses from the destruction of stock by wolves and coyotes in the western United States amounting to millions of dollars annually . . . practical means of preventing these losses are urgently needed." Those methods included locating dens and "destroying the young" or waiting at the den at dawn or dusk and shooting the adult wolves or coyotes when they come around to care for the pups. But trapping and poisoning were by far the preferred methods with a "No. 4 double spring trap with a heavy welded chain" recommended for wolves (and No. 3 for coyotes). The poison of choice was "pure sulphate of strychnine," and the preferred method was to fill gelatin capsules with four grains of the poison for wolves (two grains for coyotes), stuff them in chunks of beef suet, and "dropped from horseback along a scented drag line made by dragging an old bone or piece of hide well saturated with the fetid scent. . . ." Interestingly, he also discussed constructing the nonlethal deterrent method of constructing a wolf- or coyote-proof fence, although noting it was not practical for large areas. But the killing methods were certainly effective. A strychnine-laced carcass could kill sixty wolves in one night. Bailey's Circular No. 63 reporting the results of the bureau's wolf and coyote eradication program for the year 1907 showed 1,658 wolves and 23,193 coyotes killed in eleven western states.

Inevitably, tales of legendary, marauding wolves arose out of the wolf-killing campaign that served to amplify the perceived threat the animals posed to civilization and burnished the reputation of the men who destroyed them for a living. The Sycan Wolf of southern Oregon was said to have killed "many" horses and cattle over a twelve-year period before it was trapped near Fort Klamath. Montana's Pryor Creek Wolf was famous for his cunning in eluding traps and expertise in killing calves and Shetland ponies. Arizona stockmen accused the Agulia Wolf of killing a calf every four days between 1916 and 1924, when he finally met his demise. In the Black Hills, the Custer Wolf was said to have killed twenty-five thousand dollars' worth of livestock, and it took the trapper who finally caught him seven full months of work over the course of 1920 to complete the task. The hunter who killed the South Dakota renegade wolf Three Toes was presented with a gold watch by a grateful citizenry.[9]

It wasn't only wolves and coyotes that were targeted—all in service of the livestock and agriculture industries. Mountain lions, bears—including both grizzly and black bears—bobcats, eagles, hawks, even rodents, were targeted. Poison was applied liberally across the Western landscape, and tremendous numbers of nontarget species were killed.

Before their release into Yellowstone National Park, the wolves were acclimated in pens like this wolf in the Rose Creek pen. Photo by Barry O'Neill, National Park Service

Hunters and trappers were bitterly opposed to the federal government's mass poisoning campaign. Although no friends of wolves and other predatory animals, they viewed the poisoning program as a criminal waste of furbearing animals, robbing them of income they could derive by trapping them in a sustainable manner. That outrage was expressed by V. E. Lynch, a prominent outdoorsman and author of the day, who wrote, "The trapper is not only being robbed of thousands of dollars of furs that rightly belong to him but he is forced to help maintain the poison pill slinging gang in the way of paying taxes. This biological poison gang is a disgrace to our nation. Every hunter, sportsman, farmer, trapper and tax payer who loves to hunt or who has children who love this sport should exert every effort to have this poison menace stopped before our wild life is exterminated throughout the West."[10]

Western outdoorsmen had an unlikely ally in their distrust and dislike for the federal government's predator killing campaign. By the mid-1920s the American Society of Mammalogists had become suspicious that the Bureau of Biological Survey's end game was not predator control but complete extermination of wolves and other native carnivores. In fact, the Survey's 1926 annual report flatly stated that its goal in New Mexico (and while unstated, in the rest of the western states as well) was to "get the last one [wolf] in the State." The same report also proudly announced that in 1926, for the first time since the agency began its killing program, not a single wolf was killed in Colorado because its hunters and trappers couldn't find any. The mammalogists, who were beginning to make some connections between predators and their function within ecosystems, such as coyotes helping to control rodent numbers, tried to pressure the Survey into reforming their predator-killing program. In 1930, 148 mammalogists signed a letter to the Bureau of Biological Survey calling for an end to the extermination program, but a group of East Coast academics, much less the unorganized hunters and trappers, were no match for the agency and its politically powerful backers in the Western livestock industry; the extermination program continued.[11] But as Thomas R. Dunlap notes in his history of wildlife conservation in the United States, *Saving America's Wildlife*, ". . . the Survey was not responsible for the policy of killing off predators; ranchers had been doing that for years and the Survey was only continuing what they had done, more carefully and on a more rational basis." By the 1930s wolves in the West were largely gone, save for a few remnant packs and lone individuals here and there.

Immediately following World War II there was a surge in wolf killing by hunters in the Upper Midwest—the only place left in the lower forty-eight states at that time with a viable, reproducing wolf population—who called them the "Nazi of the forest" that "takes the deer and some small fry," and demanded to know why "deer meant for human consumption should be fed to the Nazi." (The wolves' little cousins, the foxes that "takes the choice morsels of game and the song birds," were "sly Japs.")[12]

Interestingly, there was an increase in wolf killing in Eastern Europe right after the war as well, perhaps fed by fresh remembrances of wolves feeding on war dead who had been hastily buried in shallow graves. In Ukraine's Transcarpathia region, wolf numbers were reduced to about twenty animals, although they have since rebounded to as many as four hundred.[13]

Minnesota continued its wolf control program, which included shooting them from aircraft, until 1956, and the bounty system remained in place in the Upper Midwestern states until the mid-1960s. Wolf populations were probably at their lowest during the 1960s, with 350 to 700 living in extreme northeastern Minnesota and about 20 on Isle Royale (and perhaps a few still surviving in Michigan). In 1966, wolves in the lower forty-eight states were listed as endangered under the Endangered Species Preservation Act, although it only provided limited protection and wolves continued to be killed in Minnesota. Wolves outside of Alaska were finally given complete protection as endangered with the passage of the Endangered Species Act of 1973.[14]

Besides the mammalogists, wolves had other defenders, notably the twentieth-century conservationist and advocate of modern, scientific wildlife management, Aldo Leopold. In a 1945 *Journal of Forestry* review of Stanley P. Young and Edward H. Goldman's book *The Wolves of North*

America, he noted the second to last statement in the book proposed there were a few places left in the United States large enough to allow some wolves to remain but criticized the USFWS (formerly the Bureau of Biological Survey, its name changed in 1940 and consolidated with the Bureau of Fisheries) for taking "no responsibility for implementing this thought before it completes its job of extirpation."

Since both authors were longtime employees of the Bureau of Biological Survey during the Western predator eradication campaign, the idea of leaving some wolf populations alone or relocating others to suitable areas did not very likely occur to them. The most obvious place that met the criteria as a "wolf refuge," Yellowstone National Park, had its wolf population killed off by 1923, when the last known den and its pups were destroyed.[15] Leopold noted that with virtually all of the Western wolves killed off at that point, the only wolves remaining to use as seed stock for eventually repopulating selected regions such as Yellowstone were Mexican wolves in Arizona and, presciently, "the sub-arctic form of the Canadian Rockies."[16] The idea of restoring gray wolves, especially to Yellowstone National Park, survived the livestock industry and federal government's great Western gray wolf pogrom and would eventually be revived and expanded upon nearly half a century later.

It was the passage of the Endangered Species Act of 1973, and their designation as endangered the following year, that saved gray wolves from very likely extirpation in the lower forty-eight states and paved the way for the their restoration in the northern Rocky Mountain region, since the law proposed that they be restored to as much of their former range as possible. The first wolf restoration efforts focused on the small population in Minnesota and developing a plan to expand their numbers in the Upper Midwest. By 1978 all wolves, and all wolf subspecies, in the lower forty-eight states had been designated endangered—even where there were no wolves currently present—except for the Minnesota wolves. They were listed as threatened, which allowed some to be killed if they caused problems and was intended to make the expansion of their numbers more palatable to wolf recovery opponents.

The USFWS was also looking at the declining red wolf population in the southeastern states, where by the mid-1970s it was apparent they would not make it without intervention. Biologists began trapping the few remaining wild red wolves left in the swamps of the Gulf states and had them all in a captive breeding program by 1980. In 1986 the USFWS released eight red wolves in the Alligator River National Wildlife Refuge in North Carolina, and the following year one pair had pups.

Wolf recovery planners had identified the northern Rockies, including the Greater Yellowstone area, as the best region to restore wolves to the West because of its large expanses of wild lands and abundant elk and deer populations that wolves would require as a prey base. But the historical and cultural animosity of ranchers toward wolves in combination with their significant political influence made wolf restoration in the northern Rocky Mountain states more than a little problematic. Still, since the 1960s, wolves' public image had been rehabilitated and they were increasingly seen as a valuable part of America's wildlife heritage. Non-profit conservation groups, Defenders of Wildlife and the National Wildlife Federation in particular, began to campaign for their reintroduction in the West, and especially to Yellowstone National Park.

The Rocky Mountain Wolf Recovery Team, composed of representatives from the USFWS, National Park Service, USDA Forest Service, Bureau of Land Management, Montana and Idaho wildlife commissions, National Audubon Society, and a University of Montana wolf biologist, developed a draft wolf recovery plan in 1976. It wasn't circulated for comment until 1978, and when the final plan was completed in 1980, the document was not especially detailed and expressed doubt that wolves could ever be returned to the Rockies due to local opposition.[17]

But public pressure to restore wolves to the West continued to build. Between 1987 and 1990 a series of bills were introduced into the US Congress to bring back wolves to Yellowstone National Park, but were all defeated by the considerable influence of Wyoming, Montana, and Idaho politicians, who successfully stymied any progress by wolf reintroduction advocates. Finally, wolf advocates broke through the opposition's political barrier and, in 1991, the USFWS was directed by Congress to develop an Environmental Impact Statement (EIS) for reintroducing wolves into Yellowstone National Park and central Idaho. Environmental Impact Statements are required by the National Environmental Policy Act of 1969 and are part of the federal planning process that identifies the problems and considerations involved in proposed management action, identifies important issues, determines the information needed to address and solve problems that will arise in implementing the plan, and develops a series of alternative actions and recommends the best alternative.

The Reintroduction of Gray Wolves to Yellowstone National Park and Central Idaho Final Environmental Impact Statement was approved on April 14, 1994, and signed by US Secretary of the Interior Bruce Babbitt a month later. The completion and approval of that document by the USFWS entailed extensive input from the public through 130 public meetings and about 750,000 comments received from every state in the United States and more than forty countries.

The EIS proposed five alternatives for wolves in the Northern Rocky Mountain Recovery Region. Three were variations on reintroducing wolves to Yellowstone National Park and central Idaho; one alternative would take a nonactive role in wolf recovery by allowing the natural dispersal of wolves into the region from Canada over time; the final alternative would direct the USFWS to oppose all wolf recovery in the northern Rockies, including natural repopulation. The USFWS recommended an alternative that would actively reintroduce wolves into the two areas. Both were large enough and had enough prey species to easily support a population of wolves. At the time, the Greater Yellowstone region, consisting of more than 40,000 square miles, with 5,300-square-mile Yellowstone National Park at its epicenter, had more than 95,000 ungulates—mostly deer and elk—while central Idaho, with more than 33,000 square miles of mostly national forest lands, had about 241,400 deer and elk.

There were also about 412,000 sheep and cattle grazing in the Greater Yellowstone area and about 307,000 livestock in central Idaho. In addition, hunting—especially elk hunting—was, and is, extremely popular; hunters killed an average of 14,300 ungulates each year in the Yellowstone area and about 33,400 in central Idaho. Reintroduced wolves would prey mainly on deer and elk, but could also be expected to occasionally kill livestock. The EIS estimated that minimally recovered population of one hundred wolves in the Greater Yellowstone Area would kill up to twelve hundred deer or elk, and as many as twenty cows and seventy sheep each year. The figures for a central Idaho wolf population were sixteen hundred ungulates, ten cows, and sixty sheep. For this reason, any wolves reintroduced by the federal government would be designated a "nonessential, experimental population." Even though the wolves would still be protected under the federal Endangered Species Act, this special designation would allow more management flexibility, intended to make the recovery program more palatable to its opponents, that eventually included allowing ranchers to shoot wolves they caught killing or harassing livestock on their properties and, in some cases, on public lands as well.[18]

But the EIS required that the northern Rockies reintroduction plan could go forward "only if two or more naturally occurring wolf packs were not located in either area before October 1994," and in 1994 the northern Rockies were not strictly wolf-less.

Between 1973 and 1977, the University of Montana's Wolf Ecology Project tallied 315 wolf reports in Montana it considered reliable, most coming from either the northwestern or southwestern parts of the state. Other researchers had found 130 wolf reports from Glacier National Park (where wolves had been systematically killed by agents of the Bureau of Biological Survey up through the early 1930s) and along the Rocky Mountain Front going back to 1910.

Then, in spring 1979, the researchers from the Wolf Ecology Team captured a female wolf in the North Fork Flathead River drainage near the US–Canada border. They put a radio collar on her, turned her loose, and watched to see where she went and what she did. For the next couple of years the researchers kept a close eye on her as she roamed the drainage alone. But in fall 1981 a set of larger tracks, one foot three-toed, turned up in the area. That winter, researchers also tracked a pair of wolves through the snowy backcountry of Glacier National Park that crossed over into Canada, where they had seven pups the following spring. Wolf tracks and sightings increased in the North Fork Flathead drainage through the early 1980s, and wolves were documented in Glacier National Park during the winter of 1983–84. By the following winter there were as many as ten wolves in the area. In 1986 wolves had established a population of fifteen to twenty in and around the park, including a pack of twelve that had come down across the border from Alberta, a suspected pair, and several lone wolves. Researchers could find no evidence of wolf packs in southwestern Montana.

Between the late 1960s and late 1970s, numerous reports of "large canids" in Yellowstone National Park were reported to authorities along with tales of wolf sightings in the Bridger-Teton National Forest, south of Yellowstone, during the 1980s. However, except for a lone wolf that was shot just south of the park in 1992, no evidence of either packs or individual wolves could be confirmed in those areas.[19]

While Idaho's wolf population was largely gone by the late 1920s, researchers collected more than six hundred reports of wolf sightings and signs in central Idaho dating back to 1975, with 238 of those considered reliable. Further analysis combined with field investigations led researchers to believe that there may have been as many as fifteen wolves in central Idaho at the time.[20] (In 1991 a black wolf was illegally poisoned in central Idaho and two radio collared wolves from Canada were tracked dispersing into the region; one went back while the other stayed.[21]) Probably dispersers from Canada, all were lone animals, and there were no signs of any established packs. With no packs verified in either Yellowstone or central Idaho by October 1994 (the naturally repopulating wolves in and around Glacier National Park, which by then were estimated at sixty-five to seventy animals, including seven breeding pairs, were out of the proposed recovery areas and didn't count), the reintroduction met the criteria to go forward.[22]

To reestablish wolves into the northern Rockies, a source of wolf "seed stock" would be required, and Aldo Leopold's suggested Mexican wolves, which he referred to as Arizona wolves, were gone from the wild. A subspecies of the gray wolf, *Canis lupus baileyei*, Mexican wolves, which historically occupied northern Mexico, Texas, Arizona, New Mexico (and perhaps even farther north), were put on the federal Endangered Species list in 1976. In 1994 there were no known Mexican wolves left in the wild. The last five known wild Mexican wolves were live-trapped in 1980 and transferred into a captive breeding program for future reintroduction. That left the wolves of the Upper Midwest, *Canis lupus lycaon*, often referred to as timber wolves, or Leopold's "Canadian sub-Arctic wolves," *Canis lupus occidentalis*, as the only available candidates.

Wolves in the Upper Midwest had responded well to recovery efforts that began in the early 1970s, and by 1994 there were about two thousand wolves in Minnesota and nearly sixty each in Wisconsin and Michigan.[23] While the level of social acceptance of wolf reintroduction to the northern Rockies was a question mark, from a biological point of view, the USFWS was much more optimistic about the odds for success than were the authors of the original 1980 northern Rockies wolf recovery plan. But it was vital to find the right wolves to release.

And the right wolves were *Canis lupus occidentalis* from the mountains and foothills of Alberta and British Columbia, which had populations of about 4,200 and 8,000, respectively, were steadily increasing, and could afford to contribute some animals to the restoration effort. They were the same genetic stock that had naturally recolonized northwestern Montana in the mid-1980s; were accustomed to killing elk and deer, the animals that would make up the bulk of their prey source in their new home; and would be released into similar terrain.

The USFWS made arrangements with the provincial governments to procure some wolves to meet the recovery plan for releasing fifteen wolves into Yellowstone and central Idaho each year for three to five years to reach an initial goal of two breeding pairs producing at least two pups for two years in each area.

When arrangements with the British Columbia government couldn't be made in time for a 1994 trapping operation, the USFWS focused its efforts in Alberta, which had offered to provide all thirty wolves needed for the first round of releases the following year.[24]

Based out of Hinton, Alberta, just southeast of William A. Switzer Provincial Park, Carter Niemeyer headed up the wolf-catching operation. The plan called for capturing, radio collaring, releasing, and monitoring the wolves, then going back in early 1995 to recapture and transport them back to the states. Local trappers were offered $1,400 for every wolf they trapped that was radio collared and released, $360 for each additional wolf they caught when it came time to transport the wolves back to the United States, and $215 for every wolf that was darted with a sedative from an aircraft and captured along their trap line (since the deal was that they had to refrain from killing any wolves on their trap lines for the duration of the trapping operation). The trappers put stoppers on their snares to prevent any wolf they caught from being strangled, as would be the normal procedure when trapping wolves for their pelts. When one of the trappers caught a live wolf, Niemeyer would go out with him, sedate the wolf, and bring it back to Hinton, where a veterinarian would give it any care it might need—the wolves were sometimes a little beat up and hypothermic from their time in the snare—fit it with a radio collar, and release it where it was caught.[25] By January 3, 1995, eighteen wolves had been captured, fitted with radio collars, and released.

About thirty USFWS agents and Canadian officials were back in Hinton in early January 1995 to locate the collared wolves and dart them from a helicopter (one wolf died when a dart pierced its abdomen), along with un-collared wolves who were traveling with them. They transported the captured wolves to a makeshift wolf processing facility at Switzer Provincial Park, where the un-collared animals were fitted with radio collars and all were implanted with a passive integrated transponder, which would allow biologists to identify individual animals much like a chip surgically implanted in a pet, and had temporary ear tags attached so they could be identified visually from a distance. Then they were put in kennels for safekeeping.

Of all the wolves captured, twenty-nine were for a variety of reasons determined to be the best candidates for the reintroduction. They were put in crates and flown by forest service cargo plane to Yellowstone and Idaho in two separate shipments in mid-January 1995 in preparation for their release. The fifteen wolves bound for Idaho included seven males and eight females; nine males and five females went to Yellowstone. The remaining radio-collared wolves not selected for the reintroduction were released back into the Alberta wilds to rejoin the "donor" population. These Judas wolves would help lead the biologists to their packs when the time came to capture more wolves for the reintroduction.[26]

There are two basic approaches for releasing wildlife into a new area: a soft release and a hard release. In a soft release the animals are kept in enclosures, preferably in the area where they will be released, to give them time to acclimate and calm down from the stress of their capture and handling by humans. A hard release is simply opening the cage door and turning the animals loose into their new environment. USFWS officials decided to handle the wolf reintroduction both ways. In Yellowstone, where there were facilities and staff available, the wolves were separated into three groups in three separate pens and would be held for up to two months before they were released. Not only would this help acclimate the wolves to the area, but the USFWS and National Park Service biologists also hoped the wolves would form packs within the enclosures before they went out on their own. Setting up holding pens and caring for the wolves while they were being held was impractical in the remote central Idaho wilderness, so those wolves drew the hard release card. Wolves released this way would probably separate, but the biologists were confident that enough would eventually reconnect to form breeding pairs and then packs.

The first four Idaho wolves were released along Corn Creek, along the edge of the Frank Church River of No Return Wilderness on January 14, 1995. A snowplow cleared the snow away from the road ahead of the procession that included state and federal wildlife officials, reporters, and lots of onlookers. Nez Perce tribal members conducted a blessing ceremony, and the wolves were turned loose into the snowy forest.[27] Six days later, on January 20, 1995, the remaining eleven Idaho wolves were released, this time at Indian and Thomas Creeks along the Middle Fork Salmon River.[28] Legal issues delayed the release of the fourteen Yellowstone National Park wolves for several more months longer than original-ly planned. But on March 21, 22, and 27, 1995, the doors to the pens were opened and the three groups of wolves, now the Crystal Creek, Rose Creek, and Soda Butte packs (named for the areas where their pens were located and they were released) departed into the Yellowstone wilder-ness.[29] Arguably the greatest, and without doubt the most controversial, wildlife restoration project in the history of the United States had begun.

Cowboys capture a wolf in an 1887 Wyoming wolf roundup. Photo by John H.C. Grabill, Library of Congress

THREE

Ranchers, Wolves, and Rural Power

Wielding their considerable political power in Washington, DC, agricultural and ranching interests had been, up until now, able to successfully stop legislation that would result in returning wolves to the northern Rockies. That included legislation authorizing the reintroduction of wolves into Yellowstone National Park, which was introduced in 1987 by Democratic Congressman Wayne Owens of Utah's Second Congressional District, the same year the federal government approved a wolf recovery plan for Yellowstone National Park.[1] That legislation was successfully stalled by its anti–wolf restoration opponents. In 1990, the year the National Park Service and USFWS had completed the first "Wolves for Yellowstone?" report, Idaho Senator James McClure, a Republican, introduced legislation to bring back wolves to the park and central Idaho. Although he was no friend of environmentalists, wolf advocates who met with McClure found his interest in reintroducing wolves to the northern Rockies to be genuine but primarily driven by pragmatism.

By 1990 wolves had already naturally established themselves in northwestern Montana in the Flathead River–Glacier National Park region, and McClure reasoned that a planned reintroduction that would provide more management flexibility was preferable to allowing wolves to colonize the rest of the Rockies on their own—with the highly protective endangered species status that would go with it—or the federal government's more expansive plan. It was an effort to make the inevitable return of wolves more palatable to the livestock industry than the Northern Rocky Mountains Wolf Recovery Plan that included a smaller central Idaho recovery area (2,600 square miles down from 12,000); a lower bar for number of wolves required for official recovery to three breeding pairs in two of three designated recovery areas; and state management

27

control of wolves outside the recovery areas.[2] But the Wyoming congressional delegation, consisting at the time of Senators Malcolm Wallop and Alan Simpson and Representative Dick Cheney, was adamantly opposed to returning wolves to the West, and to Yellowstone in particular.[3] Idaho's other Republican senator, Larry Craig, was also opposed to wolf reintroduction. Testifying strongly against the bill at its hearing were the American Farm Bureau Federation, Wyoming Wool Growers Association, and the Montana Stock Growers Association, all predicting devastating impacts from wolves preying on livestock along with land use restrictions imposed by the federal government to protect wolves. Surprisingly, the Idaho Wool Growers gave the bill a "lukewarm" endorsement, probably because they recognized the inevitability of the wolves' return and preferred McClure's plan to the alternatives. Nevertheless, overwhelming opposition killed the bill in committee.[4]

In an attempt to find middle ground, a Wolf Management Committee was formed to develop a recovery plan that would work for both sides of the wolf issue, combining the most palatable parts of the federal government's Northern Rocky Mountain Wolf Recovery Plan and the McClure bill. In May 1991 they came back with a plan that proposed to capture wolves from Canada as "seed" stock, designate the relocated wolves as "experimental, nonessential," and give states primary control and authority for managing their wolf populations. State wildlife officials liked the plan, particularly because it gave them management control. The livestock industry reluctantly signed off on it, especially approving of its provision to de-designate the wolves from ESA protections. Environmental groups, on the other hand, balked at that proposal and preferred the original plan.[5]

But the Wolf Management Committee's compromises were its undoing. The US House of Representatives rejected them and authorized the USFWS to produce the Wolf Recovery Environmental Impact Statement—the next step in implementing the Northern Rocky Mountain Wolf Recovery Plan.

Support for wolf reintroduction had continued to grow among the public, and 1990 opinion polls showed that 43.7 percent of Montana residents, 48.5 percent of Wyoming residents, and 56 percent of Idaho residents supported wolves returning to Yellowstone National Park, while 40.3, 34.5, and 27 percent, respectively, were opposed. A 1992 survey showed that 72.4 percent of Idahoans favored wolves in wilderness and roadless areas in central Idaho and 22.1 percent opposed. Nationally, Americans supported wolf recovery by "two-to-one margins."[6]

But there were significant numbers of opponents to wolf reintroduction as well, specifically ranchers, hunters, and many rural residents within the wolf recovery areas—or outlying regions where the wolves would eventually spread—who had considerable political influence, es-

Although its losses to wolves are minuscule, the livestock industry is a major opponent of wolf recovery. These cows are grazing on private land within a wolf pack's territory in Oregon. Photo by Jim Yuskavitch

pecially at the state level, where the long-term ground war over wolves would largely be fought.

Federal wolf recovery managers had no illusions that restoring wolves to the northern Rockies would be without significant controversy. They had seen extreme pushback by some anti-wolf people before. In 1974 biologists released four radio-collared wolves in Michigan's Upper Peninsula as part of the Upper Midwest wolf recovery plan, and all four were soon illegally shot. One wolf carcass was left on the doorstep of a local game warden. And those weren't the only illegal killings.[7]

Despite that a majority of people supported wolf recovery in the West, it was a highly polarized issue and people felt strongly in their positions—especially the anti-wolf factions, which held rallies protesting the planned reintroduction and carried signs comparing wolves to Saddam Hussein and terrorists. In February 1991, the year that the USFWS began work on the wolf recovery environmental impact statement, US-led allied forces had successfully driven the occupying Iraqi Army out of Kuwait. And, just as in the post–World War II years when wolves were the "Nazi of the forest," they were now equated with Middle East dictators and Muslim terrorists, at least in the eyes of some people.

Public meetings held by the federal government as part of the process of developing the environmental impact statement included telling people about the recovery plan and taking public input. These meetings were often tense, and where the meeting was held tended to determine its tenor and the attitudes of the attendees. Meetings in Boise and Seattle typically had a more pro-wolf atmosphere, while in rural areas such as Salmon and Challis, the crowd was more uniformly anti-wolf. In the early days of wolf restoration, public wolf meetings could sometimes erupt into shouting matches, usually instigated by anti-wolf people. Anti-wolf sentiments typically focused on wolf recovery as being "shoved down their throats" by an arrogant federal government, the insanity of bringing back a "destructive" animal, wasting taxpayers' money, and the opinion that the wolf eradication campaign during the first half of the last century was a good thing that shouldn't be undone.[8] Jim Holyan, a wolf biologist with the Nez Perce Wolf Recovery Program who, along with program leader Curt Mack, often led public information meetings about wolf recovery in Idaho during the early days, related: "It was frustrating for wolf managers to present scientific data only to be shouted down by those choosing to remain uninformed [about wolves]."

Mark Henjum, wolf coordinator for the Oregon Department of Fish and Wildlife during the early 2000s when public meetings were being held around the state during development of an Oregon wolf management plan, described the raw emotions that surfaced over wolves among the public: "At times it was bizarre," he told me. "Some people were so angry about having wolves in Oregon that they would weep while expressing their emotions."

The point of these public meetings was to have a "conversation with people about wolves," but Henjum often found very aggressive behavior by the anti-wolf people. In the past when state wildlife biologists held public meetings, they gave their spiel and then sat back and answered questions from the audience. But that didn't work with wolf meetings. Without a facilitator to run them, the anti-wolf faction would sometimes take over, shouting down and intimidating people who tried to speak out in favor of wolves.[9] (Jim Holyan and Curt Mack had just such an experience at a public meeting about wolves in St. Maries, Idaho, shortly after the wolf recovery plan had been implemented.) Particularly graphic and powerful displays of the intense hostility harbored by some people were the hand-lettered signs occasionally posted on roadside fences during the period when wolves were being released back into central Idaho and Yellowstone recommending that both the wolves and the people who were turning them loose be killed.[10]

On the other hand, Roy Heberger, who ran the USFWS's wolf recovery program in Idaho during its first five years, found that while there were occasional displays of anger, most public meetings about wolves he attended were orderly and he never experienced rude behavior. But there was often fear underlying many of the meetings. Heberger recalled, "Some members of the public were frightened for the well-being of their children, their livestock, their pets, and their livelihood. Little Red Riding Hood was alive and well in those early days of wolf recovery. I suspect she's still doing fine in some parts."

That fear of wolves was a driving factor for many people who lived in the proposed wolf recovery zones, driven by a lack of knowledge and even misinformation. A 1992 study gauging the attitudes of people about restoring wolves in Yellowstone National Park noted, "The interviews revealed not only polarization, but gross misunderstandings and misconceptions concerning the wolf and the [restoration] program. It was clear that people still do believe in the horror stories of the wolf and 'Little Red Riding Hood.' Many respondents stated as fact that they know wolves kill people."[11] Conrad Burns, Republican Senator from Montana at the time, somberly predicted that if wolves were reintroduced to the northern Rockies, there would be a dead child within a year.[12] (In 1995 Burns diverted two hundred thousand dollars from the Senate Appropriations Committee for the Yellowstone wolf reintroduction program to a Montana trout disease study that jeopardized the wolf releases planned for that year. In response, the Wolf Education and Research Center raised more than $120,000 from private individuals to help make up the difference.[13, 14])

Misconceptions about the threats wolves pose to people, livestock, and big game animals, as well as other aspects of wolf behavior and biology, were often deliberately spread by anti-wolf groups to further inflame the issue. They would hamper wolf restoration throughout the recovery stage and beyond.

But it was the wolves' main nemesis, the Western livestock industry—which had orchestrated their original extirpation from the region—that pushed back the hardest. Even with the wolves gone, ranchers were still in the predator-killing business to protect their stock, which continued to be grazed on public lands as in the old days but were now regulated to specific allotments for which they pay a cut-rate fee of $1.35 per cow and calf pair (or one horse, or five sheep or goats) per month to the federal government.

While coyotes had been equally targeted as wolves in the frontier years—with many, many more killed—unlike their larger relatives, the "song dogs" proved resilient to nonstop persecution, not just surviving but expanding their numbers and dispersing east of the Mississippi River, where they were not historically present, to establish new populations, filling the niche, ironically enough, left by eastern wolves that had been mostly killed off by 1900. A further irony is that some coyotes dispersing through the US Upper Midwest and eastern Canada appear to have crossbred with eastern wolves, producing a wolf-coyote hybrid larger than the coyote of the West. Coyotes remain an unprotected species that can be killed year-round with no harvest limits.

Western mountain lions, also on the ranchers' and Bureau of Biological Survey's hit list, survived in low numbers, probably because of their secretive habits, and have since rebounded throughout their western range where (except in Texas, where they are classified as nongame, "noxious wildlife") they are protected by hunting laws limiting the number of animals that can be killed each year or, in the case of California and Florida, illegal to hunt at all. Grizzly bear populations in the Rockies, on the other hand, are still suffering from the depopulation effects of past persecution.

As the Bureau of Biological Survey eventually became the USFWS—and its mission of "working with others to conserve, protect and enhance fish, wildlife, and plants and their habitats for the continuing benefit of the American people"—the job of predator control had moved to a different agency, Wildlife Services, under the jurisdiction of the Biological Survey's old home, the US Department of Agriculture.

A branch of the US Department of Agriculture's Animal and Plant Health Inspection Service, or APHIS, Wildlife Services' mission is "to provide Federal leadership and expertise to resolve wildlife conflicts to allow people and wildlife to coexist." However, among ranchers, fish and wildlife agencies, and wildlife advocates, Wildlife Services is known mainly for killing predators—about one hundred thousand each year—using methods that include traps, poison, and shooting them from aircraft.[15] Wildlife Services had long been killing coyotes, bears, mountain lions, bobcats, and a host of other wildlife at the behest of state fish and game agencies and ranchers, often subsidized by local county governments. Wildlife Services was slated to play a key role in the wolf recovery project, dealing with any animals that were deemed to be causing problems, lethally if necessary. Hence, the special "experimental, nonessential" designation that decoupled the reintroduced wolves from the strict protections normally provided under the federal Endangered Species Act. The era of wholesale wolf extermination wasn't coming back, but the government would still be able to kill wolves when it wanted to.

When the final decision to move forward with the reintroduction was made, Alternative 1 from the Final Environmental Impact Statement was chosen: reintroduction of experimental wolves. That alternative called for reintroducing forty-five to seventy-five wolves from Canada into central Idaho and Yellowstone National Park over a three- to five-year period. Even though gray wolves in the contiguous United States had been designated endangered under the Endangered Species Act in 1973, the wolves to be captured in Canada and released into Idaho and Yellowstone would be experimental, nonessential populations, treated as if they were only designated as threatened, a less-protective category under the ESA, or as if they were only proposed for listing under the act. That was an important feature of the recovery plan because it would allow wolves causing problems, such as chronically attacking livestock, to be killed if necessary—an important concession to the livestock industry. It also allowed state fish and wildlife agencies to remove wolves if they were having a severe impact on big game species, another concession to hunters, who were generally opposed to the wolves' return. However, that wasn't considered to be a potential problem. What made central Idaho and Yellowstone so attractive for wolf recovery was their extensive wilderness and abundance of elk, deer, and other prey species for wolves to eat.

In the third recovery area, northwestern Montana, the wolves would remain protected as endangered under the ESA because they had dispersed there from Canada on their own and were a naturally formed population. Wolves would be considered biologically recovered when there were "10 breeding pairs in each of the three recovery areas for three consecutive years." The biologists who developed the recovery plan felt that once there were two packs in each recovery area, "with each pack raising two cubs for two consecutive years" the wolf population would grow on its own to the official recovery level without the need for any additional reintroductions.[16]

Despite concessions to the livestock industry, permitting lethal control of wayward wolves and the USFWS's ultimately accurate estimate that the number of livestock lost to wolves would be barely statistically measurable—a far cry from the devastation of which wolves were often accused—the ranchers' cultural hostility to the animals was deeply ingrained. The federal government did not include a budget in the recovery plan for compensating ranchers for stock fallen prey to wolves, but the conservation organization Defenders of Wildlife was paying ranchers for livestock killed by wolves in the northwestern Montana recovery area from a private fund and had expanded its compensation program into Idaho and Wyoming to support the wolf reintroduction. Nevertheless, from the ranchers' point of view, their grandfathers and great-grandfathers had killed off the western gray wolves for a good reason, and they didn't want them back. So the American Farm Bureau, along with its affiliated organizations in Idaho, Montana, and Wyoming, sued.[17]

Represented by the Mountain States Legal Foundation, a Colorado-based law firm founded by James Watt, secretary of the interior under President Ronald Reagan, that specialized in conservative issues such as property rights and natural resources development, the Farm Bureau filed a lawsuit in December 1994 to stop the USFWS from transporting wolves from Canada and releasing them in Idaho and Yellowstone on the grounds that the wolf reintroduction was illegal and sought an injunction to stop the process until the case was heard.

The crux of the Farm Bureau's case for the injunction was that wolves would cause it and its members to suffer "irreparable harm" from attacks on livestock if wolves were introduced before that case was heard. Testifying before Judge William Downes of the US District Court in Cheyenne, Wyoming, for the federal government were Ed Bangs, USFWS wolf recovery coordinator; internationally recognized wolf expert and researcher L. David Mech; and Carter Niemeyer of Wildlife Services. They explained that the number of livestock wolves were expected to kill was minuscule (the authors of the wolf reintroduction EIS estimated that a minimally recovered population of one hundred wolves in central Idaho would kill about 0.04 percent of the region's livestock annually) and that there was a policy in place to remove, lethally if necessary, wolves that caused problems for ranchers. Hank Fischer, Defenders of Wildlife's northern Rockies field representative, also testified about the organization's Wolf Compensation Fund, which would pay ranchers market value for losses caused by wolves. Four ranchers testified for the Farm Bureau, and although they were sincere in their views on wolves and how their reintroduction would affect ranchers' livelihoods, "they presented only fears, not facts."[18]

Judge Downes denied the Farm Bureau's request for an injunction on January 3, 1995, allowing the reintroduction to go forward. On January 11, the Farm Bureau was able to get a temporary stay from the Federal District Court in Denver that required the USFWS to keep the wolves they had captured in their transport boxes at the Missoula, Montana, airport on January 12, where they had been flown from Hinton, Alberta, via Great Falls the day before. Because of the stay, the wolves had to remain in their transport boxes, with growing concern that dehydration and kidney damage could cause the animals problems, since the boxes weren't designed for long-term occupancy. But the court lifted the stay on January 12, and the wolves went as scheduled to their release in central Idaho and into the acclimation pens at Yellowstone.[19]

* * *

But the big question was always how would the wolves respond once they were released and what would they do—the hard released wolves in central Idaho, in particular. Wolves released this way typically scattered once they were set free, and wolves suddenly dumped into unfamiliar territory might try to find their way back to their home territory. Some of the Idaho wolves were expected to do that. But how many would go and how many would stay? Would the remaining wolves eventually find each other again and, most importantly, form breeding pairs to begin the pack-building process needed to grow the population?

After the first year's releases in 1995, wildlife biologists took to the air above the remote and mountainous central Idaho wilderness to search for the wolves' radio collar signals, and what they found was mostly encouraging. B-13, a female, traveled about fifty-five miles from where she was released, only to be illegally shot while feeding on the carcass of a dead calf on a ranch near Salmon, Idaho. (An examination of the calf found that it died of causes other than predation and that B-13 was only feeding on the carcass.) Another wolf, B-3, also a female, had vanished. However, more than five months after they had been turned loose into the wilds, thirteen of the fifteen wolves were still within the designated central Idaho recovery zone. Wolf B-10 did the most traveling—nearly five hundred miles in that five-month period. On the other hand, B-2 (a male, who would become the longest surviving of the original Idaho wolves and known by many who worked with Idaho wolves as "Chat Chaat"), wandered the least at about two hundred miles. And they were pairing up. Within two weeks of being released, B-6-F and B-8-M formed a pair. B-9, an adult male, and B-16, a young female, had been traveling together in the Chamberlain Basin area about fifty miles north of their original release site since early April; and B-10-F and B-5-M had paired up and were staking claim to a territory along the Idaho-Montana border.[20]

The Yellowstone wolves (which were given R-designations that distinguished them from their Idaho counterparts) were doing equally well for the most part. Those wolves had been in acclimation pens in groups— the Crystal Creek, Rose Creek, and Soda Butte packs—and, much to the biologists' surprise, the animals were tentative about leaving the pens when they were released in late March 1995. The biologists left food outside the pens for a time to help the wolves make the transition, and they didn't all leave their pen at the same time, hanging around for up to ten days before venturing out into the park. Even though the wolves were released after the February mating season, two of the three packs had bred while they were still in the pens. Wolf R-10, the male of the Rose Creek pair, was illegally shot in late April on national forestland outside the park. A couple of days later his mate, R-9, gave birth to eight pups— four males and four females. Without a mate to help her, park biologists supplied the widowed wolf with deer and elk carcasses for a time. Ultimately, because she was using an aboveground pit den in an area where humans might stumble upon her, she and her pups were recaptured and brought back to the Rose Creek acclimation pen, where she raised them in safety until they were all released again in October. At that point, between the thirteen surviving wolves released in March and pups of the year, the wolf population in the Yellowstone recovery area was now twenty-two. Shortly after R-9 and her pups were released, male wolf R-8 from the Crystal Creek pack joined the Rose Creek pack and became her new mate.[21]

While things on the ground were off to a very promising start, the legal wrangling was still ongoing. And, curiously enough, agriculture was not the only enemy of the wolf reintroduction. One major environmental organization, along with several smaller ones, were also suing to stop the program, but for very different reasons.

Judge Downes had actually joined three independent lawsuits attempting to stop the reintroduction, and the three cases were collectively known as *Wyoming Farm Bureau Federation v. Babbitt* (Bruce Babbitt was President Bill Clinton's secretary of the interior at the time). In addition to the Farm Bureau, the other plaintiffs included two Pinedale, Wyoming, residents, James and Cat Urbigkits. On the environmental side were the National Audubon Society, Predator Project, Sinapu, and the Gray Wolf Committee, represented by the Sierra Club Legal Defense Fund (now Earthjustice).

The plaintiffs argued that the introduction of "Canadian" gray wolves violated the Endangered Species Act by reintroducing a different subspecies of wolf, *Canis lupus occidentalis*, and it would threaten the existence of the wolf subspecies native to the northern Rocky Mountains, *Canis lupus irremotus*—which they believed still roamed the region, albeit in low numbers—by potential interbreeding. They also charged that the federal government should have released wolves outside the current range of wolves, using the occasional reports of wolves in central Idaho and Yellowstone National Park that wolves were still present in those areas where the experimental Canadian wolves were to be released, and finally that since the reintroduced wolves could not be geographically separated from the "current populations," there was no way to keep the two subspecies from interbreeding.[22]

The motive of the Farm Bureau was clearly to keep wolves out of the northern Rockies. The Urbigkitses were amateur scientists who had been devoting their time to searching for wolves in Yellowstone and Wyoming and claimed that releasing "Canadian" wolves would ruin their study of the "native" wolf. Unlike the other plaintiffs, the conservation groups' goal was different. First, they were only challenging the central Idaho wolf release, not the Yellowstone one. Their contention was that wolves had been naturally recolonizing central Idaho on their own and would eventually establish a population, just as wolves had in northwestern Montana in the mid-1980s. Drawing on opinions by USFWS biologists in the mid 1990s, who felt that there was already a population of about fifteen wolves in central Idaho, that they were probably breeding, and that packs that had formed from naturally dispersing animals would be documented within five years, the "anti-reintroduction" conservation groups contended that as the plan now stood, mixing "nonessential, experimental" wolves with naturally occurring wolves would result in the latter losing their endangered status. The conservation plaintiffs wanted the USFWS to keep naturally occurring wolves and wolf populations in central Idaho fully protected under the Endangered Species Act, as the northwestern Montana wolves were. The Farm Bureau, on the other hand, wanted all the wolves that were released by the federal government removed from protection should they prevail in their lawsuit.[23]

While the wolf reintroduction was ongoing, the term "Canadian wolf" among recovery opponents came to describe more than their geographic origin. It was meant to convey the idea that these were foreign wolves, a nonnative invasive species that didn't belong here. Even worse, opponents said, was that the Canadian *Canis lupus occidentalis* was larger, more aggressive, and vicious, making them an even greater threat to society than the northern Rocky Mountains native *Canis lupus irremotus*. Parsing the nonnative versus native issue is a little tricky.

In their classic 1944 book *The Wolves of North America*, Young and Goldman identified twenty-three separate subspecies of wolves, including *occidentalis* and *irremotus*. However, over time, wolf researchers have trended away from recognizing so many distinct subspecies of an animal capable of dispersing large distances, five hundred miles and more, to establish new packs and new territories, spreading their genes as they go. Take, for example, Pluie, a female wolf captured and radio-collared by wolf biologist Paul Paquet near Banff National Park, Alberta, Canada, on June 6, 1991. Between the time of her capture and December 1995, Pluie (French for "Rain"), traveling at least for a time with two unidentified, un-collared wolves, roamed across sixty-two thousand square miles of Alberta, British Columbia; Montana; Idaho; and Washington. In Montana she went as far east as Shelby and in Washington to the eastern outskirts of Spokane. If circumstances had been right and she had encountered a suitable mate, Pluie could have formed the first Washington wolf pack in decades—and years before the reintroduction as well. But that didn't happen, and despite that her travels took her through excellent wolf habitat with abundant prey, Pluie turned back north into British Columbia, where she was shot on December 18, 1995.[24]

"To me the issue of these being 'Canadian' wolves is garbage," Mark Hebblewhite, assistant professor and wolf researcher with the University of Montana's Wildlife Biology Program, told me when I put the question to him. "I always remind people that wolves reintroduced themselves first, to Glacier National Park and the Northern Continental Divide ecosystem from contiguous populations to the north, including Banff. These wolves from northern Montana have then gone on to send dispersing wolves themselves south into Idaho and Yellowstone, which have then gone on to send their genes as far as Colorado, Utah, and Oregon. Moreover, wolves coming into eastern Washington and Oregon could very well be from wolves dispersing south from the Coast Mountain Range in British Columbia and not even from the northern Rockies. On the Canadian side of the border, there are very few differences between wolves over thousands of kilometers in the Canadian Rockies from Waterton to Jasper, so by logical extension, because wolves were introduced from outside Jasper in 1995 to Idaho and Yellowstone, and these wolves do not differ genetically from those that recolonized naturally, there are few differences genetically between wolves in Canada and those here."

From the USFWS's perspective, the Canadian Rockies were the best source of wolves for the reintroduction because of the similarities between terrain and prey—and they were available. Further, since the wolf that we know today reinvaded North America from Asia more than half a million years ago, populating the continent with packs as they moved southward, the Canadian wolves were essentially the same stock as those pioneering animals. Additionally, given enough time, wolves from Canada would eventually move into the northwestern United States and reestablish populations on their own, as they had already done in northwestern Montana. The reintroduction would just speed that process along by a couple of decades. Finally, from a practical point of view, unlike the red wolf and Mexican wolf, the ranchers' and Biological Survey's eradication program in the northern Rockies had been deadly successful. There were simply no more *Canis lupus irremotus* left to reintroduce.

Although the lawsuit was still pending, the court had denied the request for an injunction, so the USFWS continued to move ahead with the reintroduction and the second round of releases. In January 1996, twenty more wolves, this time from British Columbia, were released near Dagger Falls along the border of the Frank Church River of No Return in central Idaho,[25] and another seventeen in Yellowstone National Park. Also, in late winter 1997, ten wolf pups from northwestern Montana were released in Yellowstone after Wildlife Services killed their parents, which were chronically attacking livestock.[26]

The reintroduction was going largely as planned, and the wolves were taking to their new homes quite nicely. Then, on December 12, 1997, Judge Downes ruled on *Wyoming Farm Bureau Federation v. Babbitt*—the reintroduction was illegal and all the released wolves had to go. The future of wolves in the northern Rockies, and the vision of a future northern Rockies with wolves, was now in serious doubt.

Extensive blocks of wild country, like the Frank Church River of No Return Wilderness, was a major reason central Idaho was chosen for wolf reintroduction. Photo by Jim Yuskavitch

FOUR

Idaho and the Nez Perce Wolves

A hard early-morning rain pounded the metal roof of the doublewide trailer on the forest service compound in McCall, Idaho, that served as the headquarters for the Nez Perce's gray wolf recovery program. It was a Monday in late June 2005, and inside, project leader Curt Mack and his crew of four biologists and technicians were in a short staff meeting before heading into the field for their next ten-day "hitches" to monitor wolf packs in the central Idaho forests. Wolf biologist Jim Holyan went over recent confirmed or suspected wolf depredations on livestock—it was summer, and ranchers had turned their sheep and cattle loose on public forestlands where they were vulnerable to attacks. Curt Mack noted that the USFWS had just put out a news release that an Idaho wolf had been illegally shot. Some Japanese tourists witnessed the crime, and although they didn't speak much English, they were able to give investigators a decent description of the perpetrator and his vehicle, but no license plate number.

By the time the staff meeting was over, the rain was coming down harder, reminding the crew they had a few more things to take care of in the office before setting out. I, a visiting writer, was assigned to tag along with Jim Holyan for the week, camping out in the Clearwater National Forest, checking in on the local wolf packs, and perhaps catching and collaring a wolf or two. USDA Forest Service workers had been reporting signs of intense wolf activity—tracks and scats—in a particular area of the Hemlock Ridge pack's territory, and Holyan thought it might indicate a previously unknown rendezvous site. He wanted to check that out. We were also going to poke around in the territory of the El Dorado pack and try to get a radio collar on one of the animals. So far, all the pack's members had eluded attempts to catch them.

41

The 1997 legal ruling that wolf recovery supporters feared had put an end to their grand plans had been overturned. The judge who ruled that the "Canadian" wolves and their progeny had to be removed from the central Idaho and Yellowstone recovery areas had approved a stay while his decision was appealed. The National Wildlife Federation and Defenders of Wildlife joined the government's appeal in support of the USFWS's recovery plan along with the National Audubon Society, which, under heavy criticism by its members for its participation in the earlier lawsuit, switched sides. On January 13, 2000, the Tenth Circuit Court reversed Judge Downes's decision, finding that the USFWS had properly followed the Endangered Species Act in reintroducing wolves in the northern Rockies, that the original wolf subspecies no longer existed and it was therefore appropriate to use wolves from Canada as a substitute, and that the possibility of a few lone wolves in the region did not constitute a population and therefore should not prevent the federal government from attempting to reestablish a new, viable population. The reintroduction had been put back on solid legal ground.[1]

The Nez Perce tribe was a supporter of bringing wolves back to Idaho from the beginning and a partner in wolf recovery with the USFWS. The federal government never needed permission from the state governments of Idaho, Montana, and Wyoming to restore wolves, since they were being released on federally managed lands—national park and national forest lands to be specific. But practically speaking, once recovered, the wolves were going to disperse outside the official recovery areas, and the plan was for the states to partner with the USFWS during the recovery period and then, once the wolf population was considered biologically recovered, take over complete management responsibility after writing wolf management plans approved by the federal government that would maintain each state's wolf population at a viable level. The recovery goal of thirty breeding pairs evenly divided among the three recovery areas in Idaho, Montana, and Wyoming for three years in a row was reached in December 2002. In mid-2005 Idaho had about four hundred wolves, well above the minimum required population of one hundred, and the USFWS wanted to take them off the ESA list. That year, the transition of wolf management from the federal government to the states was also in progress—Idaho and Montana had produced approved wolf management plans, but the feds wouldn't sign off on the Wyoming plan because it didn't meet their minimum criteria, and it was gumming up the transition for everyone. But in the early stages of wolf recovery, it was Idaho that had refused to cooperate with the USFWS. Angry at the federal government's plan to restore Idaho's wolves, the Republican-dominated Idaho state legislature rejected a plan in 1995 that would have allowed the Idaho Department of Fish and Game to take the lead role in the wolf recovery and stopped the state from having any involvement. So the Nez Perce tribe stepped forward to do that job.[2]

As I sat in his office while I waited for Jim Holyan to attend to a few things before we headed out the door and into the field, Curt Mack told me a little about the Nez Perce tribe's role in wolf recovery and their cultural connections to these creatures.

The Nez Perce tribe was involved in the wolf recovery effort going back to the early 1990s when the USFWS was writing the wolf reintroduction environmental impact statement. "The Nez Perce wanted to become involved because of their spiritual and traditional reverence for the wolf," Mack explained. "And when the state backed out, that left the door open for the tribe."

"The tribal perspective is 180 degrees from the non-tribal position on wolves," Mack continued. "The Nez Perce identify with the wolf." To the Nez Perce, wolves were an important animal that helped teach them how to hunt, raise their families, and act socially with one another. Traditional Nez Perce society was structured similarly to wolf packs, with clans that hunted separately but came together regularly and were part of an extended family. When young Nez Perce (*Nimi 'ipuu*) men went on vision quests, to have a wolf (*himeen*) become your spiritual guardian (*Weyekin*) was especially powerful. Tribal members with "wolf" in their name—still common today—often became leaders and other persons of importance.[3]

The traditional Nez Perce homeland was north-central Idaho but also included parts of southeastern Washington and northeastern Oregon—an area of about eleven million acres. In 1855 the Nez Perce signed a treaty giving up most of those lands for a 7.6-million acre reservation. But a growing population of European-American settlers, along with the discovery of gold in north-central Idaho, pressured the federal government into reducing the reservation in 1863 to about one-tenth of its original size. Ten years later, another Nez Perce reservation was established by the federal government in Oregon's Wallowa Valley but was dissolved in 1877, leading to the brief Nez Perce War and the famous running battle between US troops and Young Joseph and his band, who resisted being transferred to the Idaho reservation that culminated with their capture in Montana's Bear Paw Mountains by General Nelson Miles.[4]

Mack explained how the Nez Perce view their tribal experience as not unlike that of the wolves': persecuted and driven from their homeland. "The tribe sees a parallel with their history and the wolves," said Mack. "When the West was settled, the impediments were wolves, bison, and Indians, and they got rid of them."

It took a little doing, and lots of conversations between the tribe and the USFWS to convince officials to hand over a leading role in Idaho wolf recovery to an unknown entity, but in the end the federal government agreed, bolstered by the obvious unwillingness of the state to help. The tribe developed an Idaho wolf recovery management plan, and in 1995 the USFWS signed off on it, contracting responsibility for wolf recovery fieldwork and biology in the central Idaho recovery area to the Nez

Perce. The USFWS continued to be in charge of policy oversight and law enforcement and, along with Wildlife Services, dealing with problem wolves.

The fieldwork was a critical piece of the recovery effort, not just for central Idaho but in Yellowstone National Park and northwestern Montana as well. Counting wolves, determining where wolves were dispersing, keeping track of where and when new packs formed, how many pups were born each year, how many survived, overall mortality rates, and a running tally of population numbers were all critical pieces of information to help determine when the wolves were biologically recovered—the end game of the reintroduction effort.

In addition to the fieldwork, Mack and Holyan also did a lot of public outreach. They went out to meet with ranchers, trying to get to know them on a personal basis, and held public meetings in areas that had wolf packs to encourage local residents to work with the tribe's wolf program. "Whenever a wolf pack moved into an area, we would set up a meeting with the folks in that area," Mack explained. "When it comes to wolves, rural communities don't react well to surprises—they want to know when a wolf pack is in their area."

Despite the outreach, which Mack had thought was having a positive effect on public attitudes, Idaho was seeing a rise in anti-wolf sentiment and rhetoric, from sport hunting groups in particular. One of those groups was the Idaho Anti-Wolf Coalition, which Mack felt was being very politically effective even though "its wolf biology was all off" and was dealing mostly in propaganda. Another was Wyoming Sportsmen for Fish and Wildlife, which was playing a major role in shaping the Wyoming Department of Fish and Game's unwillingness to develop a state wolf plan acceptable to the federal government. "Their thing is trophy heads," said Mack.

What was driving this anti-wolf movement of course was the fact that wolves eat elk, and elk hunting is a very popular, traditional outdoor activity in the northern Rocky Mountains. Hunters didn't like the competition. And in Idaho, wolves were elk specialists, elk making up 80 percent of their diet.

But, Mack explained, there was much more at work here than a simple zero-sum game of "every elk killed by a wolf was one less for a hunter." Elk populations in the northern Rockies had been increasing since the great wildfires in Idaho and Montana in the early twentieth century that burned the region's mature forests and replaced it with younger growth that provided elk and deer with more, and more nutritious, food. But the forests had been growing back. The returning mature forests supported fewer elk, and their populations were slowly declining. The wolf reintroduction coincided with this decline in elk numbers, and hunters blamed the wolves. "Wolves are just a scapegoat," said Mack. "If you don't get your elk, you blame it on the wolves. It's a social issue that depends on your value system and whether you are willing to share elk with wolves. From a biological standpoint, we have wolves and we have elk. The wolves and the elk will figure it out."

Despite Mack's concern and disappointment over the increasing opposition to and deliberate politicization of wolves by anti-wolf groups, the Idaho wolves themselves had been faring quite well. By the end of that year, there were fifty-nine resident wolf packs in Idaho, ranging from almost to the Canadian border (any wolves north of Interstate 90 in Idaho were considered part of the northwest Montana endangered population) south to Interstate 84, bounded on the west by the Snake River and east to the Montana and Wyoming borders. Field researchers saw about 370 wolves and estimated the total end of the year wolf population at 512 animals. There were also eleven packs along the Idaho-Wyoming-Montana borders that spent at least some of their time in Idaho. Of the fifty-nine known packs, forty packs had a total of 123 pups that year, two of which didn't survive.

Of the forty-three wolves known to have died in 2005, twenty-six were legally killed by Wildlife Services or ranchers because they were attacking and killing livestock, ten were illegally shot, six died from other human causes, and one died of natural causes. Wolves killed, or probably killed, 26 cattle, 218 sheep, and 9 dogs over the course of the year.[5]

Mack was clearly happy with how the wolves and the wolf restoration were faring, even with problem wolves and hostility from hunters and ranchers. "The Nez Perce have always been in favor of wolf recovery and have never wavered," he said. "That translates into 110 percent support for what I'm trying to do here.

"And," he added, "central Idaho is a wolf production machine."

It was after noon before Jim Holyan and I finally got on the road. By that time, the rain had settled into a drizzle as we headed north on Highway 95 and through the Nez Perce Indian Reservation. The farther north we went, the more signs of anti-wolf sentiment we saw, with SUVs and pickups sporting bumper stickers that proclaimed "Shoot, Shovel and Shut Up" and "Canadian Wolves, Smoke a Pack a Day." At Kamiah, we dropped my truck at the USDA Forest Service district office parking lot. I dumped my gear into Holyan's silver government-issued Ford F-250, and we drove east, through Pierce and into the Clearwater National Forest and Hemlock Ridge.

Jim Holyan, in his early forties and originally from Washington State, had worked as a biologist for the Nez Perce Wolf Recovery Program since 2001, and as a seasonal before that. These ten-day "hitches" were a regular part of his summer wolf fieldwork.

The fieldwork followed the patterns and activities of the wolves. In April and May the biologists did a lot of flying to locate the signals of radio-collared wolves and find denning females. In June the packs are working out of the denning area and "rendezvous" areas, using them as a base from which they launch their hunting forays, stash the pups, and regroup. By mid-July the packs start to become more mobile, coming and going more often and traveling a little farther. The pups will weigh about forty to forty-five pounds by late July and early August and are fully capable of traveling with the adult wolves. By fall the pack will have abandoned the rendezvous site and the wolves will be roaming and hunting throughout their territory through the winter until the next breeding season.

Holyan's and his colleagues' fieldwork through this period included finding dens and rendezvous sites; finding packs and counting the number of adults, subadults, and pups; and occasionally catching a wolf and fitting it with a radio collar. During winter, if there was extra money in the budget, they might hire a biologist to do some snow tracking, but mostly that season was spent compiling and analyzing data collected during the spring and summer and writing their annual wolf reports.

It was getting to be late afternoon by the time we turned up the forest road toward where the possible new Hemlock Ridge pack rendezvous site was suspected. The rain tapered off a bit more, and although it was getting late and we still needed to find a place to camp, Holyan wanted to see if he could raise a signal from the pack on his radio receiver.

The Nez Perce wolf recovery team first became aware of the Hemlock pack in 2003 after some forest service employees reported seeing a lot of wolf sign in the Fidelity Creek area. Mack sent one of his field workers, Adam Gall, out to have a look. He found tracks, spotted pups (the den located in a broken cedar snag on the forest edge), and managed to trap and radio-collar an adult. But during the winter of 2003–04, someone illegally shot the collared wolf along with another wolf, and the pack went "off line." Without at least one pack member wearing a radio collar to reveal its position, wolf packs are very difficult to virtually impossible to keep tabs on, so Gall went back that summer and caught and collared two more adults, a male, designated B-210, and a female, B-207. B-210 was believed to be the pack's alpha male.

"Most wolves in a trap are very submissive," Holyan explained to me. "They want to hide from you and don't bark at you. But sometimes we get one that is aggressive and says, 'Bring it on.'" That was the behavior that marked B-210 as the probable breeding male.

The Hemlock pack's home range spanned the Fidelity Creek area south into the Musselshell region. (In 2005 the average pack territory in Idaho was 350 to 400 square miles, but later, as the wolf population grew and more packs formed, territory sizes got smaller.) The pack occasionally encountered domestic livestock but hadn't been inclined to cause trouble; their territory held a high population of white-tailed deer, making them less dependent on elk for prey than typical Idaho wolves. To date, no members of the Hemlock pack had been known to disperse to other areas, and they did not appear to have pups in 2004.

Pulling over on a spur road, Holyan swept the air with the radio receiver antenna, and the signal he picked up—a solid, steady series of beeps mixed with some background static—was B-210. "That's a good sign," Holyan said, giving me the thumbs-up. But it was drizzling steadily now, starting to get dark, and time to find camp.

Early the next morning, we were parked along the same spur road. A hard rain had driven us back into the truck, but not before once again finding B-210's signal. We couldn't locate the female, B-207, but the fact that the alpha male was hanging around in the vicinity of the suspected rendezvous site was enough to justify an exploratory hike through the area—at least once the rain let up a bit.

In the meantime, while raindrops bounced off the truck's hood and roof and the windows slowly fogged up, we talked about the current state of wolf management in Idaho.

Although Idaho had initially refused to cooperate with the USFWS on the wolf recovery effort and had only been minimally involved in the 1995 and 1996 wolf releases, recovery was now essentially a done deal and Idaho wanted to take over wolf management. The Idaho state legislature relented in its opposition to the state being involved with wolves and passed legislation allowing the Idaho Department of Fish and Game to develop a wolf management plan acceptable to the federal government, which it did. Montana had also written an acceptable wolf plan, but Wyoming's plan designated wolves as an unprotected predator that could be shot on sight in most of the state, and the federal government would not approve it. This was holding up delisting wolves from the Endangered Species Act in the northern Rocky Mountain recovery areas, even though the populations had met the recovery criteria. Wyoming was suing the federal government to try and force the government to approve the plan. In the meantime, to allow Montana and Idaho to transition into taking over wolf management, the federal government changed the ESA's 10(j) rule in February to liberalize when the two states with approved wolf plans could lethally control wolves, including allowing landowners and ranchers to kill wolves on the spot that were caught attacking livestock and guard dogs on both private and public lands and for states to reduce wolf numbers where they were causing "unacceptable" impacts on elk and deer populations to optimize hunting opportunities.[6]

The rule also allowed states to form agreements to manage wolves cooperatively with Native American tribes that had written an approved wolf management plan that was clearly intended to allow the Nez Perce tribe to continue its work with wolves. In May 2005 the state of Idaho and the tribe signed a memorandum of agreement giving it the right to monitor wolves within the McCall Sub-Region and Clearwater Region.[7]

The liberalization of the 10(j) rule expanding the circumstances when wolves could be killed and who could kill them worried Holyan, especially if Idaho Fish and Game wasn't willing to "stand up to Wildlife Services" when it wanted to kill an entire wolf pack in response to attacks on livestock.

"It's my personal opinion that there will be less tolerance for depredating wolves once Idaho Fish and Game takes over wolf management," he told me. "I think we will be headed in that direction. If wolves are in your backyard and eating your sheep, that's one thing; but if you have wolves running around on public land and you turn three thousand sheep out there, you are going to have depredations."

When I talked with Ed Bangs, northern Rockies wolf recovery coordinator for the USFWS, he was far more optimistic, telling me, "The states can do a better job of managing wolves than the federal government can." Steve Nadeau, wolf coordinator for the Idaho Department of Fish and Game at the time, was also happy to see the transfer of wolf management authority, especially "regarding livestock and ungulates." A particular concern then was a decline in elk numbers in Idaho's Lolo region that Idaho Fish and Game blamed on wolves. But since the wolves were not yet delisted, despite the new rule, the state still needed to develop a plan justifying killing wolves in the area and have it approved by the federal government before it could undertake any control actions.

Nadeau also told me there was a rising frustration among many people in Idaho that the wolves weren't delisted when the federal government had said they would be. It was going on three years since wolves in the three recovery areas had reached biological recovery; the delisting process was all balled up in policy and legal maneuvering, and he maintained that was leading to increasing anti-wolf sentiment. "Once we are allowed to manage and control the wolf population, there will be more acceptance," Nadeau told me. "Now that wolves are recovered, we should be managing these populations."

Abruptly the downpour stopped and we were out of the truck, dressed head to toe in our rain gear, plunging into the heavy timber and downed logs, then out onto an old logging road above a clear-cut, downslope through the logged forest into a small stream drainage, all the while homing in on B-210's radio signal. Pushing our way through a meadow that turned into dense alder thickets and wet swaths of thimbleberry, we came to a small stream at the bottom of the draw. It was just the kind of place wolves look for in a typical rendezvous site—a wet meadow with a reliable water supply along with some nearby timber for cover.

As we approached the stream, signs of wolf activity became apparent. Holyan pointed to some wolf scat at our feet, and then flattened vegetation where wolves had made trails. He put his finger to his lips, motioning me to keep quiet and stay close. Now there were tracks in the mud, first of pups, then adults, then a "large" adult track.

There was wolf sign all around us—scat, tracks, and trails. Moving as quietly as we could—difficult to do with our rain gear making that

A wolf daybed on the Hemlock Ridge wolf pack's rendezvous site in the Clearwater National Forest, Idaho. Photo by Jim Yuskavitch

swishing noise with each movement of our legs and arms—we crossed the stream, crawling under alder branches as we went, to the edge of a thick stand of small firs. On a well-used wolf trail that skirted the trees was a round, red plastic object that looked like it might have started out as some kind of container lid. The wolves had found it someplace, brought it back to their rendezvous site, and it was now a chew toy—dented, dinged, and punctured with tooth marks.

We ducked into the trees. They were so thick, blocking out so much sunlight, there was virtually no understory vegetation. "This is the perfect place for wolves to bed down during the day," Holyan whispered to me. He had barely finished his sentence when, not thirty yards away, a wolf stood looking at us, startled to find us there. It was dark gray, I think, because it vanished almost as quickly as it appeared, noiselessly into the thimbleberry and fern. This was definitely the rendezvous site we were looking for.

We sat down on the ground under the trees, which gave us some cover from the drizzle, to wait awhile and see what might happen. It was the perfect place for wolves to rest during the day. As we quietly looked around, there were day beds all over—shallow depressions on the forest floor about three feet in diameter, just the right size to accommodate a curled up, sleeping wolf. Holyan picked up a piece of hoof, maybe from a deer fawn, but he couldn't tell for sure.

He leaned over and said to me in a low voice, "There has been a lot of activity here. There have been wolves walking all over the place. There are probably wolves bedded down all around us."

He was right. About forty-five minutes into our vigil, we began to hear wolf pups squealing and barking to our backs. We sat tight, listening for another half hour or so, and then made our way upslope out onto an old, overgrown road in more-open forest. Here Holyan picked up B-210's signal not far off. So we sat down along the road, waiting to see who might come along.

We were in a forest of mostly firs and spruce, but cedars seemed to dominate some of the higher ridgelines. The forest floor was lush with thick and expansive swaths of ferns and thimbleberry. Wildflower season was coming on as well, with bunchberry, columbine, shooting stars, bear grass, and paintbrush in bloom and standing out brightly against all the greenery made even more intense and saturated by the rainy weather and subdued sunlight.

Nearly an hour later things remained quiet except for the sound of lightly falling rain on leaves. So Holyan thought he would try to rouse the wolves a little with some howling. He stood up, cupped his hands around his mouth, and let out three long, deep-throated and forlorn sounding howls. Almost immediately a chorus of responding howls emanated from the forest perhaps fifty to seventy yards off. They carried on for a full minute then quit. It sounded like a hundred wolves to me. Holyan's more practiced ear put it at two to four adults and as many pups. We hung around awhile longer, and the pack began to howl again, this time without any prodding from us. But they were farther off now, indicating they were moving away.

More than satisfied that we had found the Hemlock pack's new rendezvous site, Holyan recorded GPS coordinates in his Rite in the Rain all-weather notebook and we walked back to the rig.

We had gone in at 8:30 and were out by 2:30, enough time to drive into Pierce to look at some more detailed maps at the forest service workstation and have milkshakes at the Wink and a Smile Family Diner. Back on a spur road in the Clearwater National Forest, we spent a second rainy night sleeping in the covered bed of the pickup. Holyan wanted to make one last check of the rendezvous site in the morning before we moved on, where we would have a remarkable close-up experience with a wolf—one that he had never before experienced.

Early Wednesday morning we were back on the edge of the rendezvous site, standing along the small stream, when a gray wolf suddenly appeared on the trail that bordered the fir stand. He was perhaps twenty yards away, above us, a dark gray wolf that Holyan estimated to be a younger animal, about eighty pounds or so. Instead of fleeing upon seeing us the way yesterday's wolf had done, he stopped and cocked his ears forward, staring at us intently. Then he did a funny thing. He flat-

A member of the Hemlock Ridge pack on its rendezvous site in the Clearwater National Forest, Idaho. Photo by Jim Yuskavitch

tened his ears, lowered his head, stretched his front legs out, raised his haunches, and began wagging his tail, all the while watching us closely. When we didn't respond the way he expected, he quickly lost interest and walked down the trail, right by us and out of sight, without giving a second look. Holyan was a bit dumbfounded by the incident. "Normally a wolf will take a quick look at a person, but I've never seen anything like that before," he said.

El Dorado Creek is Lewis and Clark country, and on September 19, 1805, the Corps of Discovery had camped in a grove of cedars, now called the Lewis and Clark Grove, which was not far from where we pitched our tents near the El Dorado Creek trailhead.[8]

Not much was known about the El Dorado pack at the time. A local outfitter had reported wolf sign in the area in 2003, so Mack sent one of his biologists who heard howling and almost caught one. In spring 2005 Nez Perce biologists came back, found tracks, and set some traps, but with no results. For the most part, the El Dorado pack was seldom seen or heard.

That night, as if to purposely taunt us, the El Dorado pack gathered not far from our camp and began to howl. Holyan estimated them to be no more than one-quarter mile away and, based on the tenor of the howls, included a pup or two. They serenaded us in four separate suites through the night and early-morning hours, and I wrote it down—beginning at 10:21 p.m., again starting at 12:55 a.m., another at 3:58 a.m., and one last time commencing at 5:45 a.m.

The pack's only known rendezvous site was not far from our camp, and we decided to check it out. The weather had finally turned warm and sunny, but the hike to the rendezvous meadow was a wet one down a flooded trail, and when we got to our destination there was no sign that that pack was using it this year. But we knew they were around, and Holyan decided to set some traps.

Setting a steel jaw trap (with offset teeth to minimize injury) for a wolf is a deliberate and careful process. Leaning on a mat and wearing gloves to minimize contaminating the set with human scent, Holyan first dug a hole deep enough to hold both the trap and a grapple (the grapple being two hooks attached to a chain, which is attached to the trap—when the wolf is caught and tries to run off, the grapple becomes entangled on brush and other vegetation). The grapple goes into the hole first, the trap on top. Some plastic wrap over the pan that serves as the trap's trigger keeps dirt from getting underneath. Then he sprinkles dirt over the set, filtered though a wire mesh attached to a frame, and scatters some pine needles around that gives the whole scene a natural appearance. A bit of scent concocted from coyote gland and urine is the final touch. The idea is that the wolf will smell the scent and snoop around the hidden trap long enough to step on it. Holyan put out five sets, three on the trail and two on the road passing our camp, where we found a set of wolf tracks that weren't there the previous evening. If he caught a wolf, Holyan would use a jabbing stick to inject it with Telazol, an immobilizing sedative drug developed specifically for dogs and cats, so that he could work on the animal without harm to either one of them. But the El Dorado wolves had triumphed again. When we checked our trap line the next morning, we had caught nothing, although a wolf had left a footprint within inches of one trap's pan.

That night, my last in the field before I headed home in the morning, a single wolf began howling outside our El Dorado Creek camp—closer this time, it seemed to me. The Nez Perce biologists would eventually catch and collar an El Dorado wolf, but for the moment I lay in my sleeping bag not thinking anything in particular, just listening to the lone wolf from that elusive, mystery pack howling in the night forest. The wolf started at midnight and howled off and on for about half an hour before he stopped. Then I drifted off to sleep.

Nez Perce wolf biologist Jim Holyan sets a trap for a wolf along a forest road in the territory of the El Dorado wolf pack, Clearwater National Forest, Idaho. Photo by Jim Yuskavitch

FIVE

Pushback

The wolves surprised everyone with how well they were making a comeback in the northern Rockies, even among the professional wildlife biologists. Perhaps it was because they had been extirpated from the Western landscape when much of the country was still frontier and most wolves only remained in the wild country of Alaska and Canada, giving the impression they could only survive in remote wilderness, far removed from humans. But that wasn't quite true. The case in point was the Minnesota wolves, with seven hundred to one thousand animals in the northern part of the state and Isle Royale when wolves were listed under the Endangered Species Act in 1974. Although they lived in relatively remote country, the real reason those wolves survived as viable populations was because there were not enough domestic livestock in the region to make them worth the trouble of exterminating.[1]

Ed Bangs, Wolf Recovery Coordinator for the USFWS, summed it up succinctly when I interviewed him in 2006, telling me, "The only reason wolves became extinct in the lower forty-eight states was because people killed too many of them. The only reason they came back is that the ESA kept people from killing them off." The legal protections provided by the Endangered Species Act had been key to the wolves' survival and recovery once they were released back into central Idaho and Yellowstone in 1995 and 1996.

In 2008 there were about 1,645 gray wolves in the three northern Rocky Mountains recovery areas—an 8 percent population increase from the previous year. There were 914 wolves in central Idaho, 449 in the Greater Yellowstone Area, and 282 in northwestern Montana. Of the 217 established packs with territories, there were ninety-five breeding pairs; the eighth year there were at least thirty breeding pairs evenly distributed throughout the three recovery areas, and the population was considered to be biologically recovered by the federal government.[2]

The ranks of the original wolves released in 1995 and 1996 were thinning. In 2004 the oldest surviving wolf from those first releases died. B-2 was the second gray wolf from Canada released into central Idaho in 1995, just after B-5. A large gray wolf with streaks of beige, B-2 was about four years old when he was released. Nez Perce students had named him Chat Chaat, meaning "older brother" in their language. Although wearing a radio collar, he wandered extensively through central Idaho, and his signal was only picked up eleven times in five years, so much of his wanderings remained unknown to biologists. He and the female wolf B-66 mated and formed the Wildhorse Pack, whose territory was the upper Big Lost River and Copper basin. In January 2002 an elk killed B-66. Rather than taking on a new mate, Nez Perce wolf recovery team leader Curt Mack described to me how B-2 led his pack on a long and unusual trek. "The pack went on a big walkabout outside their territory," Mack related. "As they were moving, pack members started to drop out. As he came back out, we think the alpha male was by himself." B-2 was indeed by himself when he came out from his random wanderings, but he eventually found a new mate and formed the Castle Peak Pack in the White Cloud Mountains, where his radio collar began emitting a mortality signal in February 2004, indicating that he hadn't moved in some time and was probably dead. Biologists found him on April 15 when the snow melted enough to get up into the high country. A short distance away from his body was a dead bull elk. Whether the elk kicked him and the wolf died of internal injuries or he just dropped dead of old age, the biologists couldn't determine. B-2 was 13.8 years old—ancient for a wild wolf. At that point there were only three wolves left from the original releases.[3]

The very last survivor of those 1995–96 Idaho releases was B-7, who was found dead along a highway near Salmon in March 2007. He had been hit by a car, probably while feeding on a nearby road-killed deer. B-7 was twelve years old. That year there were about 650 wolves in Idaho.[4]

The original Idaho wolves were gone now, but their offspring, and the offspring of the Yellowstone and Montana wolves, had been carrying on splendidly. By 2010 there were at least 1,651 wolves in 244 packs, including 111 breeding pairs in the northern Rockies. The wolves were doing so well that there had been no need for any more releases after 1996 that had been called for in the recovery plan. The USFWS's 2010 wolf population estimate also included eastern Oregon and Washington, which now had wolves as well. In 2008 Oregon confirmed its first wolf pack, which had an unknown number of pups. That pack's breeding pair had dispersed into Oregon from Idaho. Washington also confirmed its first wolf pack that year, which had dispersed down from Canada and had six pups. In 2010 Oregon had two known packs and Washington at least three.[5, 6]

When wolves are around they leave lots of signs, such as these tracks in the Clearwater National Forest, Idaho. Photo by Jim Yuskavitch

Key to this success were the wolves' fecundity, adaptability, and resilience, combined with critical protection from humans with ill will toward them. Mating between January and April, wolves are prolific. In any given year, 60 to 90 percent of adult females will give birth to pups (after a two-month gestation period), which generally happens in April in the northern Rockies. Each pack may have one to three breeding females, although only one litter is typically born each year. Litter size can be as many as eleven pups, although the average is six.

Coupled with high reproductive potential is dispersing wolves' ability to travel far and fast, crossing geographic barriers that often stop other wildlife species from expanding into new areas. A dispersing wolf can make its way across large expanses of unsuitable habitat until it reaches a place it likes. Dispersal is a critical part of wolf natural history that results in new packs being formed, colonizing new areas and promoting a diversity of gene flow among various populations. Wolves typically disperse from their natal packs when they are one or two years old, although some may take off at nine months while others hang around until they are three or so. These younger animals are essentially temporary pack members who eventually peel off, while older long-term pack members become the breeding pair. Dispersing animals may be former alpha animals, low-ranking pack members, or animals that have been aggressively driven from the pack for one reason or another; they provide the foundation for creating new packs and colonizing or recolonizing new areas. Dispersing wolves may wander until they find a mate or may stake out a territory and wait for a suitable match to come along. Most wolves disperse and join or form new packs within sixty miles of their natal pack, but some travel much farther. These were the factors at work as the wolves reclaimed their old grounds in the northern Rockies and eventually began moving into the Pacific Northwest.[7]

The success of the northern Rocky Mountains restoration and the fact that the wolves were beginning to repopulate surrounding states, as was expected, was great news for wolf advocates. But there were plenty of people who had opposed the return of wolves from the beginning and had continued working to hamper and even undo the recovery. And the opposition had been getting progressively more strident, aggressive, and, in some cases, even threatening.

While there had been opposition to wolf recovery all along from established institutions representing the status quo Western power structure that is politically positioned to reap the lion's share of publicly owned natural resources, such as the livestock industry, one of the first citizen-organized anti-wolf groups in the northern Rockies was the Idaho Anti-Wolf Coalition, founded by Stanley, Idaho, outfitter Ron Gillett in 2006. Gillett, an ardent foe of wolves, has referred to them as an animal of "mass destruction" and stated that "the only way to manage Canadian wolves in Idaho is to get rid of them."[8]

The group's goal was to pass a voter initiative calling for removing all wolves from Idaho "by any means possible" and abolishing Idaho's Office of Species Conservation.[9]

The problem with that strategy was that wolves in Idaho were biologically recovered in 2006 and the federal government was in the process of delisting them and turning their management over to the state, although lawsuits by environmental groups had so far prevented that from happening. If the initiative was successful and the wolves were "removed" from Idaho, presumably shot, then the wolf population would drop below the federal wolf recovery plan's minimum population requirement and the federal government would drop its delisting process and retake management control of the wolves. But the initiative flopped because the coalition couldn't collect enough signatures to qualify for the ballot—and many of the people who signed the petition were not registered Idaho voters.[10]

A key strategy for ballot measure supporters was to get a large number of signatures from hunters angry at the toll wolves were supposedly taking on Idaho's elk, despite the fact that hunter success rates have remained in the 18 to 22 percent range, the same as it had been before wolf reintroduction. In 2006, 99,400 Idaho hunters harvested 20,400 elk— a typical 20 percent success rate.[11] Over the previous three years, Idaho's wolf numbers went from 368 to 512.[12, 13]

Nevertheless, a second attempt to get the wolf removal initiative on the Idaho ballot was launched in 2008, this time spearheaded by another group, Save Our Elk, a hunter-based organization that framed its anti-wolf position as a campaign to protect elk from wolves. But that year the wolves were delisted, although only temporarily, and the state of Idaho took over, also temporarily, wolf management. That deflated support for the initiative, since a key argument in favor of it was that the wolves would never be delisted, the federal government would always be in charge of wolf management, and this was the only way for Idaho residents to take control. As in 2006, this attempt also failed to get enough signatures to make the ballot.

Gillett's animosity toward wolves and wolf recovery advocates put him crosswise with the law on March 25, 2008, when he was arrested for misdemeanor assault against Lynne Stone, director of the wilderness advocacy and pro-wolf Boulder-White Clouds Council. Both Stanley, Idaho, residents, Stone and Gillett had had run-ins before, and this incident involved a scuffle when the two came upon each other at a bridge crossing. As reported by the *Idaho Mountain Express*, Gillette grabbed Stone's neck while attempting to take a camera from her as she was photographing him allegedly verbally abusing her. Gillett countered that he believed Stone was going to hit him with her camera and acted in self-defense. Gillett was arrested and stood trial on August 21, 2008, that ended in a hung jury. Since there were no witnesses and it was the word of one against the other, the jury couldn't reach a verdict.[14, 15]

The fact that the wolves had successfully established themselves, permanently it seemed, across the northern Rocky Mountains landscape didn't deter opponents of wolf recovery from attempts to derail the effort; they were especially focused on lifting as many protections for the animals as possible.

A plethora of anti-wolf websites were launched that presented wolves as dangerous, vicious destroyers of big game and livestock, often illustrated with bloody photos of elk, livestock, and domestic dogs that had allegedly been killed by wolves, along with close-ups of snarling wolves. The wolves, it was claimed, would put ranchers out of business, end hunting as they eradicated the region's elk and deer, attack people, spread deadly diseases, and threaten the rural way of life. The anti-wolf groups' wolf biology and natural history were often shaky and even deliberate misinformation and disinformation, underlain by a common theme of a bullying federal government and big city liberal elitists telling them how to manage their wildlife.

The anti-wolf rhetoric on these websites can be pretty strong. Thoughts on wolves from one site, Survivallife.com, and posted February 19, 2014, include such typical anti-wolf opinions as "Wolves are killing machines." "They kill everything in their path." "There are 100,000 wolves in all the lower 48 states." "They are very intelligent and cunning animals, highly dangerous and lethal." "Wolf packs are decimating the deer, elk and moose populations." "When the prey is gone, we're going to be next." "Is this the government's biological warfare against mankind?"

Chain e-mails are also a major vehicle to spread the anti-wolf message and typically include the same rhetoric found on the anti-wolf websites along with graphic photos of wolf-killed wildlife and livestock and the meme of wolves as dangerous, bloodthirsty killers. These e-mail campaigns often present exaggerated and even false notions about wolf behavior, biology, and impacts on people. One well-known e-mail that circulated on the Internet in 2011 featured a photograph of a large pack of wolves, about twenty-five animals, and put their location in various parts of the northern Rockies—near Kamiah, Idaho; in the vicinity of Soda Springs, Idaho; or just outside of Bozeman, Montana. As is typical of these chain e-mails, they were personalized and often claimed that the photo was taken by a friend or a wolf expert and the sender was helpfully passing it on to educate you about wolves. The intent of course was to frighten people with the idea that large packs of dangerous invasive Canadian wolves were prowling the northern Rockies, making it unsafe to go outdoors. The photograph was eventually identified as a pack of gray wolves in Wood Buffalo National Park, in northern Canada, taken by a British Broadcasting Corporation film crew working on an episode of *Frozen Planet*.[16]

Factual or not, this ongoing anti-wolf campaign has the desired effect of energizing people who didn't like wolves into action and probably, by stimulating fear and anger, brought a certain number of people into the anti-wolf camp that might have initially not had any strong negative feelings about them. Threats to illegally kill wolves were commonplace, with gut-shooting the recommended method, ideally with armor-piercing bullets that would pass though the animal and cause it to suffer as it died slowly. The wolf would also continue to run after being hit, putting distance between where it was shot and where it died, and with no bullet inside the body, little evidence would be left for law enforcement investigators to go on.[17, 18]

Illegal killing of the ESA-protected wolves happened, and still happens, regularly. Between 1999 and 2003 the USFWS reported more than 110 wolves killed by humans in the northern Rockies recovery area that were not officially removed for livestock depredation control purposes.[19] The illegal killing isn't limited to the northern Rockies. Nine protected red wolves were shot in North Carolina in 2013 and a tenth in January 2014.[20] Jim Holyan, the Nez Perce tribe wolf biologist, told me of a wolf pup caught in one of their traps intended for capturing wolves to radio collar; it was found dead and riddled with bullet holes. So there were, and continue to be, people who hate wolves enough to risk the penalty for killing a federally endangered species, which can be as much as a one-hundred-thousand-dollar fine and a year in prison.

But catching and successfully prosecuting wolf poachers is another story, and only a small fraction of them are caught—or even charged. Part of the difficulty in successfully prosecuting people who illegally kill endangered species is due to the US Department of Justice's "McKittrick Policy," which dictates that it will only try cases where it believes it can prove the accused intentionally and knowingly killed a protected species. The policy is derived from the case of Chad McKittrick, a Montana hunter who in 1995 shot and killed a gray wolf near Yellowstone National Park that was part of the reintroduced experimental population. Claiming he mistook the wolf for a rabid dog, McKittrick was nevertheless convicted and lost on appeal as well. McKittrick petitioned to bring his case to the US Supreme Court, but instead, in 1998 the US solicitor general adopted as a new policy for the Department of Justice that it "will not charge or prosecute individuals for the illegal killing of ESA-listed species unless the government can prove the defendant knew the biological identity of the animal he was killing at the time he killed it." This became known as the McKittrick Policy and has significantly limited who is charged for illegally killing wolves.[21, 22]

Judy Calman, staff attorney for the New Mexico Wilderness Alliance, came upon the McKittrick Policy while researching why so few people were being charged with shooting ESA-protected Mexican gray wolves. "There is significant opposition to [Mexican] wolf reintroduction and we kept hearing about wolves getting shot but not about anyone getting prosecuted," she explained to me from her office in Albuquerque. "People were shooting wolves and just saying that they thought it was a coyote because they know that's how you get out of being charged." Between 1998, the year Mexican gray wolves were reintroduced back into the wild as well as the year the McKittrick Policy was implemented, and 2014, more than fifty Mexican wolves have been illegally shot, but only seven people have been charged and just one convicted.

It's not just wolves but all ESA listed animals that are affected by the McKittrick Policy. People shoot grizzly bears and say they thought they were black bears; California condors are claimed to be mistaken for turkey vultures, which aren't legal to shoot but carry a significantly lesser penalty for killing; and whooping cranes taken for sandhill cranes, which are legal to hunt in some states. "The USFWS hates the McKittrick Policy," said Calman.

The New Mexico Wilderness Alliance, along with the Santa Fe-based WildEarth Guardians, is suing the Department of Justice to drop the McKittrick Policy. "The Department of Justice's policy is violating the Endangered Species Act," Calman said. "The ESA says that it's a general intent statute and it doesn't matter what the situation is. If you harm an ESA species, it doesn't matter what the intent was, you are responsible."

Even after wolves in the northern Rockies and Upper Midwest were delisted and designated a game animal, illegal killing continues unabated. Between April 1, 2011, and April 1, 2012, an estimated eighty-four wolves were illegally killed in Idaho alone.[23] The USFWS estimates that 24 percent of wolf mortality in the northern Rockies, 70 percent in Minnesota, and 50 percent of the currently ESA-protected Mexican wolves in the Southwest is due to illegal shooting. As much as two-thirds of all illegal wolf kills may go unaccounted for.[24]

The anti-wolf people are also well aware of the deadly effective role of poison in the twentieth-century campaign that killed off most of the wolves in the lower forty-eight states, and there were poisonings and attempted poisonings as well. In 2004 a gray wolf was found poisoned near Clayton, Idaho, on the eastern side of the Sawtooth Mountains. That same year a hiker's dog ate a chunk of meat it found along a trail in the Wagonhammer drainage near Salmon in the Salmon-Challis National Forest and became seriously ill. The dog's owner rushed it to a nearby veterinarian, who managed to save its life. Idaho Fish and Game officers searched the area and picked up a large number of—although probably not all—pieces of poisoned bait in the drainage. The forest service put out a news release warning area residents to watch what their pets ate while out hiking in the forest and that poison baits could have been spread in other parts of the forest.[25] Despite the warning, several dogs died from eating poisoned meat over the course of the year.

During 2005 more than twenty dogs in western Wyoming and Idaho were poisoned when they gobbled down pieces of meat laced with pesticide that had been scattered across the landscape. Law enforcement authorities believed that wolves were the intended targets of the poisoned meat.[26]

On May 15, 2005, biologists from the Idaho Department of Fish and Game out flying to locate radio-collared wolves picked up a mortality signal from wolf B-204 near the Clear Creek tributary of Panther Creek in the Frank Church River of No Return Wilderness. Biologists from the Nez Perce wolf recovery team had captured and collared B-204 on June 27, 2004. The wolf was estimated to be about two years old at the time. It dispersed from the Golden Creek pack sometime in mid-February 2005 and was last located alive on April 22 of that year. Its body was found just a short distance from a pack trail. An investigation by law enforcement agents from the USFWS and Idaho Department of Fish and Game found that the poison that killed B-204, mixed into balls of meat and scattered along the pack trail, was a highly toxic agricultural pesticide called Temik, to which animals and small children are especially susceptible.[27] Investigators determined that Temik was also used to poison dogs in the Salmon area the previous year.[28]

In October 2005 Tim Sundles, of Carmen, Idaho, was charged with "placing bait with intent to kill wolves and unauthorized use of a pesticide on US Forest Service land." An anti-wolf activist, his website offered instructions on how to poison wolves and claimed that in 2001 he had killed a wolf that had attacked him and his wife while they were out camping.[29] Sundles was convicted in October 2007 and sentenced to six days in jail and banned from entering public lands for two years.[30]

An editorial written and circulated to regional newspapers in 2010 by Montana anti-wolf activist Toby Bridges, who runs Lobo Watch, one of the more popular and prominent anti-wolf websites, especially outraged wolf advocates. While the editorial levied the usual grievances about the wolf reintroduction and the people who supported it—they were anti-hunting, blocking hunts needed to manage wolves; wolves were reducing some elk herds by 60 to 80 percent; the country was overrun with wolves, as many as ten thousand in the lower forty-eight states—it was the real focus of the piece encapsulated in the title "Xylitol Artificial Sweetener Is Toxic to All Canines!" that drew wolf advocates' ire. In his essay, Bridges postulated that hunters were fed up with wolves and were actively lacing their gut piles—the parts of an elk or deer a hunter doesn't want and leaves behind in the field—with the sweetener Xylitol, which is fatal to domestic dogs, wolves, coyotes, and other canines if they eat it. Written as a news story, some wolf restoration supporters felt it was really intended to "invoke fear and incite illegal activity," as one pro-wolf website posited.[31]

Whether that was the intent of the essay or if it had any influence, wolf poisonings continued, and in 2012 four wolves and six eagles were poisoned in the Bob Marshall Wilderness in Montana.[32] The previous year, four of five Mexican gray wolves released into a mountain range just south of the US-Mexico border were found poisoned within two months.[33]

While wolves killing livestock and big game animals fuels a great deal of the animosity toward these animals, fear of them is also a driving force for many people. Anti-wolf activists, and hunting and anti-wolf websites, regularly promote the idea that the wolves captured in Canada and used for the reintroduction are not only a nonnative, "invasive" species that doesn't belong here but were also larger and more aggressive than the "native" wolves—and therefore more dangerous to humans. And plenty of people believe the Little Red Riding Hood stories and are afraid of wolves.

That fear can be real and heartfelt, even if it isn't justified based on the history of wolf aggression toward humans. In September 2006 two employees from the USDA Forest Service Rocky Mountain Research Station in Ogden, Utah, were doing forest inventory work in the Johnson Creek drainage of Idaho's Sawtooth National Forest when they spotted some wolves chasing a bull elk through a meadow. Soon afterward they began to hear wolves howling—not an uncommon experience when wolves are nearby. As they made their way back to their campsite, the wolves

seemed to be all around them. Unnerved and believing they were surrounded by wolves, they radioed to be evacuated immediately and the
forest service sent in a helicopter to bring them out. A crew went in a
couple days later to break their camp and haul the gear out.[34]

I listened to the testimony of an Oregon rancher on April 5, 2011, at a
state legislature committee hearing considering wolf related bills. He described how, while out camping in 2009, his daughter and four of her
friends were "chased" back to camp by wolves as they walked out at
night to watch the moonrise. The group was so frightened by the experience that they stayed awake until dawn. "I have no doubt that if one of
those kids had panicked and run, we would have had a massacre," he
said.

The natural fear humans have for large predators has a powerful effect on us, and when those normal instinctive fears are further stoked by
anti-wolf groups, it can have an equally powerful effect on how wolves
are viewed and treated. Nevertheless, the idea that the wolves in the
northern Rockies today are the descendants of supersize, aggressive
wolves belongs in the same category as the idea that the original reintroduced animals were nonnative wolves and an "invasive" species. In his
classic study *The Wolf,* wolf specialist L. David Mech writes that typical
male gray wolves range from 95 to 100 pounds, while females weigh
between 80 and 85 pounds. Males may sometimes reach 120 pounds and
females 100, but rarely more. If you want to look at far northern wolves,
in Canada's Northwest Territories males run 90 to 116 pounds, averaging
98, and females run 70 to 110 pounds, with an average of 85.[35]

According to Jon Rachael, big game manager for the Idaho Department of Fish and Game, the average weight size for wolves in Idaho is
less than 100 pounds.[36] In Montana, adult gray wolves run 104 pounds on
average for males and 80 pounds for females.[37]

Doug Smith, senior wildlife biologist who heads up the wolf program
at Yellowstone National Park, says that skull sizes of wolves in Canada
are about 7 or 8 percent larger than the wolves that were originally found
in the Yellowstone area. However, that is within the normal range of
variation when you measure a number of skulls from different wolf populations, so the difference is statistically insignificant.[38] In any event,
slightly larger size averages are likely to have more to do with an evolutionary adaptation of northern animals tending to be bigger than their
southern counterparts because increased size offers a more advantageous
body mass to surface area for retaining heat in colder climates rather than
any purported increased viciousness.

Jim Holyan smiles when he hears people talk about how dangerous
wolves are and how unsafe it is to go out into forests and mountains of
Idaho without a firearm for protection. Holyan has spent years hiking
through Idaho backcountry surveying wolf packs, often alone, always
unarmed. He has told me about crawling into wolf dens to check on

pups, with the adults barking—not attacking—in protest nearby. I have never met a wolf biologist who carries a firearm into the field to specifically defend him or herself against wolves. And these are people who work in close proximity with wild wolves, capturing them to radio-collar and going into dens, rendezvous, and kill sites with wolves often present or nearby. Even back in the early part of the nineteenth century, when there were still hundreds of thousands of wolves roaming the West, fur trappers and explorers didn't consider wolves to be dangerous, although Lewis and Clark did report a wolf attack when one slipped into their camp along the Yellowstone River and "bit Sergt. Pryor through his hand while asleep." The wolf attempted to attack another member of the party before being shot and killed. [39, 40]

Still, wolves are large predatory animals fully capable of attacking and killing humans—and they have. A study published in 2003 looked at fatal wolf attack stories in southern Scandinavia over the past three hundred years and found credible evidence of ninety-four such attacks on humans—one in Norway, sixteen in Sweden, and seventy-seven in Finland. Most of the victims, the authors noted, were young children working in remote areas, often herding sheep. The attacks also tended to happen in particular areas over specific time periods, which suggests the predation on humans was learned behavior by particular wolves or packs of wolves. In addition, the attacks were in impoverished areas where people had killed off the wolves' natural prey, which probably made them dependent on livestock for food. In other words, these were likely wolves that had become habituated to humans and had lost their fear. [41]

A 2002 review of wolf attack records worldwide turned up more than twenty incidents in North America going back to the early 1940s. Six of those attacks were by rabid animals and at least two of the victims later died. The report's authors found that the main underlying causes for wolf attacks on humans throughout their worldwide range were rabies (the majority); habituation to people in areas where they are protected or where humans have significantly modified the environment and where their natural prey has been eliminated or they are exposed to garbage dumps, livestock or unattended children; and, lastly, where humans provoke wolves and they act in self defense. [42]

The Alaska Department of Fish and Game also produced a 2002 report on wolf-human encounters that identified fifty-one cases of aggressive behavior by wolves, including attacks, which included a number of those identified in the previously mentioned report. Of those, three were possible, but unsuccessful, predaceous attacks and eight were potential "prey-testing" attacks, where the wolves may have been trying to determine if the person might make an acceptable prey item. The bulk of the attacks and encounters were by rabid animals or those that had lost their fear of people. [43]

Up until that time, no humans had ever been killed by a non-rabid wolf in North America. But in November 2005, the body of twenty-two-year-old Kenton Carnegie, an Ontario man who was working at a mining exploration camp near Points North Landing, Saskatchewan, was found outside the camp surrounded by wolves. There was disagreement among wolf experts who examined the evidence about whether Carnegie was killed by wolves or a black bear, but a coroner's jury ruled on November 1, 2007, that wolves were responsible, making him the first documented person killed in North America by a non-rabid wolf. News stories detailing the incident reported that wolves living around the mining camp had been feeding at the camp garbage dump and had lost their fear of people.[44]

Then, in 2010, a thirty-two-year-old special education teacher named Candice Berner was jogging outside the Alaskan village of Chignik Lake on the Alaska Peninsula when she apparently ran into a pack of wolves that killed and partially ate her. Personnel from the Alaska Department of Fish and Game shot at least two of the involved wolves, although why they attacked was never determined. They were healthy animals that did not appear to have been habituated to people. That same year, Alaska Fish and Game killed an entire pack outside Anchorage after it had taken to following people and dogs around.[45] Becoming too used to people is probably the primary cause of wolves, and other large predators, acting aggressively toward people, and in some cases they can become dangerous. Wildlife managers regularly kill habituated large predators for human safety reasons. In 2011, national park staff euthanized a Yellowstone wolf because it was boldly approaching people attempting to get food from them.[46]

As tragic as those fatal attacks were, the threat posed to humans by wolves and other large North American predatory animals is very small. Between 1890 and 2005, mountain lions killed nineteen people; black bears killed sixty-three people from 1900 to 2009. Between 1872 and 2011, six people were killed by grizzly bears in Yellowstone National Park (in a seventh fatal incident in 1942, the species of bear wasn't identified). In that context, gray wolves are hands down the least dangerous of North America's large native carnivores.[47, 48, 49]

Still, you can find recent news reports of wolves approaching people in the northern Rockies. There have been instances when wolves came around while hunters were calling elk or after they had killed one. Often presented in the media as near attacks, or attacks narrowly averted, they are more likely instances of what the Alaska wolf report called non-aggressive, investigative approach encounters, where wolves not accustomed to seeing people were trying to find out what the humans were and what they were doing—a not uncommon occurrence in remote wilderness areas.

One of my own such encounters with wolves was on the Koyukuk National Wildlife Refuge in remote interior Alaska in the early 1980s. Alone, I was absorbed in the task of pulling teeth from a moose skull while a pack of eight or ten wolves gathered on the gravel bar on the other side of the river. Instead of crossing the stream to have me for lunch, which they could have easily done, the wolves instead spent the afternoon lounging on their side of the river, taking short naps in the sun and occasionally rousing themselves to nuzzle and groom each other or sit and watch me work, curious as to what I was all about. I never once felt threatened by them.

But wolves as an existential threat to human life is a core component of the campaign to kill them off, and there are plenty of stories about dangerous wolves on anti-wolf and antigovernment websites, such as the article "Wolves Kill Female Hikers, Liberals Cover it Up," purporting that two women who died of hypothermia while hiking in Idaho's Craters of the Moon National Monument in September 2013 were really the victims of killer wolves.[50,51] With reports of aggressive and dangerous wolf encounters concentrated on anti-wolf websites, it would appear that wolves mostly only bother people who don't like them.

The animosity toward wolves among ranchers, hunters, and many rural residents of the northern Rockies festered throughout the early 2000s. Ever since the wolves had met the USFWS's population recovery goals by the end of 2002, the federal government had been proposing to delist them, which was being stymied by lawsuits from environmental groups. To many residents of the region, it was interfering with an implicit deal between the feds and states that once the wolves were recovered the latter would be given management jurisdiction over the wolves. Conventional wisdom within the USFWS and state wildlife agencies was that once wolves were state-managed, the citizenry would feel they were in control and much of the anti-wolf fervor would recede.[52] The model for this hypothesis was the mountain lion. Like wolves, these big native cats were also persecuted for much of the twentieth century because they too killed livestock and big game animals. But over time, their numbers increased under state management. In most states where they are found, they are now a protected game animal with healthy populations and are largely viewed as a normal part of the Western landscape. But predictions that the wolves would follow a similar trajectory to acceptance proved to be spectacularly overoptimistic.

This young Oregon gray wolf was illegally shot a month after wildlife biologists put a radio collar on him. Photo by the Oregon Department of Fish and Wildlife

SIX

Shoot 'em on Sight

The USFWS tried to delist the experimental population of northern Rocky Mountain wolves a number of times after it had met the targeted recovery criteria in 2002 but was continually stymied by the courts. The wolves throughout the lower forty-eight states had been designated as "endangered," which meant they were considered to be at risk of extinction in all or a significant portion of their range. But as an experimental population, the northern Rockies wolves were treated as if they were designated threatened, which held that a species is likely to become endangered if no conservation actions are taken. A less-restrictive category, it was further amended by Congress to allow the wolves to be killed for management purposes in a greater number of situations than would normally be allowed.[1]

In 2003, with a total of 761 wolves in the three-state recovery area,[2] the USFWS determined that the wolves were biologically recovered and should be removed from protection under the Endangered Species Act and management jurisdiction turned over to the states. To begin that process, in April 2003 the USFWS designated Western, Eastern, and Southwestern Distinct Population Segments, or DPSs. A DPS is a provision of the ESA that identifies a particular portion of a species' population that is separate by distinct genetics and range of other populations of the same species. In the 2003 action, referred to as a rule, the Western and Eastern DPS wolf populations were downlisted to Threatened and the Southwestern DPS kept as Endangered, while the northern Rockies wolves and the reintroduced Mexican gray wolves continued to be "experimental populations."

Conservation groups challenged the downlisting and DPS designations. Not only did they feel that the northern Rockies wolf population wasn't yet large enough to be considered sufficiently recovered to be out of danger of potential future extinction, believing that at least two thousand wolves would be needed, but they also opposed the downlisting of wolves outside most of the Western DPS (which stretched from the West Coast; north to the Canadian border; east to the eastern borders of the Dakotas, Nebraska, and Kansas; and south to the southern borders of Nevada, Utah, and Colorado) from endangered to threatened.[3]

"The northern Rockies wolf recovery plan was developed in the 80s before there was the concept of conservation biology," Noah Greenwald, endangered species director for the Center for Biological Diversity, a group that has been actively involved in wolf-related lawsuits, told me. "I don't think there is a conservation biologist in the world who would agree that thirty breeding pairs is enough." In 2005 two federal courts ruled that the way the federal government determined the geographical range of wolves when setting the DPS boundaries violated the ESA, and the wolves regained their previous protections.

Then, in 2008 the USFWS created a DPS that encompassed just the three northern Rocky Mountain states plus a portion of eastern Washington, eastern Oregon, and a small part of northern Utah and delisted the wolves within that DPS. However, there was a major complication in that proposal, called Wyoming.

The states of Montana and Idaho had developed wolf management plans that described how wolves would be managed in those states and had passed muster with the USFWS, since the federal government wouldn't delist the wolves and transfer management responsibility unless the states could show they would not allow their numbers to slip back into Endangered status. (Even though wolves were still ESA-listed, both Montana and Idaho took over limited management of wolves in their states under federal oversight.[4]) Idaho's final approved plan, developed in 2008 (after modifying a 2002 plan that contained anti-wolf language and proposed objectionably steep cuts in the state's wolf numbers), would maintain a statewide wolf population of 518 to 723 wolves. The Idaho Fish and Game Commission eventually overruled the population goals set by the Idaho Department of Fish and Wildlife in the plan by increasing the planned future hunting harvest that would reduce the Idaho wolf population to 150 animals—just enough to keep them from being eligible for ESA listing. (Once the wolves were removed from ESA protection, the USFWS required that the states each maintain a wolf population of at least 150 animals and fifteen breeding pairs.) Montana's 2002 plan took the approach of managing for about fifteen breeding pairs of wolves rather than an overall population goal.

While Montana had moved ahead and developed a good plan that recognized the value of wolves, largely because it was created with a great deal of public involvement, and Idaho—with a good deal of pradding from the federal government and the Nez Perce—managed to put together something acceptable, Wyoming was in flat-out rebellion and refused to cooperate.[5]

Wyoming wildlife officials, heavily influenced by the Wyoming state legislature, had written a wolf management plan, but how it proposed to deal with wolves was a problem for the USFWS. The plan divided Wyoming into two wolf management zones. In the area around Yellowstone National Park, Grand Teton National Park, and the Rockefeller Memorial Highway, wolves were trophy animals that could be killed based on state-set hunting seasons and bag limits, while in the rest of the state they were classified as a predatory animal with no protections whatsoever. Under Wyoming law at the time, the predators could be killed by a variety of ways "including shoot-on-sight; baiting; possible use of poisons; bounties and wolf-killing contests; locating and killing pups in dens including the use of explosives and gas cartridges; trapping; snaring; aerial gunning; and use of other mechanized vehicles to locate or chase wolves down." For Wyoming wolves in the predator zone, it would be the no-holds-barred nineteenth- and twentieth-century slaughter all over again. A couple of other problems included the definition of a pack of wolves as five traveling together whether or not there was a breeding pair present, along with the state's refusal to adjust its management boundaries in the event that wolf populations began to fall to too-low levels—something called adaptive management, where adjustments are made in managing wildlife or other natural resources to address changing conditions. The Feds said no, and the state of Wyoming sued to have the plan approved but lost in both Wyoming federal district court and the 10th Circuit Court.[6]

In 2007 Wyoming made changes to the USFWS's satisfaction—but still included 84 percent of the state in a shoot-on-sight zone—and on February 27, 2008, wolves in the newly created northern Rockies DPS were taken off the Endangered Species list. A month later, when the delisting rule went into effect, Wyoming hunters began shooting wolves in the predator zone.

One of the first wolves killed in Wyoming was wolf 253M, a wolf from Yellowstone's Druid Pack known as Limpy by the park's dedicated following of wolf watchers, a cohort of park visitors that spontaneously came into being after the 1995 and 1996 reintroductions. These people spend days, even weeks, in Yellowstone watching the wolves through spotting scopes and getting to know them, keeping track of packs and pups, their travels and activities, wolf kills, and wolf deaths, their long-term observations eventually becoming a valuable source of information for researchers and park managers.

Limpy, a black wolf, got his nickname from his severe limp, the result of an injury during a fight with a wolf from the Nez Perce pack whose territory was adjacent to the Druid's, before he was even a year old. His fame grew even more in 2002 when he dispersed from his natal pack and

Oppositon to wolf recovery has included illegal shootings and poisonings. Photo by the Oregon Department of Fish and Wildlife

ended up in a coyote trap in Utah—the first wolf known to enter that state since at least the early 1930s. As with B-45 in Oregon in 1999, the USFWS transported Limpy back to his previous territory.

Limpy, who had wandered out of the safety of the park, was shot dead on March 28, 2008—the very day that shooting wolves in the predator zone became legal in Wyoming—at an elk feeding station near Daniel, one of nearly two dozen in that state. Common in the West, elk are regularly fed by wildlife management agencies at designated areas through the winter. Elk populations are managed for high population levels to provide hunters with as many elk to hunt as possible, but this often results in more elk than there is winter range available to accommodate them. Then the animals will move onto private ranch and farmlands, where they can have a significant financial impact, eating hay crops meant for livestock and doing physical damage to hay yards, fences, and other structures. The feeding stations draw the elk away from areas where they would end up in conflict with humans; otherwise elk numbers in many areas would have to be decreased, and that would mean fewer elk for hunters. Wyoming hunters, traveling by snowmobile, were staking out these feeding stations and having weekend wolf-hunting parties.[7] By mid-May, hunters had killed sixteen wolves in the Wyoming predator zone.[8]

* * *

A month earlier, the environmental law firm Earthjustice challenged the delisting in court on behalf of a dozen wolf advocacy groups. The pro-wolf groups' particular concern was whether there were enough wolves in the recovery region and sufficient safe travel corridors to allow wolves from different areas to interbreed and maintain a healthy gene pool. Small isolated populations of wolves might eventually become inbred, threatening the population's viability.

"The emphasis was on the numbers since the wolf population grew rapidly," explained Tim Preso, managing attorney for Earthjustice's Bozeman, Montana, office. "But there was little connectivity between the Yellowstone population and the rest of the population. But the [US Fish and Wildlife] Service looked at the numbers and said 'We're done.'" Preso also noted that some of the Wyoming wolf killing was being done with a certain amount of prejudice and glee by at least some hunters.

On the question of adequate gene flow among wolf populations, the District Court of Montana agreed with the conservation groups and rejected the government's delisting decision; the wolves were once again put back on the list of endangered species.

Wyoming's marginal protections for wolves and the killing spree that commenced after the 2008 delisting had influence in the court's decision to reinstate ESA protections, and the states of Montana and Idaho, anxious to have wolves delisted once and for all, were becoming exasperated with Wyoming's recalcitrance gumming up the works.[9] So the USFWS tried one more time; on April 2, 2009, it delisted wolves in the northern Rocky Mountain DPS except for Wyoming, where wolves would remain an experimental population until they made their plan a little more wolf friendly. But in August 2010, the court also rejected that delisting, which had again been challenged by a coalition of pro-wolf conservation organizations, ruling that a DPS had to be delisted in its entirety and Wyoming could not be pulled out from the rest of the northern Rockies DPS. (During this same time period, the federal government was attempting to delist wolves in the Great Lakes DPS, which was also being challenged by wolf advocacy organizations.)[10]

Some of the conservation groups that challenged the 2009 delisting, including the Center for Biological Diversity, Natural Resources Defense Council, Cascadia Wildlands, and Oregon Wild, had made a deal with the USFWS that would reinstate the delisting of wolves in Idaho and Montana but would not include the eastern Oregon, eastern Washington, and northern Utah portion of the DPS, as well as set some higher recovery goal numbers, but it fell apart in March 2011 when some of the other organizations involved in the legal challenge opposed delisting under any circumstances and wouldn't agree to the settlement.

Mike Phillips, a Democratic Montana state senator and member of the Mexican Wolf Recovery Team who also led the Yellowstone wolf recovery and is director of the Turner Endangered Species Fund, told me from his office in Bozeman that while the USFWS and National Park Service did an excellent job with wolf recovery on the ground, the federal government tried to cut corners on the administrative and legal aspects of delisting, while the region's residents had expected wolves to be delisted years earlier and were feeling "hoodwinked" and the environmental groups were concerned with whether the law was being applied. "Even the US Senate got fed up with the USFWS's failure to effect delisting," he said.

In April 2011, a rider requiring the secretary of the interior to delist wolves in the northern Rockies under the 2009 "rule" was attached to the Defense Department budget that was signed by President Barack Obama on April 15.[11] It was the first time in the Endangered Species Act's nearly forty-year history that a species was politically removed from the Endangered Species List. It may have also been the first time that gray wolves helped reelect a US senator.

Montana Senator Jon Tester, a Democrat, was up for reelection in 2012 and being challenged by Republican Congressman Denny Rehberg. Testor had only won his seat in 2006 by 3,500 votes. The Democrats held the US Senate majority by just four seats, and Rehberg was in a dead heat in the latest polls (and would eventually pull ahead).[12]

Wolves had become an issue in the election, especially with the anti-wolf faction, and Tester had to show his credibility on the issue to Montana's farmers, ranchers, and rural folk, who were increasingly frustrated by the lack of progress in getting wolves off the Endangered Species List.[13] Breaking that deadlock would go a long way toward securing his reelection, and Tester was able to convince his Democratic colleagues that delisting legislation would do the trick. On April 12, 2012, Tester and Republican Idaho Representative Mike Simpson placed a rider onto the federal budget bill that was all but guaranteed to pass. It's unlikely that Simpson was interested in helping Tester's reelection campaign, but Idaho's state government was as desperate to have wolves delisted as the Democrats were to keep their majority in the Senate. The rider delisted wolves in Montana, Idaho, and parts of eastern Oregon, eastern Washington, and northern Utah but kept Wyoming's wolves on the Endangered Species List until its wolf management plan was improved.[14] Tester kept his seat that November.

Environmental groups sued to have the delisting overturned, but Judge Molloy ruled that Congress's action was legal. "I'm still a little bitter about it," Greenwald related, speculating that if their deal with the Feds had gone through, it might have prevented the political delisting. "I think those guys [the conservation groups that opposed the deal and wanted to keep the wolves listed] were just being purists and didn't have any plans for after the rider was passed. I think it was apparent then that there were some good reasons for the settlement."

In August 2011, just four months after Congress delisted wolves, the state of Wyoming and the USFWS made a deal that allowed wolves in that state to be delisted as well. Wyoming agreed to modify its wolf management plan, which included maintaining at least ten breeding pairs and a total of at least one hundred wolves outside of the national parks and Indian reservations (with those areas providing additional wolves for a statewide goal of 150 wolves and fifteen breeding pairs) and developing better wolf population monitoring methods and less aggressive management of wolves within the Trophy Game Management Area, which makes up 16 percent of the state, although the wolves in 84 percent of the state would still be classified as unprotected predatory animals.[15, 16] Wolves were federally delisted in Wyoming on September 30, 2012 (and the state opened a wolf-hunting season on October 1).[17] Seventeen years after they were reintroduced into the northern Rockies, wolves were finally taken off the Endangered Species List and would stay off it as long as none of the states allowed their populations to drop below federally mandated minimum levels, although whether they were truly biologically recovered, rather than having just met an administrative numerical goal, depended on who you asked.

That Wyoming was able to keep its draconian shoot-on-sight, the-only-good-wolf-is-a-dead-wolf management attitude—the same philosophy that got the wolf extirpated from most of the lower forty-eight states in the first place—is testimony to how much influence the livestock industry has over wildlife and wildlife management in the West. For the Wyoming Game and Fish Department, classifying wolves as unprotected in most of the state was just a simpler way of dealing with potential wolf-livestock conflicts. As Wyoming Game and Fish Department large carnivore biologist Ken Mills explained at the International Wolf Symposium in Duluth, Minnesota, in October 2013, an event that attracted about five hundred wolf researchers, managers, and advocates, "You can wait until the wolves kill livestock and call Wildlife Services or you can get people to do it for you, which is going to happen anyway. That's the state's prerogative."[18] Wyoming is hardly the only state in the West where the ranching industry remains as hostile to wolves as it was during frontier days, but was the only state that managed to turn that traditional animosity into legitimate wolf management policy.

Of course coyotes in the West have always been managed that way—shot on sight, trapped, and poisoned—even before there was such a thing as professional wildlife management. The clever song dog not only survived the predator destruction programs from the late 1800s into the mid-1900s but continue to thrive even as they continue to be persecuted, expanding out of their historical range west of the Mississippi River all the way to the Eastern Seaboard, where they are now common. Coyotes have been able to persevere while constantly being hunted and killed by humans through both biological and behavioral adaptive responses. For example, in areas where coyotes are heavily hunted by people, females will compensate by having more frequent, larger litters; the animals will travel less in daytime hours, live in smaller groups, and avoid areas where they may be shot at, such as near roads; and they will have more dispersing coyotes moving in to fill the void left by those killed.[19]

Hunters kill coyotes regularly, including highly controversial coyote contests, typically organized by hunting organizations and clubs, where prizes are awarded to hunters or teams of hunters who kill the most coyotes over a certain period of time. But it is Wildlife Services that systematically kills coyotes to protect ranchers' livestock.

Unlike wolves, coyotes aren't too much of a threat to cattle, but the much smaller and less robust sheep are vulnerable. Although coyotes eat mainly rodents and hares, they will attack sheep when the opportunity arises and are responsible for a little over 80 percent of all domestic sheep killed each year by predators. Overall, though, all species of wild predators combined are only responsible for about 4 percent of total domestic sheep deaths anually.[20, 21]

Trapping and snaring, along with aerial gunning—shooting coyotes from aircraft—are some of the ways Wildlife Service "controls" coyote numbers in the West. Between 2001 and 2007, Wildlife Services shot more than 210,000 coyotes from aircraft—along with 312 wolves. (It wasn't only mammals that were targeted from aircraft. Government agents shot about two hundred thousand golden eagles from the air between 1941 and 1961 to "protect" livestock. Ultimately, studies showed the birds of prey were not the threat that ranchers had claimed, and in 1962 an amendment was added to the Bald Eagle Protection Act of 1940 that included golden eagles as well.[22])

Poisons also figure prominently in Wildlife Services' coyote-killing arsenal, including sodium cyanide and sodium fluoroacetate, the latter more commonly known as Compound 1080. The former comes in pellet form, which is loaded into a sort of booby trap called an M-44 that is buried in the ground and baited. When a coyote or other animal, wild or domestic, disturbs the bait, the spring-loaded device shoots the poison pellets into the animal's face and mouth and it runs off to die. From 2003 to 2007, M-44 bait stations killed more than sixty thousand coyotes and four gray wolves—more than sixty-eight thousand mammals total. Compound 1080 is used with livestock protection collars, where collars with a poison packet attached are put on livestock, most commonly on domestic sheep. If a coyote attacks, it bites into the poison packet and swallows a lethal dose of sodium fluoroacetate. The Nixon administration banned Compound 1080 in 1972.[23] In 1985 the ban on Compound 1080, along with bans on a number of other poisons used against predators, was overturned by the Reagan administration. However, Compound 1080 can only be used in conjunction with livestock protection collars. Currently only eleven states allow the use of Compound 1080, including Idaho, Wyoming, and Montana.[24]

One of the more gruesome ways Wildlife Services kills coyotes is called den removal, or denning. Gas cartridges containing sodium nitrate, charcoal, and other ingredients are detonated inside a coyote den, releasing carbon monoxide that suffocates the pups.[25] The pups may also simply be dragged out of their den and strangled or clubbed to death. Denning was, and is, so controversial that Cecil Andrus, secretary of the interior for the Carter administration, made denning illegal in 1979; but three years later President Ronald Reagan's secretary of the interior, James Watt, reinstated the practice.[26] There are more than a few ranchers in the West who would like to see wolves treated the same as coyotes.

But coyotes, wolves, cougars, and other predators aren't the only wild animals the livestock industry has problems with. Ungulates, dear to the hearts of hunters, are on the list as well; disputes involving competition between elk and cows for grass on public lands, crop and property damage, and threats of transmitting diseases between wild and domestic animals can be divisive and politically charged. These issues go way back and, in the context of ranchers' reaction to wolf restoration, there is no shortage of ironies.

"Are we going back to the days of the rattlesnakes and the Indians?" said Jay Dobbin, a Wallowa County, Oregon, rancher and president of the Oregon Woolgrowers Association. "Is the wilderness with game in the forests and valleys without homes better than a civilized development of the range and the farming lands?" But Dobbin wasn't talking about the recent return of gray wolves to Oregon. The year was 1912, and he was expressing his opposition to a plan by the Oregon Game Commission to reintroduce elk back into Oregon, whose native herds had been virtually extirpated by overhunting—and market hunting for meat in particular. "The elk bring benefit to no one. They harm many," Dobbin went on to say. Wallowa County ranchers' opposition to the reintroduction was simple: They didn't want to share grass on public lands with elk that they viewed as rightfully belonging to them and their livestock.

Faced with a vanishing elk population, the Oregon state legislature ended recreational elk hunting in 1909 (it had banned commercial hunting for elk a decade earlier). Despite opposition from the livestock industry, the reintroduction plan was wildly popular with the public, and between 1912 and 1913 thirty Rocky Mountain elk—sometimes called Canadian elk in the first decades of the twentieth century[27]—were brought in from Wyoming and put in an enclosure on USDA Forest Service lands to serve as breeding stock for repopulating the state's herds.[28]

Dobbin and the livestock industry remained unalterably opposed to the reintroduction of elk into Oregon, further writing, "His [the elk's] place is in parks and museums, preserving the memory of Oregon unde-veloped. Civilization and savagery cannot occupy the same ground. The one must give way to the other." Despite the stockmen's opposition, elk were eventually released around the state, sometimes while being ha-rassed by ranchers. In 1933 the state opened its first, limited three-day elk-hunting season, twenty-one years after the first reintroduction. Rath-er than having no value, as the ranchers had claimed, Oregon's elk popu-lation is a tremendous economic resource both for hunting and wildlife watching.[29]

The ranchers were right about one thing, though—elk can, and do, cause significant harm to the livestock industry; between eating a couple cuttings of hay crops and knocking down fences, the animals can easily cost an individual rancher twenty to thirty thousand dollars or more each year.[30, 31] High elk numbers in Wallowa County in the 1980s brought about what are referred to as the "elk wars," where local ranchers put political pressure on the Oregon Fish and Wildlife Commission to set higher harvest limits for elk than state biologists recommended so that there would be more grass available where they grazed their cows on public land, and occasionally gut-shot elk that parked themselves in one of their alfalfa fields for too long.[32]

Elk remain a serious, ongoing problem for ranchers and farmers throughout the West. A 1992 study estimated that deer and elk damage cost Montana ranchers and farmers $12.2 million that year.[33] A typical scenario is playing out in Washington State's Skagit Valley, where a herd of elk numbering about 1,500 to 1,700 have cost area farmers an estimated one million dollars over a several-year period by damaging fences and eating their hay and potato crops. One farmer estimated that the elk were costing him about five hundred dollars each week, and another threat-ened to illegally shoot them if they kept causing trouble. In 2013 the Washington Department of Fish and Wildlife brought in agents from Wildlife Services to kill some of the offending animals, a move that an-gered Washington hunters.[34] Washington State wildlife officials trans-planted elk from Wyoming into the region during the early and mid-twentieth century to bolster declining native herds. Interestingly, some farmers in the Skagit Valley believe that elk are not native to the area and regard them as an invasive species introduced by the state.[35, 36, 37]

For all the claims that wolves are a dire threat to the ranching indus-try, a look at some comparative numbers is revealing. Between 1996 and 2005, Defenders of Wildlife paid Idaho ranchers $135,933 to compensate them for wolf depredations to their livestock.[38] During the same span of years, Idaho ranchers claimed $649,243 for damage caused by elk to their crops, fences, hay yards, and other property.[39]

The possibility of transmitting brucellosis from wild ungulates to live-stock is a major issue in the northern Rockies, especially Montana. Brucel-losis is a bacteria-caused infectious disease, originally brought into the region by infected cattle that introduced it into the wild ungulate population. It can now be found in elk and bison, and keeping a state's livestock herd brucellosis free is economically important.[40] This has resulted in an ongoing battle between the Montana livestock industry and conservationists over bison that migrate out of Yellowstone National Park in winter and is a major obstacle to expanding wild bison populations. Migrating Yellowstone bison have been shot or captured and sent to slaughter over fears that they might infect cattle outside the park. Bison advocates dispute ranchers' contention over how great the disease threat is to livestock.[41] The Montana state legislature has also attempted to give the livestock industry more control over elk, which also can carry and transmit the disease.

Just the opposite situation, transmitting disease from domestic livestock to wildlife, has bedeviled efforts to maintain and expand bighorn sheep populations in the West. The problem is an ovine pneumonia that domestic sheep are largely unaffected by but is deadly to wild sheep. It has killed thousands of bighorns throughout the West, often wiping out entire herds. The threat is so great that wildlife managers will kill bighorns that have come into contact with domestic sheep rather than risk the possibility they have been infected and will spread it to other herds.[42, 43]

This has caused some serious conflicts with sheep growers who graze their stock on public lands. In 2010 forest service staff at the Payette National Forest in Idaho approved a management plan that put 70 percent of the forest off-limits to domestic sheep grazing, specifically to protect Rocky Mountain bighorn sheep. Flexing their political muscle, the Idaho sheep growers made their voices heard in Washington, DC, and Idaho Congressman Mike Simpson—who cosponsored the rider that delisted wolves in April 2011—tried the same trick again, attaching a rider to the House Interior and Environment Appropriations Act for 2012 that would have kept the forest service from spending any funds that would reduce domestic livestock grazing. This would have prevented the three sheep operations that grazed on the Payette National Forest from losing their grazing leases. When that approach failed, the Idaho Woolgrowers Association and other sheep industry groups sued the forest service but lost in a 2014 federal court ruling.[44, 45]

But it is wolves that bring out a militant reaction from ranchers. Acknowledging that they are "beautiful animals," a rancher testifying before the California Fish and Wildlife Commission in 2014 against legally protecting wolves in California once they recolonize that state went on to say that "they're also vicious, brutal and efficient killing machines and a threat to people, livestock and pets."[46]

Unsuccessful at stopping wolf reintroduction at the federal level, the livestock industry had moved to state legislatures and county governments to pass laws trying to stop the wolves from reestablishing themselves and to make it easier to kill them. Defenders of Wildlife, an organization that has been a leader in wolf restoration, tallied at least twenty local resolutions passed, variously prohibiting wolves from being introduced or reintroduced in a county; ordering any present or dispersing wolves to be removed or destroyed; removing them from the Endangered Species List; granting local county government authority to kill wolves regardless of their ESA status, declaring them to be an "unacceptable species"; and holding the federal government responsible for any damage they did.[47] But trying to stop wolf recovery through local or state law is a standard tactic. In 1994 North Carolina State Representative Zeno Edwards, a Republican, tried to derail red wolf recovery by attempting to pass, unsuccessfully, a bill allowing them to be shot on sight—despite the state legislature's legal counsel determining that the proposed law was both unconstitutional and in direct violation of the Endangered Species Act.[48] While none of these local resolutions—most of which were passed in the early 2000s, when wolves in the northern Rockies were still protected under the Endangered Species Act—were legally enforceable, they certainly highlighted the intense anti-wolf feelings running throughout rural ranching communities.

But if you look at the overall impact wolves actually have on the livestock industry, ranchers' reaction to wolves and wolf recovery and the time, money, and political capital they have been willing to spend trying to stop it seems well out of proportion to reality. It is true that wolves kill cows, sheep, and other domestic animals and that some individual ranchers can be faced with chronic wolf attacks on their stock. But most ranchers in wolf range don't have problems with wolves, and on an industry-wide basis, the number of livestock killed by wolves is statistically minuscule.

In 2010 the national cattle inventory was ninety-four million head. Just over 5 percent of those animals died over the course of 2010. Of that total, respiratory, digestive, calving, and other heath- or injury-related problems accounted for about 80 percent of cattle deaths, with weather contributing another 12 percent. At the opposite end of the scale were predators, which accounted for 5 percent of total cattle deaths. Coyotes topped the list at 3 percent. Wolves were second to last at 0.2 percent. (Bears at 0.1 percent were dead last, and wild cats—cougars, bobcats, and lynx—killed 0.5 percent.) Domestic dogs killed 0.6 percent of all cattle during 2010, considerably more than wolves. Carnivores killed a total of 0.23 percent of the total US inventory of cattle that year. Sheep, being more vulnerable to predation, fared a little worse, with 4 percent of the national inventory lost to carnivores.[49]

While those figures reflect the national picture that includes many areas where there are no wolves, livestock losses in the northern Rockies don't look very different. In 2011 there were 6,040,000 cattle in Montana, Idaho, and Wyoming. Of that total, the USFWS verified 188 head killed by wolves—0.003 percent of the total number of cattle in those three states. The agency verified that wolves killed 245 sheep in 2011—0.03 percent of the 830,000 sheep in the northern Rockies that year.[50]

There were 6,260,000 head of cattle in Montana, Idaho, and Wyoming in 2013, with 137 wolf kills verified by the USFWS, which is 0.002 percent of the total inventory. Of the 845,000 domestic sheep in the northern Rockies that same year, just 0.06 percent, 470 animals, were confirmed wolf kills. From 1987, when the first wolves reestablished themselves in northwestern Montana, to 2013, wolves have killed 1,990 cattle and 4,192 sheep in the Northern Rocky Mountains Wolf Recovery Area.[51, 52]

Despite the grave threat wolves are said to pose to the livestock industry in the northern Rockies, potentially putting ranchers out of business, they continue to do just fine. In 2010 the Idaho sheep industry made $22.7 million, a 38 percent increase from the previous year and its biggest profit since 1984—eleven years before wolves were reintroduced to the state.[53]

Unlike their counterparts in European countries where wolves are also repopulating former territories, wolf managers in the United States are inclined to reach first for the lethal option.[54] From 1987 to 2013, 2,107 wolves were killed in response to predation on livestock, usually by Wildlife Services, but some were lawfully shot by ranchers protecting their stock.[55]

Killing animals to "control" them is neither a tidy nor pretty sight, and Wildlife Services has come under scrutiny for questionable practices that included killing animals in a cruel fashion (agency trappers have been documented siccing dogs on coyotes caught in steel traps) and killing protected wildlife, such as eagles, and covering it up. In a three-part investigative report for the *Sacramento Bee*, reporter Tom Knudson found that between 2000 and 2014, Wildlife Services has killed almost a million coyotes along with millions of birds and other mammals from starlings and shorebirds to porcupines and wolves.[56] At least four wolves have been poisoned between 2003 and 2007 in sets intended for other animals.[57]

The American Society of Mammalogists passed a resolution in 1999 calling for Wildlife Services to stop its indiscriminate killing of wildlife and another in 2012 urging the agency to reduce its killing of wildlife, especially mammals. By the society's calculation, from 2000 through 2010 Wildlife Services agents "have killed more than 2 million native wild mammals in the United States in those 11 years, including 915,868 coyotes, 321,051 beavers, 126,257 raccoons, 83,606 skunks, nearly 70,000 ground squirrels, 50,682 red and gray foxes, 43,640 prairie dogs, 29,484 opossums, 25,336 marmots and woodchucks, 19,111 muskrats, 4,559 bears, 4,052 mountain lions, and 3,066 endangered gray wolves, nearly all of these intentionally."[58]

But Wildlife Services' control actions will likely continue to play a primary role in wolf management for the foreseeable future. Stanley,

Idaho, wolf advocate Lynne Stone described how the Basin Butte pack in the Sawtooth Mountains was reduced by Wildlife Services from thirteen members to one in 2009, a result of Idaho's liberal policy in dealing with wolf depredations that includes individual wolves and entire packs being killed for chronic livestock depredations, even if a long period of time has elapsed; wolves can be killed if they are lying in wait, following, or watching livestock.

In what wolf advocates call the "Thanksgiving Week Massacre," Wildlife Services killed seven Basin Butte wolves, a pack that was labeled as involved in chronic livestock depredation, even though they only killed a few livestock every year or so. Agents set up bait stations to attract the wolves onto private ranch property and then shot them from a helicopter and fixed-wing aircraft. "People could see them being shot from the road," Stone told me. "Wildlife Services didn't care." One of those wolves was a favorite of Stone's—B313, whom she named Angel. Angel's sister, Mary Mag, was found dead of unknown causes in September 2009. Wildlife Services agents wounded B313 on their first try and finished her off as she ran into the mountains. Stone went to look for Angel a few days later, finding her frozen stiff in minus-twenty-degree cold, legs sticking up into the air. "She was a perfect wolf and the hands-down next alpha female," said Stone. "She died at the edge of a beautiful meadow."

But even a fierce and outspoken supporter of wolves like Stone recognizes that the issue of wolves killing livestock can't be ignored and that ranchers' problems with wolves need to be incorporated into wolf management, including sometimes eliminating wolves and packs. "If ranchers don't want to cooperate with wolves, it's pretty hard to keep wolves," Stone told me.

The question is: Are more wolves being killed than necessary to protect livestock? Wolf researchers estimate that 20 percent of wolf packs kill some livestock over the course of a year.[59] For the small number of ranchers that suffer from wolf attacks, one option is to pay ranchers compensation for livestock killed by wolves.

In 1987 Defenders of Wildlife started a privately funded compensation program, the Wolf Compensation Trust, to pay ranchers in the northern Rockies the market value of livestock lost to wolves. From 1987 to October 2009, the organization paid out $1,368,043 to 893 livestock producers for 1,306 cattle, 2,421 sheep, and 105 other livestock that were killed by wolves.[60] Part of the reason for the compensation program was to increase the level of ranchers' tolerance for wolves by cushioning the financial blow from wolf depredations. But in September 2010, with a cumulative payout over twenty-three years of $1.4 million, Defenders of Wildlife ended its compensation program to focus on working with ranchers to develop ways for them to coexist with wolves, emphasizing nonlethal techniques to discourage wolf attacks on livestock.[61]

To make up for the loss of the Wolf Compensation Trust, in March 2009 the US Congress created a five-year, $5 million Wolf Livestock Loss Demonstration Project that would be used both for paying for wolf kills and for implementing nonlethal methods for reducing attacks for ranches and on Indian reservations in the northern Rockies, Oregon, Washington, the Upper Midwest, and the Southwest. In 2012, out of $80,000 received from the federal government, Idaho paid out $72,000 in loss claims for 12 cows, 44 calves, 138 ewes, 66 lambs, 2 rams, and 1 dog.[62] For 2013 Montana received $70,000, Idaho $80,000, and Wyoming $33,750 for depredation payments. For nonlethal prevention projects Montana got $100,000, Idaho $50,000, and Wyoming $0.[63]

One problem with the compensation program is false claims, along with wildlife agents who may be too eager to confirm that a cow or sheep has been killed by wolves. A confirmed kill will get a rancher full market value compensation for his lost stock, a probable kill will garner 50 percent of market value, and livestock that died of other causes earn nothing. Misidentifying wolf-killed livestock not only gets a rancher compensated for a cow or sheep that died of something else but can also get individual wolves or entire packs killed for something they didn't do.[64]

Spring is typically the peak time for wolf depredations on livestock. The ranchers are putting their cows and calves out on the range, elk and deer are getting stronger and harder to catch, and the alpha males are preoccupied with their pups, leaving less-experienced pack members to fend for themselves and maybe finding that cows and sheep are easy prey. Some of the ways biologists determine if a cow or sheep has been killed by a wolf is to look for bite marks and hemorrhaging wounds that indicate the animal was attacked while it was still alive rather than scavenged, if there are any wolf tracks nearby, or if radio-collared wolves were recently in the vicinity. Wolves will often pull out and eat the stomach, and remains and bones will be scattered away from the main carcass.[65, 66]

In Oregon Wildlife Services agents were confirming livestock as killed by wolves where Oregon Department of Fish and Wildlife biologists said the cause of death could not be determined, prompting an independent scientific panel to convene in 2011 to look into the discrepancies. Their report, issued in early 2012, found Wildlife Services agents "to be inconsistent with evidence presented and in a number of instances appeared to be the result of misidentification of evidence." And, "The panel found it difficult to understand how [Wildlife Services] investigators reached their conclusions from their written reports."[67] In other words, Wildlife Services agents are more likely to erroneously blame wolves for dead livestock based on faulty or misinterpreted evidence. It's a problem that's likely common in the northern Rockies, and the consequences of those errors are even more dead wolves in a region where one wolf has been killed by Wildlife Services or ranchers for every three cows or sheep killed by wolves.

Domestic sheep are especially vulnerable to predation by wolves and coyotes. Photo by Jim Yuskavitch

SEVEN

A Wild Wolf Chase

In mid-August 2011, four months after Congress delisted wolves in the northern Rockies, I was back in Idaho with Jim Holyan, wolf biologist for the Nez Perce tribe's wolf recovery program, for another hitch in the field surveying wolf packs. This time we were headed into the Nez Perce National Forest to search for three different wolf packs—two wilderness packs and one new pack discovered by a Nez Perce biologist just a couple of weeks earlier. No wolves in any of the packs were wearing radio collars, so finding them was going to be a challenge.

Since my last visit in 2005, Idaho's wolf population had grown to at least 705 wolves in eighty-seven packs, along with another twenty-two packs along the borders with Washington, Wyoming, and Montana, with at least some of their territory in Idaho. The Hemlock Ridge pack was still around. Nez Perce biologists had put a radio collar on a male pack member in 2010, designating him B493, who dispersed from the pack in November of that year. They weren't able to get a count of how many wolves were in the pack in 2010, but the biologists heard at least three pups howling on several occasions, so the Hemlock Ridge pack was considered to include a breeding pair for the official 2010 count. The El Dorado pack was alive and well also. There was one wolf in that pack with a radio collar, a male designated B281, but they had lost contact with him. He may have dispersed a long distance where no one picked up his signal, the collar may have malfunctioned, or he could even have been illegally killed, with the perpetrator disposing of the collar. The Nez Perce biologists tried to catch another one numerous times over the course of 2010, but the wolves were being exceptionally elusive, and efforts to put a collar on another pack member were so far unsuccessful. They did find the pack's rendezvous site and confirmed seven pups (one later found dead along the side of the road in the Yakus Creek drainage), so the El Dorado Creek pack was also counted as a breeding pair for that year.[1]

Since my previous visit, the wolf recovery team had moved its offices into new digs in McCall, Idaho, a few blocks from their previous location, and before we hit the road, Jim and I, along with program leader Curt Mack, sat down in the conference room to talk about the present and future of Idaho wolves. While the tribe, like everyone else, wanted to see the wolves delisted once they were recovered, Mack told me, "The delisting was a little disappointing. The tribe wants to make sure that wolves are managed based on science and would have preferred that it had gone through the ESA process for delisting rather than the legislative process." But now that it was a done deal, the tribal biologists were more concerned about how wolf hunting was going to affect the Idaho wolf population and, in particular, how it might hamper their ability to keep track of population trends.

It was no secret that Idaho's political establishment, especially ranchers and hunters, were anxious for the opportunity to begin killing wolves, and when the USFWS delisted wolves in 2009, they saw their chance. The Idaho Fish and Game Commission immediately approved a wolf-hunting season that began on September 1, 2009, with statewide harvest limit of 220 across twelve management zones, with a specific quota for each zone. Tags were $11.50 for residents and $186 for nonresidents. Speaking before a group of cheering, camouflage-wearing hunters in Boise in August of that year, Idaho's Republican Governor C. L. "Butch" Otter declared, "I'm preparing to bid for the first ticket to shoot a wolf myself."[2] It was those kinds of scenes and that kind of talk that made wolf advocates very nervous about the states taking over wolf management from the federal government and what their version of wolf conservation would look like.

The hunt ended on March 31, 2010—five months before the court ruled in favor of the wolf advocates' lawsuit challenging the 2009 delisting. During the seven-month open season, Idaho hunters killed 188 wolves out of the statewide 220-wolf quota. Most of the wolves killed, 58 percent, were males and 15 percent were juveniles less than one year old. The tags, which were freely available over the counter, no bidding required, were popular. Idaho Fish and Game sold 31,400 resident tags and 781 nonresident tags. Of the 188 wolves killed, 12 were wearing radio collars, leaving 142 radio-collared Idaho wolves in early 2010.[3]

When the wolves were relisted in August 2010, Idaho once again refused to participate in wolf management. In October of that year, Governor Otter sent a letter to US Secretary of the Interior Ken Salazar terminating the state's agreement with the federal government as a Designated Agent and complaining that the wolf reintroduction was a "reminder of how far we have strayed from the Founding Fathers' original intent of a national government with limited, enumerated powers be-

Nez Perce Tribe Wolf Recovery Program wolf biologist Jim Holyan searches for radio collared wolves with a radio receiver in the Nez Perce National Forest, Idaho. Photo by Jim Yuskavitch

stowed by the states." He wrote that wolves were forced on "our people, wildlife and livestock" and referred to wolves as "your wolves," meaning the federal government's, distinguishing them from "our wildlife."[4] Implicit throughout the letter in tone and words, with its emphasis on hunters and big game, was that Idahoans who want wolves—whether hunters or nonhunters—had had no legitimate say in shaping Idaho's wildlife heritage.

After the final 2011 delisting, Idaho once again took over wolf management in the state. Reflecting intense anti-wolf attitudes among politically influential groups, including hunters and ranchers, the Idaho Fish and Game Commission lowered the statewide wolf population that Idaho would manage from 518 (based on the 2005 wolf population level) down to 150 wolves or ten packs as directed in the state's 2002 management by increasing the permissible yearly harvest—just enough to keep Idaho wolves from being relisted under the ESA.[5, 6, 7] "What other species comes off the Endangered Species List and people say that we need to kill them back to minimum levels?" Holyan asked.

Both Mack and Holyan felt that Wyoming's pushback against the federal government's wolf plan requirements and its eventual agreement to allow unregulated killing of wolves in most of the state along with the delisting by Congress had significantly emboldened anti-wolf forces in Idaho. "They said, 'Wyoming didn't play ball and the government backed down. Idaho said that 'if Wyoming doesn't have to play ball, we're not going to either,'" Mack told me. The whole legislative delisting tactic demonstrated to the anti-wolf forces that they could work toward their ends through politics, rather than law and science.

"It has shown the anti-wolf people that they can get things done through politics and that they have the upper hand in the wolf debate. They can go directly to the governor, Fish and Game Commission, and state legislators," Mack continued. He mentioned that at the time, "There is evidence that there are regular direct exchanges of e-mails between anti-wolf people and [Idaho] wildlife commissioners," which would indicate the possibility that people opposed to wolves in the state were having significant behind-the-scenes influence on the state's wolf management plans without benefit of the public process.

State fish and game, or fish and wildlife, commissions are made up of volunteers, generally appointed by a state's governor, and serve as an advisory and rule-making body to the state's fish and wildlife agency; therefore they have substantial influence on wildlife management and conservation policy. People with backgrounds in hunting and the extractive industries, including ranching, typically dominate commission membership in the Western states, and wildlife policies inevitably end up being skewed toward the benefit and aims of those groups.

When I asked if all the lawsuits filed by environmental groups blocking previous delistings had forced a political solution—a common hypothesis among hunters, ranchers, federal and state wildlife managers, and even some pro-wolf people at the time—Mack pointed out that wolf advocates kept winning lawsuits because their positions were found by the courts to be the right ones, both legally and scientifically.

In the middle of all of this was the Idaho Department of Fish and Game, the state agency charged with managing Idaho's fish and wildlife resources. Established in 1899, its mission statement is: "All wildlife, including all wild animals, wild birds, and fish, within the state of Idaho, is hereby declared to be the property of the state of Idaho. It shall be preserved, protected, perpetuated, and managed. It shall be only captured or taken at such times or places, under such conditions, or by such means, or in such manner, as will preserve, protect, and perpetuate such wildlife, and provide for the citizens of this state and, as by law permitted to others, continued supplies of such wildlife for hunting, fishing and trapping."[8]

Mack described the agency as the "whipping boy" for the governor and the fish and game commission, and said it doesn't get much respect from state legislators either. "Idaho Fish and Game tries to be accommodating, but what they don't realize is that causes them to be pushed harder," he said.

The main group currently pushing Idaho Fish and Game were hunters, who were now leading the anti-wolf charge in Idaho. Although most hunters were never supportive of wolf reintroduction, it was the livestock industry that fought the initial, unsuccessful battles to derail the reintroduction. But over the previous five or six years, anti-wolf sentiments had been growing among hunters, convinced that wolves were decimating big game herds despite assurances from professional wildlife managers that was not happening.

"Now it is the hunters who are saying that the wolves are destroying the elk herds and that in five years we won't be able to hunt. I don't know how long that intense level of anti-wolf rhetoric can continue," Mack told me. "How long can you continue to beat that drum when the predictions are false? We're talking about attitude changes, and those take time." Mack also thought that Idaho outfitters and the state had missed a big opportunity with wolves. Hunting outfitters had been complaining about how wolves were "killing off all the elk, decreasing their business by chasing customers away," oblivious to the economic opportunities offered by wolves by promoting them as a prized trophy animal, much the same way many states presented bighorn sheep and Rocky Mountain goats as exclusive, once-in-a-lifetime hunts that bring in significant revenue for wildlife agencies and hunting guides. Instead, not only Idaho but Montana and Wyoming as well decided to manage wolves as a problem, as varmints, rather than as an asset, to be killed by purchasing an inexpensive wolf tag with the limit set by how many dead wolves they could legally and politically get away with.

In August 2011 Idaho Fish and Game was in the process of developing its upcoming wolf hunting season and harvest limits, which now would allow wolves to be "harvested" by a variety of methods, including rifle, archery, traps, and snares. Mack and his biologists were waiting to see what the details of the season were going to be for a couple of reasons. One was to see what the season's harvest limit would be and how aggressively Idaho Fish and Game intended to reduce the wolf population. The second was to determine how the hunt would affect their wolf-monitoring program.

During the wolf recovery phase, a significant part of the Nez Perce Wolf Recovery Program was to keep track of the wolf population so the USFWS would know when the wolves had reached their recovery goals. Now, with the wolves delisted, it was important to count wolves, packs, and breeding pairs to make sure they did not decline below the minimum population threshold and, much preferably, maintained at biologically viable population levels. To accomplish that for the central Idaho area, where the Nez Perce tribe has an agreement with Idaho Fish and Game to co-manage wolves, wolf recovery program biologists look at twenty different packs they locate from the radio collars worn by at least one pack member. They look at pack size, sex makeup, number of pups born, and other information, then use statistical models to extrapolate the overall wolf population.

During the 2009–10 wolf-hunting season, they lost a dozen collars. With a regular wolf-hunting season, they were guaranteed to lose more collared wolves, and perhaps eventually all of them. While wolves can be very elusive, there are so many people out in the mountains and forests during hunting season that wolves are vulnerable in many areas. On top of hunter harvest, wolves responsible for livestock attacks also continued to be killed by Wildlife Services—seventy-eight in Idaho in 2010, plus another thirteen legally killed by ranchers in 2010.[9]

"One of our concerns is that if we lose a lot of collars during harvest and depredation, our ability to determine population sizes is really decreased," Mack explained.

His biologists were not catching as many wolves as they used to, and whether that meant the wolves were getting smarter and harder to trap or there were not as many out there as everyone thought was hard to know. Trapping and collaring wolves was too expensive and labor intensive to continue doing if the animals were going to eventually be shot out from under them. Anticipating ongoing losses of radio-collared animals by hunters, Mack and the Nez Perce Wolf Recovery Program were working with researchers at the University of Montana to develop alternative techniques to accurately survey and count wolves, whose territories in Idaho ranged between 270 and 300 square miles, without the benefit of radio collars to track them.[10]

* * *

That was Jim Holyan's and my challenge as we drove east from Grange-ville into the Nez Perce National Forest on Highway 14 along the South Fork Clearwater River, then up the Red River into what we assumed was the territory of the Bat Rock wolf pack. Until a couple of weeks earlier, the existence of this pack had been unknown. Kari Holder, one of Hol-yan's colleagues, howled them up while she was surveying the area in early August and then managed to sneak in close enough to see wolves and confirm pups. Holyan had brought along his trapping gear and was hoping we might catch one of the Bat Rock wolves and put a radio collar on it.

By the time we reached the upper forest, it was late in the day. Holyan pulled down a forest road and stopped at an overlook, where he got out of the pickup and howled four times in four different directions then waited a few minutes. No response, which he noted on his notepad along with the location coordinates. Then we drove off, looking for a suitable campsite, surprising a small black bear in the middle of the road as we rounded a curve.

We eventually set up our tents at the edge of a meadow along an unmaintained forest road, which eventually became impassable, to serve as our base of operations. That night I dreamt about wolves. They came silently out of the forest and gathered outside the door of my tent. They didn't howl, bark, or growl, but I could hear their breathing, feet shuf-fling on the ground, and scratching noises as they brushed up against my tent. They wanted to come inside, and although they weren't acting hos-tile, I couldn't tell their intentions and wanted them to go away. They began pressing harder against the tent door, bending it inward. I pushed back, feeling the contours of their shoulders and necks—and teeth. The harder I pushed back, the more the wolves, still perfectly silent, leaned in as the tent's seams began to tear. Then, suddenly, morning light filled the tent and I was awake. Later, over the roar of my camp stove as I cooked Ramen noodles for breakfast, I mentioned my dream to Holyan and idly wondered why someone who likes wolves and hoped they succeeded would have such a tense subconscious encounter with them. He just shrugged and said he heard me mumbling in my tent last night and thought I was talking to myself. After breakfast, we filled our packs with gear for a long hike into where Holder had reported seeing the wolves. Before the day was over, we would find a Bat Rock wolf, but under circumstances we hadn't anticipated.

By late morning, after six miles of hiking forest roads and lots of stops to howl—a basic, and effective, technique for locating wolves if they are around and in the mood to answer you—our efforts had rewarded us with a lot of old, dried wolf scat and a single wolf track that wasn't especially fresh. Breaking for lunch, Holyan spread a forest map out on the ground and, studying it, said to me, "There are wolves all over the place." Then indicating their locations on the map with an outstretched hand, palm down, he rattling off the names of wolf packs. "The White Bird Creek pack here, the Pilot Rock pack here, the Earthquake Basin pack here, the Red River pack here, the Coldwater Ridge pack here. It's good," he said.

One of the things I had learned on my last field trip with Holyan, and reinforced on this outing, was that in any area used by wolves, even if they weren't around at the moment, you would find wolf scat, and probably lots of it. That was certainly true on this excursion. Wolf scat is similar to coyote scat but larger, one-half inch to an inch and a half in diameter, usually with ungulate bone fragments and hair embedded, and tapering at one end—a characteristic of wild canid scat.[11] Weirdly enough, wolf scat, or more accurately what is sometimes found in wolf scat, is used by anti-wolf groups to try and frighten people into further believing that wolves are dangerous and undesirable animals to have around.

Echinococcus granulosus is a quarter-inch-long tapeworm that lives in the intestines of wild and domestic dogs, including wolves. The tapeworms lay their eggs in the intestines, which are then passed into the environment with the feces. The eggs are transferred to ungulates such as elk or deer while they are grazing. The eggs then develop into cysts, called hydatid cysts, which usually lodge in the ungulate's lungs or liver. When a wolf kills an infected elk or deer, or a coyote scavenges on a carcass, it swallows the cysts and the parasite's cycle begins anew. The parasite doesn't harm either of its host animals.

The wolves captured in Canada and released into Yellowstone and central Idaho in 1995 and 1996 were treated for *E. granulosus* and certified free of the parasite before being reintroduced. However, a high percentage of wolves in the northern Rockies are now infected, which means the parasite was already in the system or brought in later by other wild canids or domestic dogs. When anti-wolf groups say that wolves carry a deadly parasite or are spreading disease, *E. granulosus* is what they are talking about.

In rare cases, humans can be infected with hydatid cysts, which are treated with drugs or surgery to kill or remove them. The parasite is most common in areas where sheep are raised, and the majority of people are infected through contact with domestic dogs. Basic hygiene and not handling wolf, dog, or other canid feces is the simplest way to avoid encountering *E. granulosus*.[12] But the parasite still plays a role in anti-wolf disinformation campaigns, and I have even heard people say that the hydatid "spores" will float around in the air and that you can breathe them in and become infected just by walking down a trail where wolves have been.

By the time we had hoofed it back to the truck, we still had the entire afternoon to look for wolves. We drove up another forest road where

Holyan thought the pack might be traveling if they were on the move—in August the wolves would be starting to move off their rendezvous sites and the pups would be big enough to keep up with the adults, at least on short treks. When we flushed a couple of turkey vultures from the side of the road, Holyan pulled over thinking we had found a road-killed deer that might make a good place to set a trap. Instead we found a dead wolf pup where the birds had dragged it out from under a nearby tree. When Holder discovered the Bat Rock pack, she noted that one of the pups was small and sickly. So here was our Bat Rock pack wolf. Holyan said that it would have weighed about fifteen pounds when it was alive, less than half of what a wolf pup born in April should weigh by mid-August. He estimated the pup had been dead for two or three days. Looking over the carcass, he couldn't find any obvious causes of death, no bullet wounds or broken bones that might indicate it was hit by a vehicle, so he wrapped it up in a black plastic garbage bag and put it in the bed of the pickup to bring back to McCall for a necropsy. But we needed to find a freezer to store the carcass in until Holyan's hitch was over in another week. We stopped at the Red River Ranger Station, where an Idaho game warden lived, but he was in the process of moving out, and the young guy sunbathing in a lawn chair on the front lawn of the forest service house next door told us he had no refrigerator or freezer. We had struck out, and there was no way the wolf carcass was going to last for a week in the hot weather we were having. Our best bet now was to drive into Elk City to see if the forest service's district office could loan us some space in their walk-in freezer.

* * *

Elk City is a small mountain community of 202 residents, as of the 2010 census, surrounded by Bureau of Land Management lands and the Nez Perce National Forest. It lies thirty-five miles east of Grangeville, the Idaho County seat.[13] Idaho County's economy centers on the timber industry, ranching, and farming and, as in many rural regions of the West, the county has seen its population of residents sixty-five and older rise. In Idaho County's case, it is now 21.4 percent of its current population of 16,267—up from 17 percent in 2000.[14, 15]

In what may have been the ultimate example of anti-wolf hysteria in the northern Rockies, Idaho County commissioners in September 2010, a month after wolves had been placed back on the Endangered Species List, petitioned Governor Otter to declare an ongoing "wolf disaster" that would allow people to shoot wolves on sight.[16]

The county's Disaster Declaration asserted that "the uncontrolled proliferation of imported wolves on private land has produced a clear and present danger to humans, pets and their livestock. This danger has altered and retarded historical uses of private land, dramatically inhibiting

previously safe activities such as walking, picnicking, biking, berry pick-
ing, hunting and fishing. This is an illegal government taking of private
rights on private property."[17]

The commission chairman, R. Skipper Brandt, was also a supporter of
the Idaho Anti-Wolf Coalition's petition to remove wolves from Idaho
"by any means possible" when he was a state legislator.[18]

Governor Otter declined to approve the county's resolution, but in
April 2011 he signed House Bill 343 that declared a "disaster emergency
as defined in Idaho law because of the introduction of wolves" and contained much of the same language found in Idaho County's original resolution.[19, 20] The editorial board of the *Idaho Statesman*, Idaho's paper of
record, strongly criticized the bill that equated wolves with floods, wild
fires, and earthquakes in an editorial, "Beware: Legislative 'scientists' at
work."[21] In May the state authorized sheriff's deputies to kill a pack of
about seven wolves near Elk City that locals complained were killing pets
and wildlife, the same month Wildlife Services shot at least five wolves in
the Lolo region of the Clearwater River basin from a helicopter to increase elk numbers.[22, 23] Barely a month after Congress delisted wolves,
the state of Idaho was already starting to kill them as a matter of course.

Anti-wolf paranoia had really reached a peak in Idaho County, and
Elk City in particular. Wolf horror stories circulated about how it wasn't
safe for Elk City parents to let their children outside to play and of ugly
and dangerous encounters with wolves as people were out hunting or
taking a walk on their property. One story, which follows a standard
anti-wolf theme that wolves will kill children at school bus stops, tells of
a man in Idaho County who, after seeing his kids off on the school bus,
was horrified to observe a pack of wolves almost immediately appearing
where the children had been just moments before—the wolves had been
watching the kids all along "trying to decide how best to make them
lunch."[24] A man from Grangeville told me he had heard that wolves are
attracted to the sound of children's voices.

When we got to Elk City, Holyan and I had no better luck at the Red
River Ranger District office than we had at the ranger station. Their walk-
in freezer was on the blink, so we drove into Elk City's modest down-
town, where Holyan found a pay phone in front of the Elk City Hotel (no
cell coverage in this country) to call the office for messages. Outside the
hotel entrance was a sandwich board sign that said "Wolf Reporting
Center." I wandered through the hotel door into the combination lobby
and gift shop, and after some small talk with the sixtyish woman behind
the desk, I asked what the sign out front was all about. She explained that
people in the community were collecting information on wolf activity in
the area, wolf sightings, if they found elk killed by wolves, those kinds of
things. They periodically sent their reports off to the Idaho County commissioners, who, she thought, forwarded them on to the governor. She
told me how wolves were coming into people's yards, killing off the elk,

and causing all kinds of trouble. She related how wolves were not endangered and that the government lied about it and paid twenty thousand dollars for each Canadian wolf they released in 1995 and 1996. "And the Canadians were glad to get rid of them," she said. (The actual amount the USFWS paid Canadian trappers was thirty-four thousand dollars total for all the wolves captured for the reintroduction.[25]) Even worse, she said, the nonnative Canadian wolves introduced by the government into Idaho had probably overwhelmed the native Idaho timber wolf, a smaller animal that ran in packs of two and only ate small game. I had heard this story before as wolves from Idaho began to disperse into Oregon, only in that instance it was the native Oregon timber wolves that were being muscled out by the Canadian invaders. She had a personal wolf story to tell me as well. A couple of weeks earlier a wolf had run across the road in front of her as she was driving to work. "If I had known it was going to do that," she said, smiling sweetly, "I would have sped up."

Holyan was still on the phone, so I walked across the street and into the Elk City General Store for a bottle of Gatorade and picked up a couple of free copies of *The Citizen,* a conservative "states rights" oriented newspaper published in Grangeville. WOLVES KILLING IDAHO, was the front-page headline of one issue; the lead story, "Talk about 'states' rights' in Idaho not possible while wolf crisis goes unresolved," was illustrated with a photo of a snarling wolf. The other issue's headline blared "WOLF WAR DECLARED: Lawmakers send clear message to governor to stop destruction, end threat of deadly disease." Below the fold another story blamed Idaho Fish and Game for "creating a public safety nightmare" specifically by not protecting Idahoans from a wolf-borne "difficult to diagnose disease that may not show up for 10–20 years, cutting life short, and if caught in time requiring serious and expensive surgery."[26, 27] As I sat on the bench out in front of the general story thumbing through the papers, a couple of twentyish guys—one of them carrying an AR-15 assault rifle—came out of a house across the street, got into an older model Jeep, and drove off.

By now Holyan was off the phone; but with no immediate ideas of what to do next with our dead wolf pup, he suggested we drive down the road to the Elk Creek Station and Cafe, a place he was familiar with, to refill our water bottles and come up with a Plan C over some ice cream.

Inside the cafe, a half dozen or so locals sat at the counter or in booths, while a couple of tourists mulled over the ice-cream selection. On one wall was a bulletin board with photos of local hunters posing next to big game they harvested, mostly elk but including a couple of wolves, one lying in the back of a pickup truck, another propped against a snowmobile. The locals were friendly enough, all saying hello as we walked through the doorway. Holyan doesn't generally identify himself or his work when he visits Elk City, but the people in the cafe seemed to know about us already and immediately asked if we had seen or caught any wolves, although they were under the impression we were Wildlife Services agents here to kill them. We answered that we had not seen any wolves and sat down at a table.

But one guy in the cafe knew exactly who we were and what we were up to, and he strode over and sat down with us. Holyan knew him only by his first name, Carmen. In his thirties, he was a local trapper, and Holyan seemed to genuinely respect both his trapping skills and knowledge of the backcountry. Carmen complained that there were hardly any coyotes around anymore—wolves and coyotes don't get along and when the former move into an area the latter's population generally drops, sometimes significantly. How was he going to earn money to pay for gas to keep his snow machine running if there were no coyotes for him to trap? he asked. Anticipating the state was going to open a wolf-trapping season in the fall, Carmen suggested that maybe he would just trap out all the wolves around Elk City. He didn't say it an unfriendly way, but there was a threatening undercurrent to his tone. Holyan, with a serious look on his face, acknowledged that Carmen probably had the trapping skills to pull that off.

Despite the tenor of the exchange, Holyan's past experiences with Carmen had generally been positive. After Carmen got up and walked away, he told me how a few years earlier the trapper had inadvertently snared a couple of wolves. He called Wildlife Services for the first one, and they sent someone out to put a radio collar on it. He snared the second wolf on Christmas day, and knowing that he wasn't going to get anyone to come out, let the animal go. Plenty of Idaho trappers who accidently caught a couple of wolves in traps set for coyotes would have just illegally killed them and kept quiet about it.

In the meantime, we had come up with a Plan C for our Bat Rock pup. There were a bunch of fish biologists doing chinook salmon surveys in area streams—we had run into them now and again in the course of our work—some of whom were staying at a house at the nearby Red River Wildlife Management Area. When we stopped by later that afternoon, they had extra room in their freezer; Holyan promised to pick up the carcass on his way back out in about a week.

On our way out of the cafe, Carmen intercepted us at the door. In a quiet voice so no one else would hear, he said to Holyan, "I'm getting soft in my old age. If I snare a wolf maybe instead of skinning it out you can pay me to put a radio collar on it." Holyan thought that was an interesting idea and said he would talk to his boss about it.

Making no progress at all with the Bat Rock wolves, we finally gave up and turned our attention to the two wilderness packs—the Selway and Magruder. The former's territory included the Selway-Bitterroot Wilderness, while the latter ranged through the northern part of the Frank Church River of No Return Wilderness. The first wolf Holyan caught and collared when he started his job with the Nez Perce Wolf

Recovery Program was one of the founding Magruder pack wolves. These were "dropped" packs, wolves whose territories were in remote areas, weren't causing any problems, and had very little if any contact with people. The recovery program biologists didn't worry about having collars on them, but would occasionally go out and try to check on how they were doing.

One afternoon we drove up to the top of Green Mountain, where there is a fire lookout no longer in use. From that high point, Holyan wanted to see if he could pick up signals from any of his missing wolves—wolves with radio collars whose signals had not been detected in some time and their whereabouts and fate were unknown. At the time there were about one hundred missing radio-collared wolves in Idaho, Montana, and Wyoming. He ran his finger down a list of wolf radio-collar frequencies, noting their status as he went, "dead, dead, dead," until he got to one that was not a confirmed mortality. He dialed the frequency into his radio receiver and swept the antenna through the air, hoping to pick up the signal. After going through eight or ten missing wolf frequencies without success, we got back in the pickup and left. "As you can tell, we have a lot of missing wolves," said Holyan. "It's the greatest feeling to find a missing wolf. We find about two a year."

After three more days of hard trail hiking, bushwhacking, and howling from ridgetops, we came up empty. Wherever the Selway and Magruder packs were, we could not find them. I packed up and drove home. Holyan stayed on a few more days to finish his hitch.

As anticipated, Idaho Fish and Game added trapping to its 2011–12 wolf season, and trappers killed 124 wolves in addition to 255 killed by hunters.[28] Montana also had its second wolf hunting season in 2011 that lasted into February, with 166 wolves killed,[29] although there was no wolf trapping allowed, and Wyoming had not yet authorized wolf hunting in that state's trophy zone.

Jim Holyan e-mailed me after he got back from his hitch to tell me that after three more days of hard ten-mile hikes he had seen and heard absolutely nothing of either pack, making me feel less guilty about leaving early and the possibility of missing out on something. I forgot to ask him if he remembered to pick up his frozen wolf pup from the fish biologists' freezer.

Nez Perce Tribe Wolf Recovery Program wolf biologist Jim Holyan howls for the Magruder pack wolves in the Frank Church River of No Return Wilderness, Idaho. Photo by Jim Yuskavitch

EIGHT
Gray Wolves, Black Helicopters

Wolves, it seems, have always been highly symbolic animals for humans. And not surprisingly, since wolves are almost as widely distributed across the planet as humans, people have lived alongside these powerful predators for a long time. While they hunted and killed wolves, tribal hunter-gatherer and warrior societies tended to have positive views of wolves that represented spiritual power, wisdom, courage, and even similarities in social structure and behavior. That attitude changed as human societies became settled and their economies centered on agriculture and, in particular, animal husbandry. Livestock, especially those of nomadic sheepherders, were vulnerable to attacks by wolves, and the stature of wolves rapidly went from admired and respected to hated. There were some exceptions—ancient Greeks and Celts had positive views of wolves in their mythologies, and Japanese farmers appreciated that wolves helped control the numbers of deer and other crop-eating animals and prayed to them at their shrines, although that ended in the late 1860s, when the Japanese started to adopt Western agricultural practices, including poisoning wolves.

The widespread adoption of Christianity throughout Europe, combined with the previous shift to agriculture-based societies, sealed the wolves' fate as an animal to be hated, feared, hunted down, and destroyed. For a thousand years the Catholic Church promoted the idea of wolves as evil and aligned with the devil (along with human enemies of the Church), while mythology such as werewolves helped keep wolves linked to the supernatural. So pervasive and ingrained was the negative view of wolves that it wasn't until the middle of the twentieth century that Western scientists even considered there might be value in studying them.[1]

Although science has revealed more and more about the lives of wolves, and modern views of nature and wildlife have swept away the negative myths along with fear and loathing of wolves for most people, there are still some who see wolves little differently from how they were perceived in the Dark Ages, with some contemporary modifications, and these people have had a significant influence on wolf restoration.

A good deal of the opposition to wolf recovery has been practical—competition between wolves and hunters for big game and attacks on livestock. But there is another perhaps more powerful force driving the opposition to bringing the wolves back. Just as the medieval Christian church linked wolves to its enemies, rural people have linked wolves with those they perceive to be actively hostile to them and their way of life. With 47 percent of the western United States—including 61.7 percent of Idaho, 48.2 percent of Wyoming, and 28.9 percent of Montana[2]—publicly owned and managed by various federal agencies that hold natural resources rural residents often regard as really theirs, laws that limit their ability to extract those natural resources, often for environmental protection purposes, are seen by the more conspiratorially minded as blatant attempts by the federal government and environmentalists to drive rural people from their lands.[3]

On my first trip to visit the Nez Perce wolf recovery team in 2005, team leader Curt Mack told me that in economically depressed Idaho counties, the federal government was a convenient boogeyman, and that "there is a lot of federal government paranoia in rural counties," something that is common throughout the rural West.

That antigovernment paranoia boiled over in the mid-1990s when right-wing paramilitary groups were proliferating across the country. In 1994 paramilitary organization members in Idaho claimed that armed agents from the US government, and specifically the USFWS and National Marine Fisheries Service, were flying into Idaho in black military helicopters to enforce the Endangered Species Act at gunpoint and believed that 50 percent of the United States was under "the control of the New World Order." Another rumor floating around was that federal officers were at Fort Bliss, Texas, training to invade Idaho and other states, prompting then Idaho Republican Senator Larry Craig and Republican Senator Lauch Faircloth of North Carolina to contact the Justice Department to ask if it was true. In 1995, probably not coincidentally the year wolf restoration hit the ground running in the northern Rockies, late Idaho Republican Congresswoman Helen Chenoweth sent out a press release charging that the federal government was utilizing "armed agency officials and helicopters" to enforce various environmental regulations and that if those operations did not cease, she would be then Assistant Agriculture Secretary Jim Lyons's "worst nightmare for at the least the next two years." All the claims of black helicopters and armed fish and wildlife agents, as well as imminent invasions, were of course false, if not ridiculous.[4]

More recently, Noah Greenwald of the Center for Biodiversity, who regularly peruses anti-wolf websites, told me: "It's unbelievable the things they blame on wolves." Some of the things wolves have been drawn into as agents of a tyrannical federal government by states' rights and antigovernment people include gun rights, private property rights (often extending onto public lands as a right by proximity or heritage), taxes, the Endangered Species Act, the Environmental Protection Agency, antihunting, a plot to push ranchers off the range, and a host of other perceived affronts.

Those were the people Idaho Governor Butch Otter was talking to in his 2014 State of the State and Budget address when he declared, "One form of growth we don't want to encourage is the wolf population that was imposed on Idaho almost twenty years ago. With your unflinching support, we were able to fight through the opposition of those who would make Idaho into a restricted-use wildlife refuge and take back control of these predators from our federal landlords." In the same speech he also called for a two-million-dollar allocation from the state legislature to set up a Wolf Control Fund to pay the expenses for killing wolves that would then be sustained by regular contributions from hunters and the livestock industry.[5]

Jim Beers, retired from the USFWS with an impressive résumé of credentials, including wetlands and wildlife biologist and chief of National Wildlife Refuge Operations, has been an active and outspoken critic of wolf reintroduction—and the more tolerant views of large carnivores that have evolved over time—and has charged that his former employer stole forty-five to sixty million dollars from state hunting and fishing funds to pay for gray wolf recovery. In his widely circulated 2011 essay called "Why They Love Predators," Beers gives a pretty complete treatment of the threats some people see in accepting and managing large carnivores as part of the natural landscape rather than viewing them as dangerous adversaries.

In that worldview, the "enthusiasm and support" for predators including wolves, mountain lions, grizzly bears, and coyotes is part of the core belief system of animal rights by environmental radicals who are sworn to end hunting, fishing, trapping, livestock grazing, ownership of animals, the overall use of natural resources, private property rights, rural economies, and state and local governments that stand in the way of their intent to impose "national hegemony" on us all.

Conservation of predators like wolves is nothing more than a wedge to insert the government into the affairs of American citizens, and rural residents in particular, by controlling their ability to protect themselves and their property and continually designating more land and natural resources as protected rather than managed for and used by people.

Eventually government will dictate "how and where we live and what we will be allowed to eventually 'control' but not own at government sufferance."

The "predator lovers" and their allies in the government lie about the impacts of predators, which really do spread disease, destroy big game herds, bring ranchers to bankruptcy, and attack people—the latter being one way to frighten people off their lands—and pass regulations that protect predators but not the people. In Beers's experience, this trend toward the misguided valuing of predators had its beginnings in the 1950s, when some wildlife managers were beginning to question whether predator control was necessary and effective. By the 1960s the "common-sense" view of natural resources as something to be managed for timber, wildlife, grazing recreation, and other human uses was being challenged by those who wanted to preserve public lands for "whatever 'native' species that government designates based on the 'science' bought and paid for by government and radical groups." Furthermore, the government's hiring preference given over the past thirty years to "women and other urban government-designated minorities" who don't relate to, or even oppose, rural lifestyles has put more and more government employees in the position of doing harm. Meanwhile, there is a "pervasive disenchantment with and growing disdain for US Constitutional government among universities and bureaucracies" that value animals over humans and produce predator studies that are "lies" with "truly evil purposes." Beers wraps up his analysis with a warning that if the "predator pendulum is not reversed" rural America may well end up resembling a central Asian dictatorship where the "pernicious effects" of wolves and other large predators are everywhere.[6]

The path that begins with reintroducing wild wolves to a small portion of their former range and ends at the abyss of dictatorship and loss of freedom follows a rigid, hierarchal path where "man" is indisputably second only to God and the wolf is an usurper of that rightful natural order. At the 2013 International Wolf Symposium, I sat in on a lecture by Jessica Bell, a PhD student with the Department of Sociology at Michigan State University, whose research into online discussions of wolves provides some revealing insights into why some people so intensely dislike—even hate—wolves.

Bell analyzed comments about wolves posted between 1999 and 2013 on the online editions of two magazines oriented to ranchers' interests, *Beef Magazine* and *Cattle Today*, and two hunting publications, *American Hunter* and *Outdoor Life Magazine*—all of which either have high circulations or receive large numbers of comments. She found the dominant theme of discussions about wolves, besides that they were overwhelmingly anti-wolf, was that "man" was the only legitimate apex predator and views of nature followed the traditional Christian dominion over nature theology. In that context, wolves are invaders and symbols of unwanted interlopers, specifically environmentalists and federal government employees.

Under that worldview, humans—usually referred to as "man" in the comments—are the only ones capable of balancing nature (because nature is viewed as a hierarchy with us at the top, just below God) and rejects the idea put forward by wildlife biologists, ecologists, and environmentalists that reintroducing large native carnivores like wolves can have a positive effect on ecosystem dynamics.

One of the most powerful ways to justify anti-wolf feelings is to delegitimize the animals' very existence. In that view, animals such as elk and deer are the property of humans and their purpose is to benefit us, and we are "the managers of nature, and animals are viewed primarily as objects and resources." Because game animals belong to us, when wolves prey on deer and elk, it is not a natural function of nature and they are instead "committing the criminal act of theft." The belief that wolves will eventually wipe out big game species is equally strong among people with this hierarchal, man-dominated perspective of nature. So killing wolves, preferably to extirpation but at the very least to control their numbers, is our God-given role, which is to manage nature and to protect and "save our wildlife"—a category that does not include wolves.

The anti-wolf faction also seeks to delegitimize people, environmentalists in particular, who like wolves and support wolf recovery. The usual grievance is that outsiders are telling "us" how to manage "our" wildlife, essentially saying that while wildlife belongs to people, it doesn't necessarily belong to everyone, especially those with differing views of wolves and humans' role within nature. Further delegitimizing the "wolf lovers" are claims that they anthropomorphize and romanticize wolves and have no clue how dangerous and destructive the animals are. Yet anti-wolf people apply plenty of human traits to wolves themselves, but all negative. They are "remorseless killers" that "kill for fun," proving that wolves, unlike humans, inhumanly kill their prey, making wolves unethical animals. Bell notes that "ascribing compassion to wolves is seen as anthropomorphic; ascribing malice and sadism to wolves is not seen as anthropomorphic." She also says that many online commentators who condemn wolves for "sport hunting" hunt for sport themselves, arguing that hunting by humans is ethical but hunting by wolves is not, and that photographs posted online of wolf-killed big game animals are often tagged with warnings about the graphic nature of the photos, while pictures of hunters posing with their kills never carry similar disclaimers.

Another important theme of online anti-wolf comments is the wolf as an intrusive animal, portrayed through the ideas of property rights and states' rights and symbolizing the federal government as not only forcing wolves on rural populations but also establishing rules and regulations that hamper the "ability of states and property owners to defend their livelihoods and interests" and that wolves and their advocates are "intruders who threaten the social and economic stability of rural Western communities." Ultimately, to be against wolves is to defend and "preserve Western culture and independence" and to remedy the "social injustice in which the segments of society that benefit from wolf reintroduction (urbanites, liberals, the federal government, East Coasters) do not have to suffer the costs of this conservation initiative." These are all emotionally powerful themes that inform anti-wolf discussions, and you can find many of them embedded in the two brief sentences about wolves in Idaho Governor Butch Otter's 2014 State of the State address.

But not everybody posting on those online forums dislikes wolves. Bell found ranchers who argued that they are able to live with wolves by making changes in their cow management operations that minimize the odds of wolf depredations, and hunters who view wolves as a natural part of the ecosystem who have no problems hunting alongside them for the same prey. But those are minority viewpoints that were generally "shouted down" and marginalized—a technique often used on online forums to quell dissent and establish the dominant viewpoint as the obvious, correct, and "commonsense" position.[7, 8]

There are many parallels between the online world of wolves and the reality-based one. Driving out to the Elkhorn Wildlife Area near Baker City with Oregon Department of Fish and Wildlife wolf coordinator Russ Morgan in April 2011 to check on wolf tracks recently reported there (although all we eventually found were the scattered bones of a winter-killed elk), he reminded me that "there is a cost to wolves, and ranchers are the ones who stand to lose something, whether it's property or a night's sleep worrying about their livestock." Despite that, ranchers can also have complex views about wolves, and Morgan told me about one such rancher he was working with. "He asks me about livestock and wolves, but he also asks questions about their biology and says 'that's fascinating.' As I drove away I thought, *He really likes wolves.* There are ranchers who don't want to get rid of wolves, but they aren't too forceful about it because the standard line for ranchers here is to get rid of them."

There are actually many rural residents, like Morgan's rancher, who are okay with wolves, and even welcome their return. But in small Western communities, people who challenge the prevailing worldview may find themselves, as online commenters often do, targets of pushback and sometimes hostility. Diana and James Hunter certainly discovered that when they sought a conditional use permit from Wallowa County, Oregon, in 2011 to expand their Barking Mad Farm Bed and Breakfast onto a section of land they owned that was zoned for exclusive farm use near the city of Joseph. The hearings before the Wallowa County Planning Commission and county commissioners were packed, and opposition to the proposal was heavy. While some opponents testified to their concern about the compatibility between the buildings and the tourists the B&B

would serve with surrounding agricultural activities, the bulk of the testimony centered on wolves. That's because the Hunters had been trying to develop a wolf-watching tourism industry in the area and were working closely with Oregon Wild, one of the state's high-profile wolf advocacy organizations, and were bringing in pro-wolf visitors as guests to the B& B. That rankled a lot of longtime residents. One rancher testified that he objected to the Hunters promoting tourism that was detrimental to ranching and didn't like their association with Oregon Wild. Another said that it put the Hunters on the side of people "who do not have the best interests of ranchers at heart, and it's a big indicator that her bed-and-breakfast activities and her support of tourism will not contribute to peaceful coexistence with surrounding ranchers." The opposition was intense enough that friends and supporters of the Hunters and wolf recovery were too intimidated to come forward. Despite Wallowa County having approved similar requests for conditional building permits in the past, the Hunters' application was eventually denied.[9, 10, 11]

That kind of polarization over wolves makes them ripe for fund-raising, and wolf-advocacy groups use the animosity of anti-wolf groups as well as the killing of wolves by hunters and Wildlife Services to bring in money from wolf supporters worried that the animals are on their way to re-extirpation, although that is an unlikely outcome. But when it comes to creativity and boldness in fund-raising over wolves, in this case fear that not enough of them will be killed, the grand prize has to go to the Utah-based Sportsmen for Fish and Wildlife and its spin-off organization Big Game Forever.

Between 2011 and 2014 the two organizations received a combined total of eight hundred thousand dollars from the state of Utah to lobby the federal government to remove gray wolves from Endangered Species Act protections nationally and prevent the USFWS from releasing wolves into the state—something there are absolutely no plans to do. Sportsmen for Fish and Wildlife got a hundred-thousand-dollar grant in 2011, while Big Game Forever scored one hundred thousand dollars in 2012 and later two additional three-hundred-thousand-dollar payments selling the Utah State Legislature and Utah Department of Natural Resources on the specter of wolves destroying the state's big game herds and hunting economy if they ever gained a foothold.[12]

Both organizations emphasize predator control, and Sportsmen for Fish and Wildlife was successful in lobbying the Utah state legislature into raising hunting license fees and appropriating general fund dollars to increase the state bounty on coyotes to fifty dollars (between September 2012 and May 2013, Utah hunters turned in more than six thousand coyotes for payment).[13, 14] Don Peay, founder of Sportsmen for Fish and Wildlife, helped pass Proposition 5 in 1998 as finance chairman of Utahns for Wildlife Heritage and Conservation. The proposition requires a two-thirds majority vote to approve any voter initiative that changes wildlife management rules specifically affecting hunting and fishing methods and limits. The law was promoted as necessary by Peay, its primary proponent, to keep out-of-state antihunting groups from influencing wildlife management in Utah at a time when a number of Western states were passing voter initiatives banning or limiting hunting methods for mountain lions and black bears.[15]

Peay raised eyebrows, even among some hunters, when he told the *Anchorage Daily News* in a March 3, 2012, story that the American tradition of wildlife as a publicly owned resource was socialism and needed another look, and advocated privatizing America's wildlife. In 2012 Sportsmen for Fish and Wildlife was trying to convince county commissioners in Montana to "circumvent the state wildlife commission on predator management" and in Arizona and Idaho was "lobbying legislatures to allow landowners to own and sell hunting privileges."[16]

The grants to the two groups were not without controversy. A spate of newspaper stories in 2013 questioned the value Utah was receiving in return for the money. State Senate Majority Leader Ralph Okerlund, who recommended the second three-hundred-thousand-dollar appropriation for Big Game Forever, and Utah Governor Gary Herbert, who approved the budget, both Republicans, had previously received campaign contributions from officials of both organizations.[17]

An accomplishment report submitted to the state in 2013 by Big Game Forever was vague in its details, and an audit by Utah's legislative auditor general found that because the group comingled Utah funds with private money, it was difficult to determine how the state's grant had been spent.[18] The report also noted that Big Game Forever, "the sole applicant, was awarded the contract. In our opinion, this language specifically describes BGF and gives the appearance that it [the contract] was tailored to meet their experience and expertise."[19] As of 2014, Utah had no known wolf population.

The conservative political organization Americans for Prosperity is tapping into wolves as the symbol of an intrusive federal government and a vehicle to advocate for conservative views on natural resource management, which included an October 2013 symposium in Salt Lake City on reforming the Endangered Species Act and the film *Wolves in Government Clothing* by filmmaker and Americans for Prosperity California State Director David Spady. The film's website explains: "*Wolves in Government Clothing* is one man with a camera exploring the consequences of mixing an apex predator with civilization. True conservation cannot come at the expense of mankind. When civilization is forced to regress to accommodate a bygone ecology the results are simply . . . unsustainable." One photograph on the website shows children in cages that local people built at a bus stop in the Southwest where Mexican gray wolves have been reintroduced. It's a brilliant and powerful visual that makes the persistent myth that wolves deliberately stalk children waiting for the school bus seem real.[20]

There are also more personal, individual antigovernment statements made through the medium of dead wolves. One of the more famous ones, which started out on the Facebook page of a Wyoming hunting guide service then spread across the Internet in 2013, was a photograph of eight hunters, each clutching rifles and wearing facemasks cut from white sheets. Two hunters hold an American flag, while a third hoists a dead wolf by the neck. The caption reads: "Fed Up in Wyoming." Comments on the Facebook page included "Kill all federally funded terrorists," "To some, the reintroduction of wolves represents Washington's treason against civilization itself," and "Yet another bleeding heart program . . . reestablish the bloodthirsty critter that every civilization since the dawn of time has tried to eliminate."[21]

Wolf conspiracies aren't limited to the federal government. One myth that has floated around the Pacific Northwest since at least the 1970s has it that timber giant the Weyerhaeuser Company was for years releasing wolves onto its tree farms to control deer and elk that were eating young tree saplings. John Stephenson, a USFWS biologist, told me he once talked with a man who claimed that a friend of his witnessed such a release decades ago. The wolves, he said, were in metal cages dropped out of an airplane, floating to earth by parachute. Once the cages hit the ground, their doors automatically flew open and the wolves bounded off into the forest.

The strong opinions, polarization, and high-profile nature of wolf reintroduction has made it a major focus of reporting in the media, which has often contributed to spreading negative opinions and inaccurate information about wolves as fact. Reporters often allow people they interview to make exaggerated claims about wolves' impacts on the livestock industry or big game herds without checking to see if they are true, or engage in "he said, she said" journalism to give the impression of balance to a news story that may do just the opposite by putting less-knowledgeable people on the same standing as experts. An example is a 2013 news report that featured interviews with a hunter who believed that wolves were causing Montana's elk population to decline opposite a professional wolf biologist with Montana Fish, Wildlife and Parks explaining the nuances and complexities of predator-prey relationships. The story not only presents the hunter's personal opinion about wolves' impacts on Montana's elk as equal to the wildlife biologist's professional knowledge, experience, and access to current scientific data about elk and wolves but also gives the edge to the wolves-decimate-elk narrative by headlining the story "Hunter: Wolves mean less game."[22]

The headline of a wolf-related news story published in Oregon newspapers in early 2014 screamed "Wolf pack blamed in elk and deer deaths" and proceeded to tell the story of how many were killed ("at least one deer and one elk . . . over the past two weeks") and the attempt to identify the wolves who did it, as if it were a criminal investigation. If there was ever a headline that conveyed the idea that wolves' killing their natural prey is illegitimate, even criminal, that was it.[23] It's unlikely you will ever read a story about the deer season opener titled "Hunters suspected in spate of weekend deer shootings."

As Ralph Maughan, president of the wolf advocacy organization The Wolf Recovery Foundation, who also runs The Wildlife News blog, told me: "The drip, drip, drip of wolves killing livestock stories in the media was deadly to our cause in Idaho. They even republished old livestock depredation stories. There really needs to be some way to break through the reporting of livestock deaths as if it is the same as a child being run over by a hit-and-run. They can make seven dead sheep, three calves, and one cow over a year or two sound like a mass slaughter."

While the print media can be guilty of false balance in its reporting, television and movies can be outright sensational when it comes to wolves, such as the film *The Grey*, where oil workers stranded in Alaska are stalked by wolves. In 2014, in response to public complaints, Discovery Channel canceled a planned "Man-Eating Super Wolves" show that sensationalized wolves as extremely dangerous animals and promoted false stereotypes and myths about them.[24]

Although there is plenty of good, solid reporting on wolves, the media tends to follow the status quo narrative that wolves are killing large numbers of elk, deer, and livestock and over time gives the public the impression that wolves are causing far more trouble than they really are.

This negative news reporting about wolves isn't limited to the northern Rockies. Researchers from Ohio State University and the University of Minnesota analyzed news reports about wolves in the United States and Canada published between 1999 and 2008 and their impacts on people's attitudes towards them. They found that over a ten-year period, reports about wolves became increasingly negative. The most negative reporting came from states with relatively new wolf populations, while the states and provinces that have had wolves for a long time, or never lost their wolves, had the least. Interestingly, negative news reports about wolves were also high in states that were in wolf recovery zones but did not yet have wolves, suggesting that just the idea that they would eventually recolonize had an effect on how they were portrayed in the media. However, once wolves arrived in an area and people became more knowledgeable about and used to the animals' presence, negative attitudes eventually decreased—with the exception of hunters and livestock producers, whose negative attitudes tended to increase.[25]

For wolf advocates, this is all problematic, and potentially discouraging. While there is significant popular support for wolves across the United States, as researcher Jessica Bell points out, wolves are an exceptionally symbolic and value-laden animal tied deeply to a person's worldview and moral universe, where minds are not easily changed, making the controversy over wolves extremely resilient. It's the reason that compensating ranchers for wolf depredation has not made them more tolerant of wolves and predator hunters still don't support wolf recovery, even though by hunting them they are supposedly controlling their numbers, just as they have demanded. She notes in her research paper: "A small minority with strong antipredator biases can exert a disproportionately harmful impact on predator populations."[26] Many wolf advocates would say that is exactly what has happened since the wolves were delisted in 2011.

Residents of Elk City, Idaho, demonstrate their opposition to wolves by collecting information on wolf sightings and complaints and forwarding them to the county government. Photo by Jim Yuskavitch

NINE

Wolves versus Elk

"Wolf Wars" was the cover story for *National Geographic* magazine's March 2010 issue, which featured an inside photograph showing an anti-wolf demonstration by hunters in front of the Kalispell office of Montana Department of Fish, Wildlife and Parks who carried signs that said "Does Anyone Care About Our Deer & Elk Herds" and "Animal Genocide." While anti-wolf bumper stickers proclaiming "Canadian Wolves, Smoke a Pack a Day" speak more to an anti–federal government sentiment with wolves as the proxy, roadside signs pleading "Don't Let the Wolves Do Our Hunting for Us" pretty clearly communicated who hunters thought was entitled to kill and eat deer and elk and who wasn't, vividly paralleling the view of Upper Midwest hunters of the 1940s, who saw wolves as killing deer meant for human consumption. Many hunters really do believe they are at war, and I have heard them describe themselves as in a battle with wolves.

Hunters and hunting organizations took a little longer to mobilize against wolves than ranchers and the livestock industry, but when they did their opposition was widespread, aggressive—even militant—directing their ire at the federal government who released the wolves in the first place, state wildlife agencies that weren't doing enough to fight the threat they believed wolves presented to big game, and the environmental groups who used the courts to stymie attempts to remove their ESA protections.

Viewing wolves as vicious killing machines, many hunters were, and still are, angry over the release of wolves into what they consider their own hunting territories, the delays in removing wolves from Endangered Species Act protection, and their belief that wolves were decimating big game populations throughout the northern Rockies that one day would result in so few elk and deer that there would be nothing left for people to

111

The northern Rocky Mountains' abundant prey species such as elk made the region ideal for restoring wolf populations. Photo by Jim Yuskavitch

hunt. They pointed to declines in the elk population in the Clearwater region of central Idaho and the Northern Range in northern Yellowstone National Park and southern Montana that seemed to coincide with the arrival of the wolves as proof of the damage the predators were doing to the northern Rockies big game herds. In 2010, when the *National Geographic* magazine article was published, there were about 1,650 wolves (down from 1,733 in 2009)[1] in the northern Rockies, well above the minimum recovery goal of three hundred distributed evenly over the three recovery areas, and hunters wanted an aggressive wolf-hunting policy to kill as many wolves as possible before all their fears were realized.

Not the type to mince words, hunters and hunting groups laid out their case against wolves bluntly on websites and Internet bulletin boards. HuntWolves.com's "Help preserve wolves . . . take one to a taxidermist" welcome page explains, "For years, hunters have watched as deer and elk populations have been decimated and ranchers have stood by while their livelihood was eaten before their eyes." The SaveElk.com website explains that wolves kill two animals each month for food and two more for sport, or "thrill kills," and they are "killing out the future of our herds." SaveElk estimates that there are three thousand wolves in Idaho, Wyoming, and Montana (although the USFWS says there were 1,691 in the region at the end of 2013[2]). Big Game Forever calls wolf recovery "unsustainable predation" that is "dramatically damaging pop-

ulations of moose, Rocky Mountain elk, and other large ungulate populations in the northern Rockies and western Great Lakes."[3] The landing
page for Montana Sportsmen for Fish and Wildlife informs its visitors:
"This year a Minimum 43,500 Elk will be Eaten Alive by Wolves in the
northern Rockies? Do You Have a Problem With That?[4] The opening
page for Lobo Watch's website serves up the header "Good Big Game
Conservation Begins With Predator Management," a succinct summation
of what many hunters view as the fundamental threat to elk and other
big game—wolves, bears, cougars, and coyotes—and that the best way to
ensure abundant big game populations is by killing those predators.[5]

Elk are the second-largest deer in North America after moose, and an
adult bull Rocky Mountain elk can weigh as much as seven hundred
pounds and cows up to five hundred pounds. Elk historically lived in a
variety of habitats including mountains, forests, meadows, plains, and
desert scrub, migrating seasonally between summer range at higher ele-
vations and moving downslope to winter range where snow cover is less
deep and the weather less severe, although human development has
complicated elk migration in many areas and reduced the amount of
winter range available to them.[6]

Rocky Mountain elk, *Cervus elaphus nelsoni*, which range through the
northern Rockies and is the primary object of hunters' concern, is one of
six elk subspecies that historically inhabited North America as far north
as northern Alberta, Canada, and south to the Mexican state of Hidalgo.
Elk once roamed the West Coast from Vancouver Island down to Southern California. They were abundant throughout the Great Plains up into
Canada and east almost to the Eastern Seaboard, and before the arrival of
European-American settlers may have numbered as many as ten million.[7]
Two of those subspecies, Merriam's elk and eastern elk, are extinct. Merriam's elk, whose range included southern Arizona, New Mexico, and
western Texas, were killed off in the early 1900s, mainly from overhunting by humans and a combination of hunting and habitat destruction by
overgrazing domestic livestock in Mexico. Eastern elk began disappear-
ing in the southeastern United States by the mid-1700s; their extinction
was completed when the last of them expired in Kansas in 1892.[8]

Four subspecies of North American elk are still with us. The population of Tule elk, endemic to California, declined precipitously between
1800 and 1840, killed in large numbers by market and tallow hunters; by
the 1870s only a remnant number remained out of an estimated historical
population of five hundred thousand. Saved beginning in the mid-1870s
by the efforts of a California rancher who protected the few elk on his
property, the population has increased today to about 3,800 animals in
twenty-one herds.[9] The formerly northern plains–ranging Manitoba elk
subspecies was driven to near extinction by overhunting in the nineteenth and twentieth centuries and are now restricted to some provincial
and national parks in Manitoba and Saskatchewan, Canada.[10]

Roosevelt populations are robust throughout their historical range in the Pacific Northwest into northern California, and Rocky Mountain elk are widespread and abundant in their historical range down the Continental Divide in Canada through the United States. But the current abundance of Rocky Mountain elk belies their past difficulties—and it had nothing to do with four-legged predators.

Wyoming had the Rocky Mountain subspecies in its western mountains and the Manitoban subspecies on its eastern plains, the latter killed off by the same meat and hide hunters that nearly drove the American bison to extinction. Human settlements, and especially sheep and cattle grazing, pushed elk out of most of their traditional winter ranges and cut off migration routes, and it was only the fastness of Wyoming's wild mountain country that kept them from statewide extirpation. Wyoming's remaining Rocky Mountain elk herds were preserved through a combination of setting aside habitat, including Yellowstone and Grand Teton National Parks, and an artificial feeding program by the federal government, begun in 1909, to get the elk through the winter, since there wasn't enough winter range to go around and migration routes were blocked, that is continued today by the USFWS at the National Elk Refuge in Jackson Hole, Wyoming. By 1976 the state's elk population had grown to sixty-five thousand. Rocky Mountain elk from the Yellowstone region have long been used as stock for transplanting to other states to start new elk populations, including into the former ranges of the extinct Merriam's and eastern elk subspecies and the regionally extirpated Manitoba elk.

Idaho also had an abundant historical population of Rocky Mountain elk, but when gold miners and settlers began pouring into Idaho beginning in 1860, hunting eventually whittled the elks' numbers down to an estimated 610 animals on national forestlands by 1918. Between 1915 and 1946, 675 elk from Yellowstone National Park and the National Elk Refuge were released in Idaho, and by 1976 the state's elk population had risen to fifty-one thousand animals.

Lewis and Clark noted large numbers of elk in what is now Montana, especially in the river bottoms, when they passed through the region in 1805 and 1806. Rocky Mountain elk inhabited all of Montana, but as the number of settlers in Montana increased, elk numbers decreased until, by the turn of the last century, they were extirpated from eastern Montana and only a few small herds hung on in the west. A reintroduction program in the early 1900s began to bring their numbers up again, and the best estimates put the 1968–69 Montana elk population at forty-eight to sixty-four thousand.[11]

But hunters are right: Wolves do eat lots of elk—an average of 15.3 elk per year per wolf in Yellowstone's Northern Range, for example.[12] Yet the northern Rockies herds are a long ways from decimation, and for all the angry accusations and hearsay accounts of elk destruction by wolves—along with wolf advocates who sometimes seem to argue that wolves have no impact at all on elk—the situation on the ground is much more complex, nuanced, and dynamic.

Despite the insistence by so many people that wolves are the ultimate killer, sowing destruction and wiping out deer and elk populations wherever they go, claims of their ability to bring about wildlife Armageddon leave much to be desired. As successful predators as they are, wolves also suffer from significant handicaps affecting how much impact they have on prey populations. These limitations have determined what they hunt and how that is directly attributable to the animals' morphology—how their bodies are built—that extends literally from their nose to their toes. It's what Dan MacNulty, assistant professor in the Wildland Resources Department at Utah State University calls, "the limits of wolf predatory power." MacNulty, who has studied wolves and their interactions with prey species extensively, particularly in the Yellowstone region, took some time one afternoon to explain to me what he meant by that.

Surprisingly, the business end of a wolf is where its limitations on killing begin. "The morphology of a wolf's jaw is the weak point in the predatory power of wolves," MacNulty told me. The distance between their killing teeth—canines and incisors—and the joint where the jaw connects to the skull is relatively long; this affects their biting power and prevents them from locking their jaw, as compared to a cougar, which has a shorter nose that allows for superior biting leverage and force. "Prey can wiggle away from a wolf's jaw," MacNulty said. "It's not uncommon for an elk or bison to escape after having been grabbed by a wolf." Wolves are also fairly small relative to their typical prey of large ungulates, as opposed to African lions, for example, that can muscle their victims to the ground. They don't have muscular legs, "just sticks for running" as MacNulty put it. With neither retractable claws nor the ability to rotate their legs at the elbow, wolves can't grapple with their prey as cougars or bears can.

All together, these factors have had a profound effect on how wolves go about hunting. "Wolves can't kill anything they want because they have these limitations," MacNulty explained. That's why wolves hunt in packs and target the very young, the old, and physically disabled or diseased animals. "If a wolf tries to kill a healthy adult elk, there is a real high risk that it [the wolf] will be killed," MacNulty told me.

At the 2013 International Wolf Symposium, conference-goers were treated one evening to some clips of wolves in action at Yellowstone National Park, taken by wildlife filmmaker Bob Landis and introduced by internationally known wolf biologist L. David Mech, who suggested that we pay extra attention to one short film following a pack of wolves on the hunt. The wolves walked or galloped in and out of a Yellowstone elk herd making its way across open sagebrush terrain. Sometimes the wolves would break off a small group or individual animal from the main herd and chase it for a short time before peeling off. Periodically an elk confronted by the wolves would stop and defend itself, and the wolves would test and worry it, then back off. Suddenly the wolves focused on a bull and chased it away from herd. Only then, as the wolves rapidly closed ground, could the human audience detect the limp from the bull's injured rear leg.

Research by MacNulty and others in Yellowstone shows that wolves primarily kill elk calves and cows; they don't start targeting the adults until they are ten to eleven years old, with most killed being older than thirteen. Because older cows are less likely to reproduce, when wolves take these animals it doesn't have much impact on the elk population over the long term. A winter wolf and mountain lion predation study conducted by Idaho Department of Fish and Game wolf biologist Jason Husseman in the Salmon region from 1999 to 2001 found similar predation patterns. Although wolves mostly killed elk calves, the cow elk they killed averaged 12.6 years old compared to cows killed by hunters, which averaged 7.3 years and would have been more likely to breed and produce more elk into the population. Those are important statistics, because more than 80 percent of breeding-age cow elk generally need to survive to maintain the population—and those are the cow elk human hunters, not wolves, are most likely to kill. Interestingly, the study also found that of all the elk that died in the research area during the study period, wolves were only responsible for 7 percent, while hunters killed 52 percent. For deer the figures are 9 percent for wolves and 18 percent for hunters, with mountain lions making up 32 percent of the predation— similar to the percent of elk they killed as well. Hunters continually accuse wolves of killing far more prey than they can consume just for "sport," but Husseman found that 80 percent of the wolf-killed carcasses were at least three-fourths eaten, and all carcasses were fed on to some degree. While surplus killing, which is what wildlife biologists refer to when carnivores deliberately kill more prey than they can eat, does happen among wolves, it is typically in unusual situations, such as in deep snow when prey is more easily killed and the wolves may not be able to suppress their killing instinct as they encounter more vulnerable elk or deer than expected. Because wolves regularly return to a kill site multiple times to eat more of the carcass, photos of lightly consumed deer or elk that appear regularly on anti-wolf websites to prove wolf sport killing as fact were more likely just taken between feedings.[13, 14]

Surplus killing by humans—poaching—has a much greater effect on big game animals than "sport killing" by wolves does. A mule deer mortality study conducted by Oregon Department of Fish and Wildlife researchers between 2005 and 2010 found, much to their shock, that poachers were killing as many deer as were legal hunters in the central part of the state. Even more alarming, the poachers are having a far greater impact on the mule deer population because they are mainly shooting does in their reproductive prime.[15] In northern Idaho, state wildlife officials believe that poachers are killing more big game animals than wolves do—about 600 elk, 80 moose, 260 mule deer, and 1,000 white-tailed deer each year. Making matters worse is that government-suspicious locals often aren't willing to report poachers or cooperate with wildlife law enforcement officers trying to catch them.[16] Poaching of elk, deer, and other big game animals is almost certainly widespread throughout the rural West, and likely throughout the entire United States as well. In 2005 the National Park Service calculated that poaching contributed to the decline of twenty-nine wildlife species in national parks and other lands it manages.[17]

Wolf behavior and social structure also serve to shape and limit their predatory power. Wolves spend time holding onto their territories and fighting and killing one another. These factors, MacNulty explained, can have a huge impact, limiting the number of wolves and wolf packs in an area that, in turn, reduces predation on elk and other prey species. Interestingly, large wolf packs don't necessarily have a significant hunting advantage over smaller packs. In fact, research has shown that hunting efficiency peaks in packs comprising four wolves, and having more wolves in the pack does not translate into significantly greater success. This is due to what MacNulty calls "free riders"—older pack members that hold back and let the younger or more skilled hunters among them do the work and take the risks. In other words, larger packs kill less prey per wolf than smaller packs.[18]

Hunter websites commonly present figures tallying how many elk wolves will kill each year, using one of the many estimates of wolf kill rates, of which there are many due to the considerably varying factors affecting predation in different areas with different environmental conditions and different predator and prey species. Take the 15.3 elk predation rate per wolf per year for each of the ninety-five resident Yellowstone National Park wolves at the end of 2013, and that adds up to 1,454 elk taken per year. Make that calculation for the 450 wolves living in the Greater Yellowstone ecosystem and you get 6,885 elk.[19] Apply that formula to the roughly 1,700 wolves in the northern Rockies and you come up with a figure of 26,010 elk killed every year by wolves. Whatever multiplier you might use and how you go about it—anti-wolf websites often significantly overestimate the northern Rockies wolf population, sometimes more than doubling it—you can end up with some big numbers. Hunters look at those numbers and see a lot of economically valuable elk lost to predators and far fewer animals they can harvest for themselves. Except it isn't quite so simple.

For one thing, wild ungulates hardly need humans to protect them from native carnivores. Elk have been around for a long time, evolving alongside a fearsome lineup of very large predators that roamed North America tens of thousands of years ago years ago that included saber-toothed cats, dire wolves, American lions, American cheetahs, and short-faced bears—all of which elk, along with deer, moose, bison, pronghorns, muskoxen, caribou, and mountain sheep and goats, have outlasted.[20]

The evolutionary strategies that animals wolves prey on have adapted to survive include both morphological and behavioral. Exceptional alertness is a common trait of most animals that are hunted by wolves, along with the ability to run fast or navigate steep and difficult terrain adeptly and quickly. Larger prey species may stand their ground and fight back with antlers, horns, and sharp hooves when confronted by wolves, and are capable of killing them. Fleeing into deep water is a common defensive tactic against wolves, as long-legged ungulates can stand in deeper water than wolves, putting the latter at a disadvantage. Gathering in herds offers more eyes to watch for predators, and a large number of moving animals helps confuse hunting wolves and, in the crowd, reduces the odds that any individual will be the one the wolves ultimately catch. Elk and other ungulates often herd up in the winter, a time when they are most vulnerable to being killed by wolves. Migration puts distance between prey species and wolves and makes the wolves spend more time looking for them. Some ungulates such as caribou spread out over large areas, which makes each individual animal less likely to be discovered by wolves. Elk and other species of ungulates give birth to their young during the same brief period each year, "swamping" wolves with far more vulnerable baby animals than the wolves can possibly find and ensuring that enough will survive to reach adulthood and reproduce.[21]

The effectiveness of these various survival strategies against predators is readily seen in how northern Rocky Mountain elk populations adapted to the sudden appearance of wolves in the mid-1990s, an animal their species had evolved with but today's animals had no previous experience dealing with. In fact, elk populations in Montana, Wyoming, and Idaho have been generally increasing over the past half-century. In 2011—sixteen years after wolves were reintroduced and before intensive wolf hunting and trapping were instituted to "control" their numbers—there were 371,000 elk in the three states combined, up more than 20,000 from the previous year. Montana's elk population had grown by 20 percent over the previous five years to 150,000, while Wyoming's population of 120,000 was 50 percent higher than Wyoming Game and Fish considered desirable at the time. With just over 100,000 elk, Idaho's statewide population had declined about 20 percent, mainly in the central part of the state and mostly driven by natural changes in habitat that were less desirable for elk. Overall, though, elk numbers for most of the state were at or above Idaho Fish and Game's goals.[22, 23]

MacNulty had pointed out to me the obvious regarding wolves and their natural prey—something that doesn't occur to people who keep insisting that wolves will eventually destroy all the big game animals: If wolves were inclined to do that, they would have done it thousands of years ago, and deer, elk, and other wild ungulates would now be among the ranks of the extinct. That hasn't happened, and it is not going to—at least not because of wolves.

But elk in the West are managed to provide hunters with maximum hunting opportunities, and that completely changes the context by which elk populations are defined as ample and healthy. To that end, state wildlife agencies mange elk (as well as deer and other big game animals) under the concept of maximum sustainable yield to produce an ongoing harvestable surplus of animals for hunters to kill.

In the case of elk management, maximum sustainable yield is the maximum number of animals that hunters can harvest out of an elk population without reducing it over time. Determining the maximum sustainable yield, and therefore the harvestable surplus, is calculated by the mathematical relationship by which elk, deer, and many other wildlife populations grow. Imagine an "S" curve, called a Sigmoid Growth Curve, that represents an elk population. At the bottom of the curve is a small, struggling population, where every animal that dies from disease, starvation, predation, or other causes has a disproportionate effect on the population as a whole since there are so few individuals. At the top of the curve is a population at equilibrium, with the maximum number of animals the habitat will support and where the number of animals that die each year is about the same as the animals that are born, maintaining a roughly stable population at carrying capacity. In the middle of the curve is where the population growth is happening as cow elk increase the number of calves they give birth to in response to the additional available habitat and food that can accommodate more animals.[24]

If you are an elk manager charged with providing as much hunting opportunity for as many hunters as possible, for obvious reasons you don't want to be at the bottom of the curve. But you don't want to be at equilibrium either, because there are no surplus animals to harvest. But in the middle of the curve is just right—where the elk cows will eternally pump out calves intended to take the population to an equilibrium they will never reach because your hunters will shoot them first.

This is called abundance management, where populations of wolves, mountain lions, bears, and coyotes are manipulated downward for the purpose of producing the largest possible number of big game animals for hunters to harvest, and that goal often takes precedence over other wildlife values. State wildlife agencies divide their state into administrative districts, variously named hunting districts or game or wildlife management units or zones, and establish management objectives, or "MOs," for different game species in each of those units. One of the primary ways wildlife biologists estimate elk populations is through winter and early-spring aerial surveys; they then use statistical formulas and computer models to calculate total elk numbers and population trends. Elk management objectives are set for each unit or area, taking into account a number of factors such as hunting demand, social tolerance by people—usually dictated by how much damage elk do on private property—predation levels, and habitat carrying capacity. That MO will likely include not just an overall population target but also desirable levels of calf birth rates and numbers, ratios, and age ranges of bulls and cows.[25]

However, maintaining those management objectives and keeping the elk in the middle of that Sigmoid Growth Curve is far easier said than done, simply because there are so many things affecting wildlife populations over which humans have little or no control. Weather is a big one, with huge and wide-ranging impacts on wildlife. Severe winters can kill large numbers of elk and deer as they deplete fat reserves, starve if food is too difficult to find, and struggle in deep snow that makes them more vulnerable to predators. Drought conditions can suppress spring and early-summer green-up of grasses and other forage plants that ungulates need after expending fat reserves through the winter, and elk calves born to undernourished cows may be less likely to survive.

Habitat is the other big factor. While wildlife habitat can be protected from development, and hunters' organizations such as the Rocky Mountain Elk Foundation, The Mule Deer Foundation, and others have invested many millions of dollars in improving and protecting elk and deer habitat, those efforts generally affect relatively small areas. Across the larger landscape, human development and activities have a huge, and usually negative, impact, especially on wildlife such as elk that need large wild areas to roam, high-elevation summer range, low-elevation winter range, and secure, barrier-free migration corridors to travel between the two. Predation and harvest by hunters are the other two significant factors influencing elk populations.[26]

Setting hunting season lengths and limiting the number of elk tags available are ways hunter harvest is controlled. Depending on the status of the herd and management goals, an unlimited number of tags might be sold for some areas, while in others only a limited number may be available that are awarded through a lottery system.

Wildlife managers have a variety of metrics they use to determine how well elk herds are faring, but a basic one is how many elk calves are born, or recruited, into the herd each year, measured by the number of calves per one hundred cows. If you have overall good survival of calves and cows, a ratio of thirty calves or more to one hundred cows is a pretty good place to be; but if you start dropping below twenty, your herd may be having a problem.[27] When recruitment and overall elk numbers begin to fall and that maximum sustainable yield is threatened, wildlife managers start looking at what might be the cause. Inadequate nutrition due to environmental factors often turns out to be the major reason for poor calf survival, but sometimes predators, including wolves, are part of the mix. But that, also, is not so simple.

That's because of a predator-prey relationship concept known as compensatory and additive mortality, which refers to whether an animal killed by a predator would have otherwise died of something else. Vulnerable elk—an elderly cow, an injured bull, or a starving calf—killed by wolves would not reduce the overall elk population because those animals were going to die soon anyway, and that mortality would be considered compensatory. Broadly speaking, in most circumstances predation on big game animals by wolves and other wild carnivores is usually compensatory. Hunters calling for the widespread killing of wolves, or any other predator for that matter, across large areas or entire states assume that is going to automatically increase elk numbers. But if predation is compensatory in a given area, then killing wolves won't have much effect on the elk, because more elk will just die of other causes to compensate for those not eaten by wolves. However, predation on big game can also be additive when the animals that wolves (or other predators) kill are not offset by fewer animals dying of other causes and therefore is additional mortality that can reduce the prey population over time. (Because human hunters usually kill healthy elk, either bulls in their prime or cows in their reproductive years, hunting by people is virtually always additive.) Big game animals are at particular risk from additive mortality by predators when their populations are near the bottom of that Sigmoid Growth Curve.[28]

That's the situation in Idaho's Clearwater region, specifically within the Lolo and Selway Elk Zones, where additive mortality by wolves is substantially suppressing elk populations and has significantly lowered hunting opportunities over time. Ever since wolves were first reintroduced into Idaho, hunters have been pointing to declining elk herds in "the Lolo" as proof of their destructive effects on big game. It's true that elk in the Clearwater region are struggling and that predation by wolves is a major factor. But the situation there is less a story about elk versus wolves than about how wildlife, weather, and a changing landscape interact over time, and this story begins in the early years of the last century.

In 1910, an exceptionally dry year in the northern Rocky Mountain states, massive wildfires swept across central and northern Idaho and in northwestern Montana as well, burning about three million acres of forest and killing more than seventy firefighters along with a number of homesteaders.[29,30] While the fires were a disaster in terms of lost lives, property, and merchantable timber, for elk, deer, and many other species of wildlife, it was the beginning of a golden age. Grasses, forbs, shrubs, and small trees began regrowing in the burned areas—the early seral stage of forest recovery, called forest succession—creating prime habitat full of nutritious food sources for grazing and browsing animals like elk and deer. In 1937 more fires in the region created even more early-stage forest successional habitat favorable to elk that peaked between the late

1940s and late 1970s. In response, the central Idaho elk herds grew and the elk population in the Lolo Elk Zone reached a high of about sixteen thousand animals in 1989.[31]

But the forests were slowly growing back, and the amount of prime early seral stage elk habitat was shrinking. Also, after the fires of 1910 the federal government began to aggressively put out wildfires on public lands, which reduced the amount of early seral stage forest that histori-cally made up as much as 45 percent of the region down to about 14 percent. Almost all of the two elk zones are within national forestlands, and for a time logging, which also stimulates early seral stage growth, filled in for wildfires. But logging levels have slowed considerably on public lands since the heydays of the 1970s and 80s.

In the early 1990s, calf recruitment began seriously declining. A hard winter in 1996–97—just after the second wave of wolves were reintro-duced into central Idaho—produced a record snow year, 200 percent above normal. Large numbers of elk in the Lolo and Selway Elk Zones— as much as 40 percent of some herds—died in the deep snow and cold. The decline in the number of elk calves surviving their first months con-tinued. By 2007 the elk population was down to 3,381 cows and 934 bulls in the Selway Zone, and by 2010 the population was down to 1,358 cows and 594 bulls in the Lolo Zone.[32] Idaho Department of Fish and Game wildlife biologists found that mountain lions and black bears were re-sponsible for most of the elk calf mortality. Increased recreational hunt-ing for mountain lions and bears helped dull their impact on the elk, but as wolf numbers increased in the two zones, they became the limiting factor for rebuilding the elk herds.[33]

When I talked with Kent Laudon, who formerly worked with the Nez Perce wolf recovery team surveying wolves in central Idaho along with Curt Mack and Jim Holyan and is now a wolf management specialist with Montana Fish, Wildlife and Parks, he questioned whether killing wolves over an expansive area would really help to any significant de-gree if the habitat that once supported large numbers of elk just wasn't there anymore. "It's well documented that the elk population in the Clearwater region was declining before the wolves came in," Laudon told me. "Then, all you heard was 'habitat, habitat, habitat,' and now all you hear is 'wolf, wolf, wolf.'"

But "wolf, wolf, wolf" is the policy direction that hunters have pushed state wildlife agencies in, and when the deputy director of Idaho Fish and Game testifies before an Idaho House Committee on a two-million-dollar wolf control bill that wolves killing elk—a native predator eating natural prey—is "depredation" on "our wildlife," it's clear that state wildlife agencies don't always need much prodding in that direction.[34]

Idaho Fish and Game has been quietly killing wolves in the Clearwa-ter region since 2010 to try and boost elk numbers. In early 2014, under the direction of Idaho Fish and Game with no public notice, Wildlife

Services agents shot twenty-three wolves in the Lolo Zone from a helicopter.[35] Aaron Miles, director of the Nez Perce's Natural Resources Department, under which the Nez Perce Wolf Recovery Program operates, called it an arrogant act that ignored the habitat issue in the Clearwater region. Prior to those shootings, Idaho Fish and Game killed twenty-five wolves in the Lolo region in six previous control actions. During the 2013–14 season, hunters and trappers killed seventeen wolves in the Lolo region out of its estimated population of seventy-five to one hundred.[36]

Wildlife politics can also send elk numbers back down that Sigmoid Growth Curve and help crash elk numbers even more effectively than predators. In 2003 the Montana state legislature passed House Bill 42, a livestock industry–driven bill sponsored by then Republican Montana representative, now state senator, Debby Barrett that effectively required Montana Fish, Wildlife and Parks to manage the state's elk herds at or below management objective—ranchers don't like elk competing with their cows for grass—that would eventually cause the state's elk population to decline.[37] But regional wildlife managers in Montana are given a lot of authority when it comes to setting management objectives and hunting seasons, and the state wildlife commissioners generally sign off on their recommendations without much concern. Most elk managers didn't take HB 42 very seriously.[38]

"The manager in Region 2, in the Bitterroot Valley, took HB 42 seriously and knocked the elk population down pretty hard," noted Bob Ream, who was a commissioner with Montana Fish, Wildlife and Parks from 2009 to 2013, served on the Northern Rocky Mountain Wolf Recovery Team from 1974 to 1988, and started the University of Montana Wolf Ecology Project, which studied the first wolves to begin recolonizing northwestern Montana in the late 1970s. "Then we had the wolves come in and mountain lions increased. So we had the perfect storm in the Bitterroot Valley and the controversy that the wolves were killing all the elk."

With the Bitterroot Valley's elk population deliberately reduced by wildlife managers, followed by an increase in the large predator population and reduction of the elk calf-to-cow ratio to an undesirable 14:100, Montana Fish, Wildlife and Parks and the University of Montana undertook a three-year study beginning in 2010 to look at elk survival in the East and West Fork Bitterroot Valley herds and whether it was the wolves' doing, as many people were claiming.[39] The study found that mountain lions were killing the most elk calves and cows, followed by bears, with wolves a distant third.[40, 41] In 2012 the calf-to-cow ratio was up to 56:100 for the East Fork Bitterroot herd, and researchers believe that it is mountain lion predation that drives those elk populations.[42] Because mountain lions are opportunistic stalk-and-ambush predators rather than coursing predators like wolves, which chase down prey after detecting a weakness, mountain lions may be more likely to cause additive mortality.

In spring 2013 state wildlife biologists counted 7,373 elk in the Bitterroot region, the highest number seen in the past forty-eight years, and the West Fork calf-to-cow ratio was up to 33:100.[43] The wolf population in the Bitterroots remains steady, and in 2014 there were fifteen confirmed wolf packs and an estimated total population of sixty to seventy wolves.[44]

But wherever there are wolves, they are regularly blamed for declines in big game, an assumption that is often refuted by good scientific research. Completed in 2013, a study of declining calf-to-cow ratios in Wyoming's Absaroka Mountains Clarks Fork elk herd by the Wyoming Cooperative Fish and Wildlife Research Unit found that increased predation by grizzly bears and habitat limitations driven by drought have lowered the quality and availability of forage, not wolf predation or stress caused by the presence of wolves. (Another popular idea among hunters is that when wolves are not killing elk and deer, they are running them to death. In fact, elk don't usually even take notice of wolves until they approach within about a half-mile or so, causing them to become more alert and perhaps shift their location slightly, but nothing remotely resembling panicked flight.)[45]

Similar scenarios are playing out in the Upper Midwest where wolves are under the same pressures and accusations as wolves in the northern Rockies. Wisconsin hunters had insisted that wolves were killing large numbers of white-tailed deer fawns in the state's northern forest region and pressured the Wisconsin Department of Natural Resources to do a study to prove it. That study, begun in 2011 and completed in 2014, found no link between wolves and fawn mortality but did determine that a large percentage of fawns were dying of starvation due to poor habitat conditions. The primary cause of deer deaths in Wisconsin's North Woods—15 percent of the does and 40 percent of the bucks—is from human hunters.[46]

It's not just the alleged "decimation" of elk and deer by wolves that has not held up to scientific scrutiny. Bighorn sheep in Yellowstone National Park have been increasing 7 percent each year since 1998, and research has shown that wolves have not affected the wild sheep population.[47, 48] Hunters and politicians have long blamed wolves for steeply declining moose numbers in the Yellowstone region over the past twenty-five years. However, the latest research shows that wolf reintroduction has had little or no effect, with wolves killing, at most, an average of three moose per year since the 1995 reintroduction, and that habitat changes from extensive wildfires in 1988, which destroyed large tracts of old-growth forest in the Yellowstone region, is the probable culprit.[49]

At the end of 2013, 70 percent of Montana's elk hunting zones were at or above management objective, as were 20.5 of 29 elk zones in Idaho; and 2012 and 2013 were record elk hunting seasons in Wyoming.[50, 51, 52] But the plethora of research, along with practical experience, showing that wolves clearly are not the ultimate predator that all but exterminates big game populations has done little to convince the anti-wolf factions, who continue to make "wolf, wolf, wolf" the management policy in the northern Rocky Mountain states. And hunters in the Pacific Northwest point to the devastation wolves have supposedly caused there as foretelling the future of "their" elk and deer herds as wolves recolonize that region.

Hunters charge that wolves are decimating elk populations in the northern Rockies; however, most elk herds are doing fine. Photo by Jim Yuskavitch

TEN

Into the Pacific Northwest

At an Oregon Department of Fish and Wildlife meeting in La Grande in mid-October 2011, a state wildlife biologist sitting next to me leaned over and casually mentioned there was a wolf in Harney County, in southeastern Oregon's high desert country. That was a juicy tidbit of news, since at the time there were only two wolf packs in Oregon—both located in the extreme northeastern part of the state—for a known statewide population of twenty-one animals. The Imnaha pack had fourteen members, while the Wenaha pack had six, plus one dispersing male wolf from the Imnaha pack whose radio collar signal had vanished somewhere in the Ochoco Mountains in central Oregon at the end of September.[1] At the moment, this particular wolf was hanging around the GI Ranch on the Harney-Crook county border. Local ODFW biologists were making area ranchers aware of his presence, but not too many other people knew about him. Less than a week later, October 24, the wolf was 75 miles to the southwest near Fort Rock.[2]

Born into the Imnaha pack in April 2009, this wolf dispersed in September 2011, heading south through the Strawberry Mountains and down Silvies Valley, traveling in a straight line, as wolves on the move do, and keeping to the timbered national forestlands before striking west into open sagebrush country.

The reason so much was known about him and his wanderings was that he wore a collar with GPS—Global Positioning System—technology that sent signals to satellites, allowing his position and movements to be tracked. GPS collars are programmed to transmit location information at certain times and intervals, and that data can be periodically downloaded for detailed information on an animal's travels.

The wolf was captured by ODFW biologists and fitted with a GPS collar on February 25, 2011. They designated him OR7—OR to indicate that he was an Oregon-born wolf and 7 because he was the seventh Oregon wolf to be captured and fitted with either a VHF or GPS tracking collar. Seven months later he dispersed from his natal pack, and by early November he was roaming the crest of the southern Cascade Mountains around Diamond Peak and Mount Thielsen in the Umpqua National Forest, just north of Crater Lake National Park, occasionally using the Pacific Crest National Scenic Trail as his travel corridor.[3] Then OR7 began moving south, toward California and worldwide fame.

It didn't take very long after the dispersing wolf B-45 was captured in late March 1999 and returned to Idaho for more wolves to make their way into Oregon—unfortunately to bad ends. On May 30, 2000, a wolf was hit by a vehicle and killed along Interstate 84 south of Baker City while it was feeding on a road-killed fox.[4] The wolf wore a radio collar identifying it as B-83, a male disperser from Idaho's Timberline pack, and just a little over a year old.[5] That same year, another wolf was found dead from a gunshot wound between Ukiah and Pendleton. Although it was not wearing a radio collar, DNA samples from the female wolf confirmed that she too originated in Idaho.[6]

But wolves from Idaho continued to disperse into Oregon, and state wildlife officials confirmed the state's first wolf pack, the Wenaha pack, in 2008. It was discovered in July of that year by wildlife biologists conducting howling surveys when at least two adults and two pups responded.[7]

The previous year the body of a badly decomposed female gray wolf was found illegally shot in Union County and was believed to possibly have been a member of the Wenaha pack.[8] Founded by a pair of un-collared Idaho wolves, their territory was in extreme northeastern Oregon, including the Wenaha-Tucannon Wilderness, and spilled over the state line into Washington.

One of the ways ODFW biologists were looking for wolves in Oregon in the early years, and specifically in northeastern Oregon, where wolves were most expected to disperse from neighboring Idaho, was by taking to the air and searching for the signals of collared wolves that had been reported as missing by Idaho wildlife biologists. That's how they found B-300, a female gray wolf from, ironically, the Timberline pack, the same pack that the ill-fated B-83 had dispersed from into Oregon eight years earlier. They finally confirmed her presence in Oregon on January 23, 2008, videoing the wolf resolutely trudging through deep snow in the Wallowa-Whitman National Forest.[9]

Unlike B-45, B-300 was allowed to stay, and her story would be much longer and more successful, at least from a biological standpoint. By the following summer she had mated with an un-collared male wolf from Idaho, and that November ODFW biologists documented ten members of the pack they had named the Imnaha pack, which roamed national forest and private ranchlands east of Joseph. Eventually biologists captured B-

300, put a new collar on her, re-designated her OR2, and captured and collared her mate as well (OR4).[10] Oregon wolf advocates named OR2 Sophie.

Wolves reintroduced in the northern Rockies had already demonstrated how prolific they were and capable of expanding their range rather quickly. The fact that wolves were already coming into the Pacific Northwest within five years of their release into Idaho was proof enough of that. During a conversation in late August 2012, Russ Morgan, ODFW wolf coordinator, told me how, based on his experience, once packs form, wolves spread quickly. "There will be more around than you think there are," he said, and they were finding wolves "all over the place" in northeastern Oregon.

Just four days later, on August 25, Morgan had an experience dramatically reinforcing that observation. He and Mark Henjum, then-wildlife biologist for the Umatilla National Forest and previous ODFW wolf coordinator, were on an early-season bow hunt for elk in the Eagle Cap Wilderness when they heard wolves howling. "As soon as he heard those howls, Russ went from elk hunter back to a wolf biologist and went running toward them," Henjum recalled. "He saw five pups in the meadow. Then two adults stood up and were about to lie back down again when they realized they had been discovered by people and they all took off." Morgan had unexpectedly discovered the Minam pack—a pack that no human knew existed until that moment. There were wolves all over the place.

By the end of 2012, Oregon had six confirmed packs, two more than the previous year, and a total population of forty-eight wolves, including some lone animals, up from twenty-nine wolves in 2011. By early 2014 two more packs had formed, for a total of eight packs and sixty-four wolves, including several wolves wandering the state on their own. Although there was one known wolf—OR7—and some suspected wolves in Oregon's Cascade Mountains, all the state's packs were concentrated in northeastern Oregon.[11]

Wolf recolonization in Washington State to the north was tracking similar to Oregon. Washington wildlife biologists confirmed the state's first breeding wolf pack in 2008 in Okanogan County. Designated the Lookout pack, it had at least ten members, four of them pups. In 2009 a second pack was confirmed in Pend Oreille County and named the Diamond pack. It had six pups that year. Biologists tested hairs from one of the pack's male members and found him linked genetically to wolves from Alberta, northern Idaho, and northwestern Montana—related to the naturally establishing wolves from Canada rather than from the reintroduced population. In December 2010 the pack had twelve members. In July 2011 the state had five wolf packs. By December 2013 there were ten confirmed packs in northeastern Washington and three in the northern

Cascade Mountains, for a minimum total wolf population of fifty-two animals and five breeding pairs for that year.[12]

Both states, as with the rest of the West, had exterminated their wolves by the 1940s, although occasional wolves were reported over the following decades; perhaps some of those reports really were wolves passing through and vanishing, their fates unknown. But in Washington's wild North Cascades region, bumping up against British Columbia, there was some early bona fide wolf activity. During the 1990s there were twenty confirmed wolf sightings, mostly in the North Cascades. Researchers eventually concluded that there may have been one or two packs that had pups in that region but had for some reason disappeared.[13] But with the confirmation of the Lookout pack in Washington and the Wenaha pack in Oregon in 2008, the recolonization of wolves into the Pacific Northwest had indisputably begun.

There were some key differences between wolf recovery in the northern Rockies and the Pacific Northwest. The most obvious difference was that in the northern Rockies wolves were transported from Canada by the federal government and turned loose in Yellowstone National Park and central Idaho as part of a deliberate reintroduction plan, while wolves in the Pacific Northwest were moving in on their own, mostly from Idaho but from Canada as well. This didn't give opponents of wolf recovery as obvious a target or course of action as in the northern Rockies, where lawsuits were filed against the federal government to stop the releases or states simply refused to actively cooperate in the recovery, as Wyoming and Idaho did. Also, both Washington and Oregon have state Endangered Species Acts under which wolves are listed as endangered, so even after the April 2011 political delisting of the Northern Rockies Distinct Population Segment, which included parts of eastern Washington and Oregon, wolves remained legally protected in the two states. Perhaps the most significant difference was the political landscape in Oregon and Washington, where the Democratic Party—much more sympathetic to environmental issues, including wolves, than the Republicans who dominated the Rocky Mountain states—often won the races for governor and controlled the state legislatures. On top of that, a majority of the region's residents looked favorably on wolves. After B-45 was captured and sent back to Idaho in 1999, a survey conducted by the Portland, Oregon, polling firm Davis & Hibbitts and funded by the conservation organizations Oregon Natural Desert Association, Defenders of Wildlife, Oregon Natural Resources Council (now Oregon Wild), and Predator Defense Institute found that 70 percent of Oregonians supported bringing wolves back to their state.[14] In Washington, support for wolf recovery is 75 percent.[15]

But there were, and are, still plenty of people in the Pacific Northwest who are against wolf recovery, the same groups that oppose wolves in the northern Rockies—hunters, ranchers, and rural residents, especially those who live in agricultural country east of the Cascade Mountains, where the wolves showed up first, and who have more culturally in common with the residents of Grangeville, Idaho, than the urban areas of their own states.

Unlike Idaho and Wyoming, both Pacific Northwest states moved forward with developing wolf management plans with a considerable amount of input by the public—twenty-three public meetings and more than sixty-five thousand public comments in the case of Washington State's wolf plan—in an attempt to incorporate a diversity of their citizens' views about wolves and how they should be managed, as opposed to the former states, whose wolf management plans really reflected only the views of the political establishment of ranchers, hunters, and other rural interests.

Because the first dispersing wolf from the northern Rocky Mountain wolf recovery region ended up in Oregon, that state was first to start moving in the direction of writing a wolf plan, beginning with a series of four workshops in 2002, presented to the Oregon Fish and Wildlife Commission, featuring a variety of wolf experts, scientists, politicians, wildlife agency personnel, and representatives from conservation, hunting, and ranching groups—all of whom had experience with wolves and wolf recovery in the northern Rockies.

Held in ODFW's former Portland office, the workshops played to a packed house—casually dressed environmentalists hoping to see support for wolves, men in tight-fitting jeans and cowboy hats worried about how wolves would affect their livelihoods, and lawyers in three-piece suits anticipating the legal and lobbying work that wolves always bring. As the presenters described their experiences and involvement with wolves in the northern Rockies, it was clear to the commissioners and members of the audience that wolf recovery would be equally contentious in the Pacific Northwest as it was in the northern Rockies.

One of the presenters, former Idaho Fish and Game director Rod Sando, told the commissioners, "There is no other resource issue like this issue. People will tell you things [about wolves] that are unbelievable. And they believe them. I've never been around any area of resource management with more crazy ideas." He also warned the commissioners that in Oregon wolves would have the support of a silent majority, while a vocal minority would oppose them. "That will be a tough position [to be in]," he predicted. "It's a political tar baby—the harder you hit it, the more you'll stick to it."[16]

Mack Birkmaier of the Oregon Cattlemen's Association gave a preview of what the position of the Oregon anti-wolf faction would be when, during his presentation, he described wolves as ". . . cruel killers and don't let anybody kid you. They run cattle and sheep to exhaustion, chew on their flesh, and eat them when they're still alive. They're not little puppy dogs."[17] An Idaho official attending one of the workshops angrily described "wolf-lovers" as "people who believe that God is dead and Elvis is alive."

The Oregon Department of Fish and Wildlife completed its Wolf Conservation and Management Plan in 2005, updating it in 2010. The Washington Department of Fish and Wildlife got a later start, completing its Wolf Conservation and Management Plan in 2011. The plans addressed a variety of wolf issues, including expected conflicts with livestock and people; impacts and interactions with deer, elk, and other wildlife species; and management objectives and strategies. Of special interest to both pro- and anti-wolf people were the criteria for removing them from the states' Endangered Species List. That would open the door for the potential of wolf hunting seasons that, depending on one's point of view, were either a vital tool for managing the animals or a threat to wolf recovery and ecologically viable populations.

For recovery purposes, Washington divided the state into three recovery regions: Eastern Washington, Northern Cascades, and Southern Cascades and Northwest Coast. Wolves could be downgraded from state endangered to state threatened when there were six breeding pairs (a breeding pair being a male and female wolf with at least two pups that survive to the end of the year the pups were born) for three consecutive years, evenly divided in the three recovery regions. Wolves could be taken off the list entirely when there were fifteen breeding pairs for three consecutive years, including four pairs in each of the three regions and three additional pairs anywhere else in the state.[18]

Oregon's plan divides the state into eastern and western recovery zones. Wolves would be considered for potential delisting from the state ESA when there were four breeding pairs in eastern Oregon for three consecutive years. (ODFW wildlife biologists believe that is the minimum number of wolves needed to maintain a self-sustaining wolf population in Oregon.) Once that population objective was reached, the focus would be on meeting a statewide population objective of seven breeding pairs for three consecutive years. Based on an average wolf population of 6.4 to 7.8 wolves per pack and 1.5 to 1.63 packs per breeding pair in Idaho, seven breeding pairs of wolves would pencil out to be ten or eleven packs and sixty-seven to eighty-nine wolves.[19] For Washington, fifteen breeding pairs would work out to be a statewide total of twenty-three to twenty-four packs and 144 to 190 individual wolves.

Even though the plans were developed with input from the livestock industry and hunting organizations, those groups weren't done opposing wolf recovery and expansion. In Oregon the Oregon Cattlemen's Association and various hunting groups tapped sympathetic, mostly rural, state legislators, just as anti-wolf groups had in the northern Rockies, to bring forward wolf-related legislation mostly intended to make it easier to kill them.

After the livestock industry lost the battle to stop wolf reintroduction in the northern Rockies, turning to state legislatures to pass laws loosening restrictions on killing wolves was an effective strategy in this rural, politically conservative region. An example is Senate Bill 200, signed into law by Montana Governor Steve Bullock, a Democrat, in 2013, which allows ranchers to shoot wolves on their property without a license if the wolf is believed to be a threat to human safety, livestock, or dogs—as is allowed in Idaho. Ranchers believe the law permits them to protect their property, while wolf advocates fear it will be used to randomly kill wolves that are not threatening anyone or anything.[20, 21] But even in the anti-wolf climate of the northern Rockies, some bills went too far. Republican Montana State Senator Joe Balyeat's 2010 bill declaring that the federal government "lacks the authority to impose wolves on Montana" and demands that "the United States agree in writing to unfettered state management of wolves with no further assertion of federal authority" died in committee.[22]

In the Pacific Northwest, wolf bills tended to try to create wolf management policy rather than make ambitious and constitutionally questionable challenges to federal authority over the states. In Oregon that ranged from trying to have wolves removed from the state Endangered Species List to allowing people to shoot wolves in "self-defense."[23] Democratic majorities in the state legislature and a more influential environmental movement than in the northern Rockies have helped kill or defeat attempts to legislate wolf management, which are introduced in just about every legislative session. The same legislative scenario plays out in the Washington state legislature as well, such as the failed Senate Bill 5187 introduced in 2013 that would have allowed ranchers to shoot depredating wolves without a special permit issued by the state (although both Oregon and Washington established administrative rules allowing ranchers to shoot wolves on the spot if they see them in the act of attacking livestock—something that seldom happens).[24]

On the pro-wolf legislation side, in 2011 the Oregon state legislature passed a law, HB 3560, that funds compensation for ranchers who lose livestock to wolves and helps pay for implementing nonlethal methods to deter wolf attacks on domestic stock. Washington passed a similar law, SB 5193, in 2013, funded by a ten-dollar additional charge on vanity license plates.

While there are not enough wolves yet in Washington and Oregon to have any detectable effect on deer and elk, they were giving ranchers a problem. In Oregon wolves began killing domestic livestock much sooner than state wildlife managers had anticipated.[25]

Barely a year after Oregon's first wolf pack formed, a rancher in the Keating Valley in Baker County found a dozen lambs on his ranch killed by predators one morning, with only a few of them eaten. Oregon Department of Fish and Wildlife wolf coordinator Russ Morgan set up surveillance cameras triggered by movement. When the wolves came back on April 13, 2009, and killed two more lambs, they were photographed by one of the cameras.[26] ODFW biologists captured one of the wolves on May 3 and put a radio collar on him, making him OR1, the first Oregon wolf to be collared.

Under Oregon's wolf management plan, wolves that chronically attack livestock can be killed, but first a rancher must try nonlethal methods for deterring attacks, and the state will help out. The rancher cooperated, adopting a range of known methods for scaring wolves away from livestock, but to no avail. By September the pair had killed twenty-nine of the rancher's stock in four or five incidents. Wildlife Services agents, in accordance with the state's management plan and the special provisions made for wolves in the federal Endangered Species Act, shot the two Keating Valley wolves on September 5, 2009. Genetic testing linked them to Idaho wolves, but it was uncertain whether they had dispersed into Oregon from Idaho or were born to an Oregon wolf pack. The animals were also a little young to be on their own, and state biologists speculated that may have been why they resorted to attacking easier-to-catch domestic animals rather than their normal prey of deer and elk.[27, 28]

While many ranchers have traditionally preferred shooting predators like wolves, advocates of wolf recovery have been promoting nonlethal deterrents, techniques ranchers can use to reduce or prevent wolves from attacking and killing their stock. Surprisingly, the first attempts at nonlethal control of wolves and coyotes were between 1907 and 1910, just as the federal government was beginning to get into the predator killing business. The USDA Forest Service and the US Bureau of Plant Industry constructed wolf-and-coyote-proof fences at Billy Meadows in what was then the Wallowa National Forest, now the Wallowa-Whitman, and on several locations in Colorado's Cochetopa National Forest—eventually split up into the Gunnison, Rio Grande, and San Isabel National Forests.[29] Interestingly, Billy Meadows was where the elk brought in from Wyoming to restore Oregon's elk populations were penned in 1912.[30] Billy Meadows was also where a hunter shot and killed Oregon's last grizzly bear in the late 1930s.[31] It's not likely that the federal government in 1907 was actually looking for ways for livestock and wolves to coexist. Rather, the wolf-proof fences were just experiments to try to further maximize the use of national forest grazing lands by cows and sheep.

But today, nonlethal deterrents are specifically being deployed to help wolves and livestock coexist and, although they didn't fend off the Keating Valley wolves, can be very effective. One ranching tradition is to dump the carcasses of cattle that have died from disease, injury, or other causes into what ranchers refer to as "bone piles." Bone piles are known to attract wolves and other predators onto a rancher's property, and getting rid of them by burning and burying carcasses instead can make a big difference in whether wolves come around. Fences, either permanent or portable, and penning livestock at night can also significantly reduce wolf predation on cattle and sheep. A less-expensive and portable alternative to fencing that can be set up to fend off wolf attacks is called fladry, where a thin rope line is strung around a grazing herd of animals and red flags are hung at eighteen-inch intervals; a fladry can be set up to protect a large area. Wolves don't like "new" things, and the motion of the flags will frighten them off. However, once wolves become used to it, a fladry may no longer work very well, although adding an electric fence can extend its effectiveness. Livestock-guarding dogs such as the Anatolian shepherd, Great Pyrenees, and Akbas are also frequently employed to protect livestock from wolves and other predators. Range riders—people on horseback—can help keep wolves away by their mere presence or chasing them off if need be. Shooting nonlethal ammunition such as cracker shells, beanbag shells, and rubber bullets can also discourage wolves from coming around. One of the more high-tech approaches is a radio-activated guard system, or RAG box. An idea developed by a Montana rancher in the early 1990s, a RAG box has a receiver that picks up the signal of radio-collared wolves when they approach, which sets off alarms and lights and collects information that identifies the trespasser.[32]

These methods do work; state wildlife personnel will help ranchers implement nonlethal methods, and federal funds are available to offset costs. And despite the hard line the livestock industry has taken on wolf recovery—often expressed as "shoot, shovel, and shut up"—there are many ranchers who are willing to give nonlethal wolf deterrents a try.

Environmental groups are also moving to help wolves and livestock coexist. In Washington State, Conservation Northwest is funding range riders in several counties to help prevent wolf attacks on livestock and keeping track of wolf pack locations through collared animals' GPS signals.[33] One of the best examples of a large nonlethal deterrent project initiated by a nonprofit conservation organization is Defenders of Wildlife's Wood River Wolf Project in Blaine County, central Idaho. The project began in 2007 when wolves from the Phantom Hill pack began killing sheep grazing on public lands in the Sawtooth Mountains region. Federal and state officials planned to destroy the pack, but the public pushed back. Defenders of Wildlife brought area sheep ranchers together to cost-share for nonlethal methods to protect their sheep from the wolves that included guard dogs, fladry, lights, noisemakers to scare wolves off, and trail cameras to detect when wolves were in the vicinity of sheep herds.

The project now covers more than one thousand square miles of public and private lands where one hundred thousand sheep graze. The number of animals lost to wolves in the project areas is 0.01 percent of the total herd, compared to a 0.54 percent loss for the rest of Idaho. "We have some ranchers who refuse to use nonlethal deterrents offered to them by our project and are experiencing significant losses," said Suzanne Asha Stone, northern Rockies representative for Defenders of Wildlife, as she described the Wood River Wolf Project during a presentation at the International Wolf Symposium in Duluth, Minnesota, in October 2013. Defenders of Wildlife is also working on developing a nonlethal deterrent approach with the Umatilla tribe in Oregon as wolf numbers expand on reservation lands.

One of the things Stone emphasized is that automatically killing wolves to protect livestock becomes an endless cycle that never solves the problem, because more wolves will move in and take the place of the wolves that have been killed. Wolves attack livestock when they are vulnerable to attack. Nonlethal deterrent techniques are designed to reduce where, when, and how livestock is susceptible to wolf predation. "If the vulnerability is there, the new wolves will start preying on the livestock and the cycle will repeat over and over again," Stone explained.[34]

* * *

But wild wolves are also wild cards, and Russ Morgan, ODFW wolf coordinator, related a nugget of wisdom about wolves passed down to him by Carter Niemeyer, former Wildlife Services agent and USFWS Idaho wolf recovery coordinator: "Wolves will never do anything to help themselves. They will always get into trouble at the wrong time and the wrong place." And sure enough, one of the earliest wolf livestock depredations in Oregon was a calf owned by the brother-in-law of the head of the Oregon Cattlemen's Association. The attack on livestock by the Keating Valley wolves served to reinforce ranchers' contention that the return of these animals to Oregon would be nothing but trouble. With that incident behind them, Oregon wolf advocates had hoped Oregon's two established packs at that time—the Wenaha and Imnaha—would behave. But true to Niemeyer's maxim, the Imnaha pack began attacking livestock.

* * *

The Imnaha pack ranges throughout a six-hundred-square-mile territory between the Wallowa-Whitman National Forest and adjacent private ranch land, sometimes traveling more than thirty miles in a single day. They tended to travel between the national forest and rangeland on the Zumwalt Prairie via a north–south ridge that goes through the "back forty" of a number of ranchers' property that locals dubbed the "Wolf Highway." A large pack at the time, it had fifteen documented members in December 2010, down to ten by the following April from dispersals, mortality, or both.[35] But the pack spent most of its time on the private land, regularly encountering livestock, and eventually the temptation became too great. In May 2010 pack members killed three cow calves on private land. By early June the pack had killed six cow calves.

Despite efforts to keep wolves away using nonlethal deterrents, the pack was determined to be chronically killing livestock. Two pack members were killed by Wildlife Services in May 2011, despite a legal attempt by a coalition of conservation groups to stop it.[36] But the pack continued to kill livestock through 2011, and in September the Oregon Department of Fish and Wildlife decided to break up the pack, which at that time consisted of four wolves—the alpha pair, a juvenile male, and one pup of the year. The breeding female, OR2 (formerly B-300), and her pup would be spared to potentially form a new pack, but killing the other two would effectively dissolve the Imnaha pack and presumably end the attacks on livestock. The conservation groups Oregon Wild, Cascadia Wildlands, and Center for Biological Diversity sued to stop the killings, arguing that Oregon had a statewide population of only fourteen known wolves at that time and killing them would be inconsistent with the state's Endangered Species Act. The Oregon Court of Appeals agreed and in November put a temporary halt to the planned killing. Instead of going back to court, ODFW, the Oregon Cattlemen's Association, and the conservation groups reached an agreement on how future wolf depredations would be handled before wolves were killed, including a requirement that nonlethal deterrents be tried first, there must be at least four attacks on livestock over a six-month period, and the decision to lethally control wolves is only valid for forty-five days.[37] Since then, the Imnaha pack, which was up to six wolves at the end of 2013, has killed some livestock, as have two other packs, but none have reached the lethal control threshold.[38]

Given the cultural and political differences, it's unlikely that a pack of wolves marked for removal could have been saved by this legal and settlement strategy in the northern Rockies. In fact, just the opposite happened in 2010 with one Idaho pack, the Blue Bunch pack, which was killed off by Wildlife Services more than six months after the lethal control deadline of sixty days had passed, possibly leaving a couple of the pack's pups orphaned and eventually starving to death.[39]

With about the same number of wolves, although more individual packs, Washington has gone harder on its livestock-depredating wolves than Oregon. During the summer of 2012, the Wedge pack, comprising eight wolves in northeastern Washington, killed at least fifteen cattle from the Diamond M herd. The attacks intensified, indicating that the pack had become habituated to preying on livestock over natural, wild prey—although wolf advocates pointed out that the rancher tried only a few nonlethal deterrents. Despite receiving twelve thousand e-mails, mostly opposing the killing, the Washington Department of Fish and Wildlife made the decision to eliminate the pack.[40, 41, 42, 43] By the end of September seven pack members had been killed from the ground or via helicopter, for a total cost of $76,500, an expense that drew criticism from at least one state legislator.[44]

Back in Oregon, the dispersing Imnaha pack wolf OR7 was managing to avoid any entanglements with livestock and, even worse, people. Being the first known gray wolf in the Oregon's Cascade Mountains since 1946, he was drawing a lot of interest, which only increased when a hunter's trail camera photographed him on November 14, 2011, near Butte Falls. That was the only known photograph of OR7 at the time, since the biologists who put the GPS collar on him didn't take any pictures as they usually do.[45]

On December 29, 2011, the two-and-a-half-year-old wolf crossed into northern Siskiyou County, California, to become the first known wolf in that state since 1924. By then he was about 300 linear miles from his starting point in northeastern Oregon, but on the ground he had traveled more than twice that distance.[46]

For the next fourteen months, OR7 wandered across northern California, going almost as far east as Nevada and south nearly to Lassen Volcanic National Park, while making occasional brief forays back into Oregon. By March 2012 he had traveled about two thousand miles through Oregon and California. During that time he became a worldwide media sensation, with articles detailing his travels often portraying him as "looking for love," which was more or less the purpose of his travels—to find a mate and start a new pack. He was photographed once in California by state wildlife biologists, and his tracks were sometimes found, but he remained largely invisible and his travels known only because he wore a GPS collar that gave away his locations. To help spread public awareness and support for OR7, the conservation group Oregon Wild held a naming contest. They received 250 entries from children from around the world, settling on Journey as the winning name.[47] The California Department of Fish and Wildlife even developed a blog to help OR7's fans keep up with his travels, and a Bend, Oregon, filmmaker made a documentary about his travels called *OR7—The Journey*.[48]

OR7's arrival in California also prompted the Center for Biological Diversity to petition the state to list gray wolves under the state's Endangered Species Act, which the California Department of Fish and Wildlife and the California Fish and Game Commission did in early June 2014, even though the CDFW opposed giving wolves that protection.[49, 50] The CDFW also began developing a state wolf management plan in anticipation of the virtual certainty of eventual gray wolf recolonization.[51] Rural northern California communities reacted with typical alarm at OR7's arrival, and Siskiyou County leaders briefly considered passing a law banning wolves from the county but thought better of the idea when community support for the proposed measure failed to materialize.[52]

On March 13, 2013, OR7 crossed the border back into Oregon—this time, except for occasional day trips back to California, to stay, establishing a territory in the southern Cascade Mountains straddling the Jackson-Klamath county line from the border north to Diamond Peak.[53] If he couldn't find a mate by roaming around, he would establish a territory and wait for one to come to him. But wolf biologists were skeptical. By then OR7 was four years old, and the odds of his encountering a female wolf in the remote southern Cascades was small. For all his thousands of miles of travel and the risk that journey entailed, it looked like OR7 was headed for a biological dead end, crushing the hopes of wolf advocates that he would start a new pack in the Cascades or perhaps even in California.

The greatest threat to wolves is humans, and the odds that OR7 would be killed either accidentally or deliberately during his travels was fairly high. Case in point was OR7's brother OR9, who dispersed into Idaho from the Imnaha pack in July 2011 and was illegally shot on January 2, 2012, by a hunter whose wolf tag, required to hunt wolves, had expired. The state of Idaho declined to charge the hunter with a wildlife violation, and Idaho's Republican Governor Butch Otter sent Oregon Governor John Kitzhaber, a Democrat, a sarcastic letter offering his "sincerest apologies" for OR9's killing and offered to send Oregon 150 wolves from Idaho.[54, 55]

Specific anti-wolf groups hadn't really developed in the Pacific Northwest the way they had in the northern Rockies, although one short-lived organization, Wolf Free Oregon, formed in Wallowa County; its business card listed a selection of suggested wolf poisons. Members, made up mainly of some part-time ranchers and local residents, testified in favor of a few anti-wolf bills before the Oregon state legislature and held a couple of anti-wolf rallies, then faded away.[56] Nevertheless, the Pacific Northwest's nascent wolf population was seeing its share of illegal killing.

In 2014 Oregon had three unsolved illegal wolf killings, including a two-year-old male wolf from the Wenaha pack that was shot in October 2010, a month after wildlife biologists had put a radio collar on it and while it was still protected under the federal Endangered Species Act. The USFWS has offered a $2,500 reward for information about the illegal killing.[57] Another wolf was illegally shot in northeast Oregon in 2012 and a third in 2013.[58] In Washington the Lookout pack, the state's first confirmed pack, had as many as five of its members illegally shot in 2009. In 2012 William, Tom, and Erin White of Twisp, Washington, were convicted of killing the legally protected wolves and fined seventy-three thousand dollars. In addition, William White was sentenced to six months of home detention and Tom White to three months. They were caught when a woman, who gave a false name but is believed to have been Erin White, tried to ship a wolf hide to Canada from the Federal Express office in Okanagan in a package that was dripping blood.[59] In 2013 big game hunters shot and killed an un-collared female wolf in Okanogan County, Washington.[60]

OR7's supporters were particularly concerned about a coyote-shooting contest being held in Modoc County, California, in February 2013. The contest was sponsored by a local gun club, and the hunter who killed the most coyotes over the weekend won a silver belt buckle. Fearing that OR7, or any other wolves that might be in the area, could be mistaken for a coyote and accidently shot, Project Coyote and other conservation organizations tried unsuccessfully to convince the California Fish and Wildlife Commission to stop the event. Fortunately, OR7 survived this threat as well.[61]

But for all the hatred, cruelty, and killing at the place where the lives of humans and wolves intersect, there is also hope and rebirth. In late 2013 two wolves were seen in the Wedge pack's old territory; and by the end of the year, the Washington Department of Fish and Wildlife determined that the pack had reformed, although it did not produce any pups that spring.[62, 63]

As for OR7, wildlife biologists using remote cameras photographed him and a black female wolf using the same trails in early spring 2014. OR7's GPS signals that used to track him ranging far and wide suddenly showed that he was hanging out in the same area, indicating that he had mated and there might be a den with pups. His mate, the black wolf, wore no radio or GPS collar, but DNA analysis from some scat samples showed she was born in Oregon, either into the Snake River or Minam pack.[64] In early June, biologists from the USFWS and ODFW stole into the suspected den site in the Rogue River–Siskiyou National Forest and spotted two pups tucked under a hollow log, later confirming a third.[65]

The previous summer, OR7s mother, B-300—founding female and matriarch of the infamous Imnaha pack—vanished along with the seven pups she had given birth to that April. Biologists monitoring the pack throughout the rest of 2013 never saw any of them again.[66] But her son Journey, just like his mother, had beaten the staggering odds all dispersing wolves face by avoiding death, finding a mate, and starting a new pack in a new territory. Now, after being gone for seventy years, gray wolves had a toehold in Oregon's Cascade Mountains. Sooner or later they will do the same in California. Wolf B-45's 1999 message to the Pacific Coast states had been fulfilled. Wolves were no longer coming— they were here.

Pups from the Wenaha wolf pack in Oregon. Both Oregon and Washington now have growing wolf populations. Photo by the Oregon Department of Fish and Wildlife

ELEVEN

A-Wolf Hunting We Will Go

Idaho's and Montana's rush to open wolf-hunting seasons after the first, temporary ESA delisting in 2009 (Wyoming was still battling it out with the federal government over its wolf plan) made clear what the thrust of wolf management would be when the states finally took full control over wolves within their borders. After the April 2011 delisting by Congress, both Idaho and Montana again opened wolf-hunting seasons, with Wyoming following suit in 2012. At the end of 2011, when the hunts began, the wolf population in the northern Rockies was estimated at 1,776 and a total of about 287 packs, at least 109 of which were breeding pairs. Montana had 653 wolves and 130 packs. Wyoming had 328 wolves and 48 packs, while the Idaho wolf population was 746 wolves and 101 packs, along with a small number of wolves in eastern Oregon and Washington.[1]

For 2011 Montana set a statewide harvest quota of 220 animals. Hunters killed 166—75 percent of the quota—including 97 adults, 35 yearlings, 25 juveniles, and almost an even split of males to females, 86 and 80, respectively. Montana Fish, Wildlife and Parks sold 18,531 wolf tags for a total of $407,389.[2] The following year Montana hunters killed 128 wolves. The state also opened a wolf-trapping season beginning that year, and trappers took 97 wolves for a grand 2012 season total of 225 wolves. In 2013 the Montana state legislature also passed House Bill 73, which allowed hunters to buy up to three wolf licenses per season, and the nonresident wolf license fee was lowered from $350 to $50. (Resident wolf licenses are $19.[3]) During 2013 ninety-five wolves were harvested.[4] Currently Montana has no statewide wolf quota limiting how many hunters and trappers can kill over the course of a season.

By the time of the final 2011 delisting, the Idaho state legislature was still fuming over the 2009 delisting and subsequent relisting in 2010, denying the state a 2010–11 wolf-hunting season. "This was a boiling point," Jon Rachael of the Idaho Department of Fish and Game told the audience during his Idaho wolf management update talk at the 2013 International Wolf Symposium in Duluth, Minnesota. "The relisting of wolves resulted in extreme frustration among hunters, and the legislature was very upset." Idaho legislators began to ask why the state had agreed to have such a high wolf population—five hundred-plus to seven hundred wolves and more than fifteen packs—in its 2008 management plan. It reverted to its 2002 plan calling for just 150 wolves, and with the 2011 delisting reopened its hunting season, adding trapping as well, with the objective of preventing Idaho's wolf population from growing. For the 2011–12 season, 379 wolves were killed, 255 by hunters and 124 by trappers. The following season hunters shot 198 wolves and trappers caught 119, for a total harvest of 314.[5, 6]

Idaho hunters can buy up to five wolf tags each year, trappers up to five each season. Idaho resident wolf tags sell for $11.50 each and nonresident tags for $31.75, down from $186. Between 2009 and 2013 the Idaho Department of Fish and Game brought in $2.3 million from selling wolf tags. Despite Idaho's push to suppress its wolf population, Rachael reiterated, "We will not jeopardize the wolf's [ESA delisted] status, but we will continue to emphasize the need to control wolves for livestock and human conflict."[7]

Wolves were delisted in Wyoming on September 30, 2012, and on the next day the state opened its wolf season. Between October 1, 2012, and the end of the year, hunters killed forty-one wolves in the Wolf Trophy Game Management Area, where the objective was to reduce the wolf population by 11 percent, and twenty-five wolves in the 84 percent of Wyoming's shoot-on-sight area, where the objective was to have no wolves at all.[8]

As called for in its delisting agreement with the USFWS, the state of Wyoming planned to manage its wolf population at a minimum of one hundred animals and ten breeding pairs outside of Yellowstone and Grand Teton National Parks and the Wind River Indian Reservation, where the state has no wildlife management authority.[9] However, on September 23, 2014, US District Court Judge Amy Berman Jackson ruled that Wyoming's wolf management plan was inadequate to protect the species, relisted Wyoming wolves under the ESA and returned management control back to the USFWS until the state develops a legally acceptable plan. Montana is managing its wolves for a minimum of 150 individuals and fifteen breeding pairs, although practically speaking it expects its wolf population to remain in the four hundred to six hundred range,[10] while Idaho intends to reduce its wolf population to as few as possible—preferably the 150 minimum that will avoid running afoul of the Endangered Species Act and triggering the federal government to reassert its management control.

To that desired end, the Idaho state legislature approved House Bill 470, signed by Governor Butch Otter in late March 2014, to create a five-person state wolf control board. The bill's proponents hope it will get the state on track to fund the eventual killing of 500-plus of its 2014 estimated wolf population of about 680 and knock it down to the minimum 150. Otter's original request for two million dollars to pay for wolf control was whittled down to four hundred thousand dollars in seed money, but that is expected to be supplemented by annual payments of $110,000 each from the Idaho Department of Fish and Game and the livestock industry.[11, 12, 13]

In response, Defenders of Wildlife, the Washington, DC–based conservation organization that has played a major part in the long battle to restore and sustain gray wolves in Yellowstone National Park and the northern Rockies, launched a summer media campaign blasting the state of Idaho for its aggressive plans to drastically lower its wolf numbers, pointing out that by the end of 2013, Idaho's wolf population had declined by 23 percent, from 856 to 659, since the state had taken over wolf management from the federal government in 2009. Since that year, 1,470 wolves have been killed in Idaho, including both recreational hunting and trapping and government wolf control, and the number of breeding pairs has dropped by 59 percent.[14, 15] The average pack size for Idaho wolves has also decreased, from 8.1 members in 2009 to 5.4 at the end of 2013.[16]

Wolf advocates decried the hunts from the beginning, pointing out the unprecedented nature, and absurdity, of hunting a species just removed from the Endangered Species List for the express purpose of drastically reducing its population. Environmentalists never trusted the states to manage wolves for viable populations, and that was a major reason for their dogged efforts to keep them ESA-listed and under federal jurisdiction. Earthjustice attorney Tim Preso pointed to Idaho as proof that their fears were not unfounded. "Idaho abandoned its original management plan of managing for a population of 520 wolves and is now decreasing them to a minimum population," he told me. "We hate to say to the [US Fish and Wildlife] Service that we told you so, but we told you so." During her keynote address at the wolf symposium, Jamie Rappaport Clark, current president and CEO of Defenders of Wildlife and director of the USFWS from 1997 to 2001, was equally blunt in her criticism of state wolf management, telling the audience: "Since delisting, the states of Idaho, Montana, and Wyoming have been systematically lowering their wolf numbers instead of maintaining healthy and ecologically valuable wolf populations on the landscape as they do with other wildlife species they manage."

She went on to say, "Furthermore, state legislatures and wildlife commissions have pressured wildlife agencies to ignore recent science about the impacts of wolves on game populations, and regardless of studies that show wolves are having only minor impacts on elk numbers or hunter harvest, they are continuing to promote more aggressive hunting regimes aimed at reducing wolf numbers. . . . Gone is the vision for restoring wolves to suitable habitat."[17]

That reversal of fortune—from the unexpectedly quick recovery under federal management to "extirpation lite" by the states—is a blunt demonstration of the formidable political influence of the Western livestock industry and hunters whose license and other fees fund a significant portion of state wildlife agencies, agencies whose views of nature are decidedly hierarchal and harvest oriented, and how little people outside that political establishment have to say about state wildlife management policy.

However, wolves are resilient animals, and their populations can absorb a significant level of killing by humans. Studies on the percentage of wolves that can be killed by hunters without decreasing the population over the long term are relatively consistent. A study of wolf harvest in Alaska's central Brooks Range found that killing 29 percent or less of the population each year didn't affect population trends.[18] Once you start killing more than 40 percent of the wolves, the population will start to decline. One study showed that a wolf population was unaffected by killing 16 to 24 percent of the animals, but after 42 to 61 percent were harvested began to decline by 20 to 25 percent.[19]

Wolves are subject to the same ecological and biological forces as their prey, including additive and compensatory mortality, so how wolf populations respond to hunting depends on a variety of factors, such as how many pups are being born into the population and whether the wolf population is at carrying capacity, and therefore, as with elk and deer, there's a limited "harvestable surplus."[20] But wolves, like coyotes, quickly build their populations back up again after being reduced by hunting, and wildlife managers that want to keep a wolf population at a reduced level need to keep hunting them. Just between 2012 and early 2013, hunting in the northern Rockies had lowered the wolf population by 16 percent in Wyoming, 4 percent in Montana, and 8 percent in Idaho. In response, Wyoming cut its wolf harvest quota in half for the fall 2013 hunting season, while Montana and Idaho continued with plans to keep reducing its wolf numbers.[21]

While wolf populations do recover from hunting pressure, it also disrupts pack social structure and behavior. A number of studies have shown that when one of the breeding members is killed, packs often cede territory to neighboring packs, and 38 percent of packs that lose one of the alpha pair dissolve. Scattered former pack members may then have violent encounters with other packs as they enter their territories, and wandering lone wolves may also be more likely to get into trouble with people and livestock. If a pack has been reduced in size, it may actually become more lethal to big game, since smaller packs kill more prey per wolf than larger packs, especially if the older animals have been killed off, leaving the younger, more effective hunters, which also require more food than older wolves. On the other hand, if a shot-out pack is made up of very young, inexperienced wolves, the pack may be more likely to turn to easier prey such as cattle and sheep.[22]

Although wolves are vulnerable in areas with lots of roads and open country, and 1,754 were killed by hunters and trappers in the northern Rockies between 2011 and mid-2014, they have turned out to be much harder to hunt than some thought, especially in more-remote, rugged, and forested regions.[23] For that reason, it is unlikely that even Idaho will ever get its wolf population down to the bare federal government-required minimum, although it may eventually be successful in substantially reducing their overall numbers. Bob Ream, former Montana Fish, Wildlife and Parks commissioner, told me that even after Montana increased the allowable number of wolf licenses to five per hunter annually, the statewide wolf harvest didn't go up. He also thought that if wolves weren't hunted at all, they would eventually reach equilibrium, but at slightly higher population levels. And while hunting can disrupt and dissolve packs, it doesn't appear to have especially negative impacts on a wolf population as a whole.[24] The more useful question may be how many wolves need to be killed, where, and for what reasons.

Some of those questions rose to the surface during the 2012–13 wolf hunt when during the first months of the wolf-hunting season, at least seven wolves from Yellowstone National Park resident packs were killed by hunters after they ventured outside the park's boundaries, including one well known by park wolf watchers, 832F, the Lamar Canyon pack's alpha female. While the killings didn't endanger the park's wolf population, wolf advocates were angered not only by the death of 832F—one of the more highly visible of Yellowstone's wolves that her wolf-watching admirers followed and nicknamed "06" for the year she was born—but also because a number of the wolves wore radio or GPS collars and were part of long-term wolf research in the park. Was the loss of those research wolves worth giving a few hunters around the park's boundaries a recreational wolf-shooting opportunity? One of the particular values of wolf research in Yellowstone is that it provides scientists the opportunity to study wolves that are unexploited by humans—that is, people didn't kill them—so their natural history is affected only by natural influences. That opportunity went away with the shootings.

Concerned that too many park wolves were being killed during the hunting season, and with Montana's first wolf trapping season set to begin in mid-December, the Montana Fish, Wildlife and Parks Commission voted to close the wolf harvest season, not permanently but just for the remainder of the current season in parts of the Gardiner hunting district adjacent to the northern boundary of Yellowstone. But that small concession to protect valuable research wolves, along with wolves important to Yellowstone's significant wolf-watching economy, was too much for some hunting groups, including the Montana affiliate of Sportsmen for Fish and Wildlife, Big Game Forever, and Montana Outfitters and Guides Association, along with Citizens for Balanced Use and Montana Republican State Representative Alan Redfield, who sued the commission to have the season reinstated.[25] The commission lost the case when on January 2, 2013, a Montana judge ruled that it did not give proper public notice prior to its decision—a decision that also prevented the Montana public from exercising its legal right to hunt wolves.[26] By that time, because the wolf season was almost over, Bob Ream, who chaired the Montana Fish, Wildlife and Parks Commission at the time, told me that the commissioners decided not to pursue the issue any further.

The following month, Montana's Democratic Governor, Steve Bullock, signed House Bill 73 into law. The law allowed hunters to purchase additional wolf permits, reduced the cost of nonresident wolf permits, permitted the use of electronic calls for wolf hunting, and had a provision that prohibited the Montana Fish, Wildlife and Parks Commission from closing areas around Yellowstone National Park to wolf hunting.[27]

By the end of the 2012–13 wolf season, sixteen wolves in Montana, Idaho, and Wyoming with ties to Yellowstone had been killed adjacent to the park, including twelve wolves from resident park packs and four wolves that spent some time inside park boundaries. Of all the wolves killed, six wore either radio or GPS collars, three were alpha animals, and three were pups.[28] The park also lost two collared wolves to hunters in 2009 and two more in 2011 (one of which was 832F's mate's brother, 754M).[29] Despite the loss of 832F, the Lamar Canyon pack remained intact, and the pack's new alpha female, 926F, gave birth to six pups in 2014.[30]

Responding to concerns about hunters and trappers killing Yellowstone wolves, Oregon Democratic Congressman Peter DeFazio requested that the Department of the Interior work with Montana, Wyoming, and Idaho to establish a "wolf safety zone" around the Yellowstone and to develop similar safety measures for wolf populations around other national parks.[31]

In December 2013 another major controversy over wolf hunting arose, specifically its purpose and location, this time in Idaho's Middle Fork Elk Zone, which is mainly the Frank Church River of No Return Wilderness. Idaho Fish and Game had been documenting declining elk numbers in the wilderness for some time. Between 2002 and 2011 the elk population had dropped 43 percent, from 7,485 to 4,229. State biologists believe that wolves are a primary cause of female and juvenile elk deaths, especially in winter, which is keeping the herd from building back up to management objectives, which is a maximum of 5,750 cow elk and 1,030 bulls. The calf-to-cow ratio has been dropping since 1995, and in 2011 was at thirteen calves per one hundred cows. Idaho Fish and Game calculates that if wolf predation is left unchecked, the elk in the Middle Fork Elk Zone will continue to decline between 3 and 7 percent each year. There are six to eight wolf packs living in the Middle Fork Elk Zone and another two or three packs whose territories overlap the zone.[32]

In 2009 Idaho Fish and Game requested that the USDA Forest Service allow them to fly helicopters into the Frank Church River of No Return Wilderness to dart wolves from the air with tranquilizers, then land and put radio collars on them to monitor the wolves' impacts on elk.[33] When the forest service, under whose jurisdiction the wilderness area falls, gave the okay, environmental groups including Wolf Recovery Foundation and Western Watershed, along with the Wilderness Society, Great Old Broads for Wilderness, Idaho Conservation League, Winter Wilderness Alliance, Wilderness Watch, and the Sierra Club sued on the grounds that helicopter landings in a federally designated wilderness were both inappropriate and illegal, but they eventually lost their challenge.[34] That winter, wildlife agents flew into the wilderness area intending to collar twelve wolves, but only managed to collar four after a dozen landings.[35]

In December 2013 Idaho Fish and Game hired a trapper to go into the wilderness area and kill all the members of two packs, the Golden Creek pack and the Monumental Creek pack. That struck a nerve with a large number of Idahoans, including many who supported wolves but accepted that lethal management could be justified where wolves were causing conflicts with humans and private property. But this lethal control action was in the Frank Church River of No Return Wilderness—2,366,907 acres of some of the wildest country in the lower forty-eight states, federally designated as a wilderness area in 1984 and named in honor of the late Frank Church, a Democrat who served as an Idaho senator from 1957 to 1981 and who played a key role in passing the Wilderness Act of 1964.[36]

It was the size and wildness of this and other central Idaho wilderness areas that made it an ideal place to restore gray wolf populations in the West, and why the USFWS chose the region along with Yellowstone for the original reintroduction. Previous surveys showed that a majority of Idahoans support having wolves in federally designated wilderness areas. The questions were: Was it appropriate for Idaho Fish and Game to kill wolves, which many people hope to see or hear when visiting wilderness, to increase elk hunting opportunities for one small group of wilderness users? And if wolves would not be left alone to interact naturally with their environment in a remote wilderness like the Frank Church, where could wolves live unpersecuted by man? To many people, Idaho Fish and Game was overstepping its bounds by wanting to manage wildlife in a wilderness area for maximum hunter benefit at the expense of other wildlife values and wilderness users.[37]

Conservation organizations Defenders of Wildlife, Western Watersheds, and Wilderness Watch sued the forest service, claiming that the action violated the limitations the Wilderness Act places on active human management of federal wilderness areas, but they eventually lost and the killing went ahead.[38] By late January 2013 the professional trapper had killed nine wolves. Idaho Fish and Game declared the mission accomplished and pulled him out.

Despite the public outcry, the Idaho Department of Fish and Game released its Predation Management Plan for the Middle Fork Elk Zone in February 2014, which calls for reducing the wolf population in the wilderness by 60 percent. That means killing fifty-three to fifty-eight wolves from the current estimated population of ninety-three, driving it down to thirty-five to forty wolves.[39] Defenders of Wildlife, Western Watersheds Project, and Wilderness Watch took legal action against the forest service and the Idaho Department of Fish and Game to stop any further wolf control in the wilderness.[40] With a hearing before the Ninth Circuit Court of Appeals scheduled for August 2014, Idaho Fish and Game instead decided in July to postpone the next round of wolf control in the wilderness area, which was scheduled to begin in December 2014, until at least November 1, 2015, while it gathers more information, although in its legal declaration the state claims that its plan to cull wolves is to "appropriately mitigate the negative effects to wildlife from wolf reintroduction into the wilderness."[41, 42] As is so often the case, wolves are defined as separate from wildlife, their natural interactions with prey species as destructive, and normal ecological responses between the two as something to be fixed—at the expense of wolves and the people who value them. At the same time, forest service officials agreed to notify conservationists about any future arrangements with Idaho Fish and Game to kill wolves in the wilderness area.[43]

A smaller wolf-hunting controversy broke out in Idaho in December 2013, notable in that it was a private initiative rather than government sanctioned, when Idaho for Wildlife, a prominent hunter-oriented anti-wolf group announced it would hold a two-day coyote and wolf derby at the end of the month around the community of Salmon. Entry fees were twenty dollars per two-man team, and prizes included one thousand dollars each for the team that killed the most coyotes and the largest wolf, along with door prizes, including for the most female coyotes killed.[44]

Some contest business sponsors received threatening e-mails or posts on Facebook pages, including death threats, from event opponents.[45] The New Mexico–based environmental organization WildEarth Guardians, along with a number of other groups, sued to stop the event, arguing that the hunt would take place on national forestlands and that the forest service was improperly not requiring Idaho for Wildlife to have competitive event permits. But the groups lost their suit and the derby went ahead.[46] More than 230 hunters participated in the event, killing twenty-one coyotes but no wolves.[47]

Wolf derbies in the western United States could potentially become as common in the future as coyote shooting contests are now—they are regular events in some Canadian provinces. In British Columbia private groups sponsor wolf-hunting derbies, and hunters who kill the largest wolves may win cash prizes of as much as one thousand dollars.[48] In Alberta private hunting and trapping groups, including the Wyoming-based Wild Sheep Foundation, are paying bounties of fifteen to three hundred dollars per wolf to encourage hunters to kill more of them.[49] The problem with these coyote and wolf contests and bounty programs is that they amount to freelance predator control that, unlike when state wildlife agencies initiate lethal control programs, are not based on any data showing that the predators being killed are having any effects on big game. Organizers and sponsors simply assume they are. Private bounties have become enough of a concern to wolf conservationists that in October 2013 the International Union for Conservation of Nature and Natural Resources Wolf Specialist Group formally requested the Alberta provincial government to outlaw the practice.[50]

Although it didn't participate in the lawsuit that prevented the Montana Fish, Wildlife and Parks Commission from temporarily closing wolf hunting and trapping around Yellowstone, one mainstream national hunter organization that opposes a wolf protection buffer around the park and has taken a leading role in pressing for aggressive wolf control measures in the northern Rockies is the 203,000-member, Missoula, Montana-based Rocky Mountain Elk Foundation.

The organization promotes the narrative that wolves are decimating elk herds and that they threaten the future of elk hunting.[51] RMEF's president and CEO, David Allen, is a controversial, lightning-rod figure who has said that "wolf reintroduction is the worst ecological disaster since the decimation of the bison herds" (a somewhat odd analogy since it was human hunters, not wolves, that nearly exterminated the American bison). Allen horrified wolf advocates when in 2012 he told a reporter from an Oregon newspaper that gassing wolf pups in their dens should be a standard part of wolf control programs.[52, 53]

RMEF has also stirred controversy with a series of large financial donations to state wildlife agencies, including fifty thousand dollars to the Idaho Department of Fish and Game in 2013 to expand its wolf radio collar program, and fifty-one thousand dollars in 2012 and twenty-five thousand in 2014 to Montana Fish, Wildlife and Parks to fund radio collaring more wolves and pay Wildlife Services for wolf-killing operations.[54, 55, 56]

Along with wolves, RMEF also wants to see more black and grizzly bears, mountain lions, and coyotes killed. It believes this will increase elk numbers and that aggressive predator control by humans is needed to maintain a balance of nature.[57, 58] Critics questioned the propriety of the donations and whether it amounted to an organization interested specifically in maximizing elk populations for its elk hunting members paying a public agency to manage publicly owned wildlife for its benefit.[59]

In July 2012, appalled by RMEF's increasingly strident support for reducing wolf populations throughout the northern Rockies, Donald Murie requested the organization stop awarding the Olaus Murie Award, which it presents to people who have made significant contributions to protecting wildlife habitat. The award was named in honor of Donald's father, Olaus Murie, a biologist who is best known for his pioneering research on elk natural history, biology, and management in the Jackson Hole, Wyoming, region beginning in the late 1920s; his book *The Elk of North America* remains a classic. (His brother Adolph conducted some of the earliest scientific wolf research in Alaska in the 1930s and 1940s.[60]) In Murie's letter to Allen, he writes: "Now we find that your organization has declared all-out war against wolves; unreasonable, with no basis in science at all, wholly emotional, cruel and anathema to the entire Murie family. . . . It is in total opposition to the findings of careful independent research by hundreds of scientists."[61] Former RMEF employee David Stalling, who conceived and created the Olaus Murie Award in cooperation with the Murie family, also weighed in, writing that his old employer, once a leader in wildlife ecology and science-based wildlife management, now under changed leadership "ignores and defies science and panders to outfitters, politicians and hunters who have little understanding of wildlife and, in particular, interactions between wolves and elk. The group has abandoned principle for income and popularity."[62]

When it comes to wolf hunting, hunter organizations such as RMEF as well as individual hunters commonly point to the North American Model for Wildlife Conservation that guides wildlife management in the United States and uses hunting as an important wildlife management tool to justify current wolf-hunting programs. It's a legitimate enough point but one that bears a closer look, because not all wildlife professionals believe that the forces driving wolf hunting meet the model's scientific and ethical standards.

The North American Model for Wildlife Conservation encompasses seven tenets that are supposed to inform wildlife management decisions and programs by wildlife management agencies: Wildlife is a public trust resource; commercial markets for game should be eliminated; wildlife is allocated by laws and the principles of democracy; wildlife should only be killed for a legitimate purpose; wildlife is to be considered an international resource; science is the proper tool for discharging wildlife policy; and hunting should be available to everyone.[63]

But some wolf researchers and ethicists believe that general hunts for wolves are at odds with a number of the model's principles. One of those wolf researchers is John Vucetich, an associate professor at Michigan Technological University School of Forest Resources and Environmental Sciences and codirector of the Isle Royale Wolf-Moose Study, who argues that general season wolf hunting violates at least three of the model's tenets: wildlife as a public trust, principles of democracy, and use of the best available science. Vucetich notes that wildlife, including wolves, are held in public trust for all citizens, not just those that hunt; but state wildlife agencies often establish wolf hunts by hunter demand, ignoring the desires of other members of the public who are opposed to wolf hunting and thereby ignoring the model's tenets of public trust and democracy.

While state wildlife agencies and hunting organizations may insist that wolf hunting is based on solid science, Vucetich questions that as well. Wolves that chronically kill livestock or pose a threat to human safety need to be dealt with by immediately targeting the offending wolf or wolves, not through a general hunting season months after the fact, hoping that some hunter will kill the "right" wolf. Similarly, if wolves are not causing a decline in big game numbers, then randomly killing wolves across large areas will not make a difference. He points out that just because wolves can absorb relatively high levels of human-caused mortality is not a reason by itself to kill them.[64]

He and other researchers have also criticized the North American Model as outdated and flawed, putting too much emphasis on recreational hunting as a wildlife management tool, not giving enough credit to the contributions of the nonhunting-oriented environmental movement to wildlife conservation, and not recognizing the full value of nonconsumptive and ecological aspects of wildlife, including wolves, which makes it more difficult for the nonhunting public to fully participate in wildlife policy decisions.[65]

Speaking at the wolf meeting in Duluth, Vucetich said, "Citizens get to decide what's a legitimate purpose to kill wolves through democracy and reasoned discourse." Reasoned discourse is something that has been in very short supply throughout the two decades of wolf reintroduction, recovery, and management in the northern Rockies.

In Wolf Country

Yellowstone wolves wearing radio collars killed by hunters outside the park sparked outrage among wolf advocates. Photo by Jim Peaco, National Park Service

TWELVE

What Good Are Wolves?

I was having trouble seeing the road in the predawn darkness and drizzle on a September morning in 2010 as I made my way from Mammoth Hot Springs out Yellowstone National Park's Northeast Entrance Road bound for the Lamar Valley to try my hand at wolf-watching. So far, it was looking like I wasn't very good at it. Driving slowly from west to east, passing through the territories of the Quadrant, Canyon, Blacktail, Lamar Canyon, Agate, and Silver packs and as I went, I stopped at each turnout along the way to scan the landscape with my binoculars and listen for howls. As first light filled the valley, I began to spot the dark forms of a few elk and bison moving about, but no wolves. At one point a chorus coming from a hillside to the north raised my hopes, but the high-pitched yelps and yaps identified the source as coyotes.

After nearly reaching the northeastern boundary of the park, I turned around, still hoping to see a wolf on my way back but prepared to concede defeat. Then, just a short distance west of Slough Creek Campground, a line of parked cars and a group of people lined up and peering through spotting scopes on a small bluff above the road was a sure sign that something involving wildlife was afoot. I had heard of these people—they were the Yellowstone wolf watchers who spent days, even weeks, in the park searching for and observing wolves, getting to know the packs and even individual animals. Clambering up the hillside, I found they were friendly and knowledgeable. A man from Boise let me look through his spotting scope at the focus of their interest—the Lamar Canyon pack alpha pair (the alpha female, "06," would be killed by a hunter a few years later) and two of the four pups the pair produced that year.[1] The pack's seventh member, an adult, was somewhere out of sight.

Exciting as it was for me to see the wolves, I had missed the real drama by just an hour or so, the wolf watchers told me. A couple of days earlier, the pack had attacked a cow elk that took refuge in Slough Creek, flowing below us, that had been able to fend off the wolves. The wolf watchers had been coming back each day to keep a vigil as the pack attacked and harassed the cow until the wolves eventual killed her. That morning the wolves were feeding on her lifeless body when a grizzly bear arrived, sending the wolves scattering. The bear helped himself to free elk meat, then wandered off when he had enough. The remarkable scene I had just missed exemplified some of the many changes in the interactions between the park's wildlife and their environment since wolves had been reintroduced here in 1995 and 1996.

In addition to the well-documented role of wolves in the culling of older, diseased, and otherwise unfit animals from prey populations that ultimately strengthens the herds, one powerful and far-reaching ecological force that wolves are credited with influencing dramatically is something called a trophic cascade.

Trophic levels refer to the flow of energy through living organisms from when it is first captured by Earth's biosphere as sunlight until it emerges as waste heat. At a simplified level, it is composed of plants, the producers; herbivores, the consumers of plants; and meat-eating predators at the top of the hierarchy through which this energy flows. There are two views on what forces have the dominant effect on this flow of energy. One is a "bottom-up" hypothesis that says herbivore numbers are limited by the availability of plants, which themselves are limited by soil nutrients, weather, climate, and other factors; and that, in turn, controls predator populations. Another view is of a "top-down" energy system, based on something called the Green World Hypothesis, which says predators regulate herbivore populations, which prevents them from becoming too numerous and overgrazing plants, and therefore are the reason the world is green. Furthermore, if you remove top, or apex, predators such as wolves from the system, the resulting overpopulation of herbivores will cause habitat damage as they eat too many plants at too fast a rate, which will alter plant communities and how that ecosystem functions, ultimately causing a trophic cascade of side effects.

One of the classic and often-cited examples of a trophic cascade is based on the work of marine ecologist James Estes, who looked at sea otters and their relationship with their environment in the Aleutian Islands beginning in the early 1970s. In areas where sea otters had been extirpated, he found that sea urchins, the otters' primary prey, proliferated; and because urchins eat kelp, the native kelp forests were gone. Furthermore, because kelp forests harbor microscopic plankton that serves as food for other sea life and provides safe havens for fish to hide from predators, those ecosystem functions were lost as well. On the other hand, where there were still healthy numbers of sea otters, there were also healthy kelp forests.[2] More-recent research has shown that this top-down effect is at work at the macro level as well. Scientists have discovered that ensatinas, a species of salamander in northern California, prey on leaf litter invertebrates, which helps increase the population of mites, barklice, and similar arthropod grazers that are a critical part of the forest terrestrial food web. Without the salamanders, the arthropod grazer population would crash.[3]

Some of the earliest work in Yellowstone to determine if the arrival of wolves on the scene had any influence on the park's ecosystem was done by William Ripple, Eric Larsen, and Robert Beschta, researchers at Oregon State University's Department of Forest Ecosystems and Society, who looked at the history of willow, aspen, and cottonwood growth in the park and how these trees have responded since wolf reintroduction. Ripple and Larsen saw that many aspen groves were made up of large trees, 70 to 120 years old and smaller trees representing newer growth. Midsize trees were absent, and that gap represented the period when the park had no wolves. Taking core samples of the trees showed that aspens stopped regenerating in the 1920s, exactly when wolves were extirpated from the park, then began to produce new trees after the wolves returned. This, the researchers believed, was a result of the "ecology of fear." When the park was wolf-less, elk browsed heavily on aspens, willows, and cottonwoods along stream corridors, suppressing new growth. After wolves came along, the elk adjusted their behavior, spending less time in those areas where they were more vulnerable to wolf attack and instead sought out more open areas where they could see wolves approaching and more easily escape. With browsing pressure by the elk reduced, these plant communities expanded and became healthier. To further test their hypothesis, the researchers went to Olympic, Yosemite, Wind Cave, and Zion National Parks and Jasper National Park in Canada and found a similar patterns—declines in vegetation coincided with when the wolves in those places had been killed off.[4] Ripple and Beschta calculated that in Yellowstone willows began coming back by 1997, cottonwoods by 2002, and aspens by 2006.[5]

The decline of aspens in Yellowstone had long been recognized, and ecologists had previously suggested there might be a connection with elk and the absence of wolves; research in several Canadian national parks in the mid-1990s made some trophic cascade connections. With the wolves' return to Yellowstone, and the subsequent recovery of aspens and other streamside plant communities, positive ecological cascading effects became apparent. More trees and shrubs along streams stabilized the banks and reduced erosion, as well as provided shade that lowered water temperatures in summer, which is good for fish. As stream corridors became ecologically healthier, the park's beaver population began to increase. The dams they built formed ponds that created more habitats for fish, wildlife, and aquatic insects; raised water tables; and improved stream hydrology. Waterfowl, songbirds, amphibians, and a host of other plant and animal species have benefitted from these positive habitat changes.[6, 7]

While wolves have had positive effects on Yellowstone's ecological processes, they have also had undeniably desirable impacts on the Yellowstone region's economic ecology. Of the many studies conducted by the National Park Service in the early 1990s, prior to wolf reintroduction, two—in 1991 and 1999—looked at how interested park visitors might be in seeing wolves, if more people would visit the Yellowstone area specifically for the opportunity to see a wolf, and what the economic benefits of wolves might be compared to their costs. Those studies estimated that with wolves in the park, visitor use would increase by 5 percent and bring in an additional twenty-three million dollars in tourism revenue each year. Cost to hunters in lost hunting opportunities from wolf predation on elk and deer along with lost hunter-related tourism income was $394,000 to $879,000, in addition to $1,888 to $30,470 in livestock losses from wolf depredation. Looking at the total picture, factoring in the economic costs of wolves, the researchers concluded that having wolves in the park would result in a net positive benefit of twenty million dollars each year for the Yellowstone region's economy.[8]

A follow-up study was done in 2005. With wolves now established in the park, 44 percent of visitors surveyed said they would most like to see one during their trip (grizzly bears were number one), and around 70 percent of people living in the Greater Yellowstone area were in favor of having wolves around. About 326,000 visitors to Yellowstone in 2005 saw wolves, and an estimated twenty thousand people come to the park each year specifically to watch wolves. Visitors in the three-state Yellowstone region were spending a little more than thirty-five million dollars each year directly attributable to wolves, with a multiplier effect throughout local communities boosting that wolf-related income to about seventy million dollars per year.[9, 10]

Despite the aggressive opposition to wolves among the people who don't like them, there are many more who have a positive view of the animals and want to see one in the wild. Those people are voting with their feet and their wallets when they come not only from throughout the United States but also the world, making wolves an economically, as well as ecologically, valuable natural resource. As Mark Henjum, former wolf coordinator for the Oregon Department of Fish and Wildlife, once told me, "I think there must be something wrong with you if you are not moved by a wolf howl."

The return of gray wolves to the northern Rockies has given scientists many new opportunities to study them, and ongoing research is beginning to uncover what other ecological benefits wolves might offer. Limiting elk, deer, and other herbivore populations by eating them—the Green World Hypothesis—keeps plant communities from being over-browsed and overgrazed.[11] It's also well documented that wolves kill the young, weak, and old of their prey species. That keeps the herd healthier by ensuring that the strongest animals with the best genes reproduce and,

Wolves are believed to affect elk behavior, causing them to spend less time browsing in concentrated areas, which allows more trees and shrubs to grow. Photo by Jim Yuskavitch

because the weak and old animals may be more likely to have diseases, also helps minimize the potential for outbreaks of chronic wasting disease, brucellosis, and other maladies to which wildlife are susceptible.[12] And it is not just wolves, but other large carnivores as well, which is why it is important to have ecologically functioning populations of all our native carnivores. A study in Colorado, for example, found that mountain lions appeared to be selecting for deer infected with the prion that causes chronic wasting disease as prey.[13]

Wolves are also known to directly affect populations of medium-size predators, known as mesopredators, and their relationship and competition with coyotes has had a significant effect on the ecosystems in which they live. Wolves suppress coyote numbers wherever they are found together by either killing them or forcing them out of their territories, and when wolves were extirpated from a region it caused a "wolf effect." Looking at trapping records from both the United States and Canada, researchers from Oregon State University found that where wolves had been eliminated, coyotes outnumbered foxes by a three-to-one ratio, but where wolf populations remained healthy, foxes had the upper hand by a four-to-one ratio. Once wolves were extirpated in the American West, coyote populations exploded, expanding their range to the East Coast and becoming a major predator on livestock, especially sheep, inflicting far more costs on the livestock industry than wolves had.[14]

Since coyotes are a major predator of pronghorn fawns, the return of wolves, which don't bother with the fawns because they are too small to make a decent wolf meal, has helped increase pronghorn populations as coyote numbers have dropped. Researchers with the Wildlife Conservation Society found that where wolves were common, pronghorn fawn survival was 34 percent, while it was just 10 percent in areas without wolves.[15]

The carcasses of prey killed by wolves have an especially far-reaching effect. In Yellowstone partially consumed carcasses are scavenged by black and grizzly bears, coyotes, red foxes, bald and golden eagles, magpies and ravens, and another twenty other species to a lesser degree. Nearly sixty species of beetles will gather at the carcasses of elk and other ungulates killed by wolves, most of them to feed on the flies and beetle species that also scavenge the carcass. That additional free food wolves provide other animals can have its own trophic cascading effects. For example, in Yellowstone having more wolf-killed carcasses of elk and other large animals provides more scavenging opportunities for grizzly bears, supporting higher bear numbers. Since grizzlies are among the most efficient hunters of newly born elk calves, higher bear densities mean higher elk calf mortality and potentially lower elk populations.[16]

One of the more fascinating associations wolves have is with ravens. Research on wolves and ravens in Yellowstone has shown that the birds, particularly in winter, constantly follow wolves expressly for scavenging on their kills. (Some researchers think that ravens follow wolves not only visually but also by listening for their howls and following their tracks in the snow.) Because the birds are almost always nearby, they discover 100 percent of wolf kills in the park within minutes, if not seconds. Ravens don't follow coyotes, apparently able to tell the difference between the two species and know that wolves are able to killer larger prey and therefore provide more food to scavenge. But the ravens' devotion to wolves isn't reciprocated; wolves will defend their kills, dispatching any ravens they might catch. Ravens have been seen "playing" with wolves, frolicking with wolf pups and pulling adults' tails; that may be the way they learn about wolf behavior, which helps keep the birds safer when they are in close proximity to wolves at kill sites.[17]

There is a host of potential ways that wolves may affect other creatures and ecological processes. Some researchers hypothesize that restoring wolves may help beef up populations of the Canada lynx, listed as threatened under the Endangered Species Act, which has seen a decline in its primary prey, snowshoe hares. The hares are being eaten by coyotes, whose populations have exploded in response to the past extirpation of wolves across so much of the landscape. More wolves on the landscape will cause coyote populations to drop and potentially a corresponding increase in snowshoe hares, to the benefit of lynx.[18]

Another study in Yellowstone found that grizzly bears had more berries in their scat after wolf reintroduction than before. This suggests that the presence of wolves, which causes elk to move around more frequently, may be preventing them from browsing too heavily in one area for long periods of time, destroying berry bushes in the process, thereby increasing the berry crop, an important food source for grizzly bears.[19]

These and other hypotheses on how wolves may affect their environment and their role in trophic cascades still need more research. Even the recovery of trees and other plant communities in Yellowstone after wolf reintroduction may not happen everywhere wolves live. Mark Hebblewhite, the University of Montana wolf researcher, was quick to remind me that wolves don't cause trophic cascades outside of protected areas like national parks and wilderness areas where human activities dominate the environment. "Humans," he told me, "cause the biggest trophic cascade, but to date people have only focused on the wolf part of the story." In other words, if the world is green inside Yellowstone because wolves and other predators keep the population of elk and other herbivores from getting out of hand and overeating their food resources, the world may be green in agricultural areas outside the park because farmers and ranchers keep planting and growing alfalfa. Even the reasons for the recovery of willows, aspens, and cottonwoods in Yellowstone are not yet settled science. Some researchers think that a warming climate may be an important player in the resurgence of Yellowstone plant communities—between 1995 and 2005 the number of days above freezing went from 90 to 110 in the park's northern range, providing for a longer growing season and better overall growing conditions—as well as changes in precipitation patterns and perhaps other factors yet to be discovered.[20]

One effect in which wolves play some role in Yellowstone that not everyone is pleased with has been the decline of the elk population on the park's Northern Range, the expansive grassland area along the northern border of the park between the Lamar and Yellowstone Rivers. By the 1930s, a decade after the last of Yellowstone's wolves had been killed off, park managers believed that the Northern Range elk herd had doubled over the previous fifteen or twenty years and that the range's carrying capacity was being exceeded. The National Park Service decided to reduce the size of the Northern Range elk herd and between 1935 and the late 1960s removed about twenty-six thousand elk by either shooting them or shipping them off to states that wanted to restore their vanishing herds. During the same period, hunters hunting on lands surrounding the park harvested about forty-five thousand elk, and by the late 1960s the Northern Range elk herd had dropped from twelve thousand to fewer than four thousand animals. The culling program was ended in the late 1960s because the public didn't like the idea of elk being shot in a national park, and park managers went to a hands-off, let-nature-take-its-course approach to the Northern Range elk. The herd rapidly increased, reaching nineteen thousand by 1988. The reintroduction of wolves back into the park in 1995, when the Northern Range winter elk population was seventeen thousand, coincided with an increase in bear and mountain lion populations, which put more predation pressure on the elk. At the same time, an extended drought decreased the quality of forage, which affected the fitness and health of pregnant cows and calf survival rates. By 2003 the Northern Range elk population had dropped to less than ten thousand, stabilizing to around six thousand to seven thousand between 2007 and 2012. (During that same period, the Northern Range wolf population declined from ninety-four to seventy-nine, mostly due to disease.) By early 2013 elk numbers had fallen to 3,915—the lowest population since the culling program ended.[21]

Because Yellowstone is primarily summer grazing range and most of the park's elk migrate outside the park boundaries to winter range, hunters killed large numbers of the elk as well, further reducing the herd. In addition to a number of rifle and bowhunting seasons, one longtime special season was the Gardiner Late Hunt north of the park in Montana, which, beginning in 1975, was intended to lower the Northern Range elk population so that there were not more elk than their habitat could sustain. To do that, the hunt was more than 90 percent targeted toward breeding-age elk cows, because killing female elk most likely to reproduce will reduce the population over time. In fact, where elk hunting is allowed, it is the major source of elk mortality and a greater limiting factor for elk populations than predation, the quality of habitat, disease, or severe winters.[22]

The hunt was so effective, Dan MacNulty, the Utah State University wolf researcher, told me that "most of the elk killed by hunters were robust, breeding-age females." Hunters were harvesting 1,500 to 2,000 elk each year during the Gardiner Late Hunt, and combined with wolves, grizzly bears, mountain lions, and drought it was what MacNulty described as "the perfect storm for the elk." The exact role of the wolves in all of this is still being sorted out, with some studies concluding that wolf mortality on elk is compensatory while other researchers believe it is additive.[23] Montana Fish, Parks and Wildlife has since ended the Gardiner Late Hunt.

Hunters and others opposed to wolves have long pointed to the precipitous decline of Yellowstone's Northern Range herd and claimed that wolves are the cause. But what we are really seeing is the messy, fluid balance of nature as different ecological forces and conditions bump up against one another, with unpredictable results within a natural system that is not being manipulated to provide specific natural resource benefits for humans. Overall, the elk in Yellowstone National Park are doing just fine, with a summer population of up to twenty thousand animals in as many as seven herds—a higher elk density than surrounding national forestlands—and a current wolf population of ninety-five in ten packs.[24] As Curt Mack, leader of the Nez Perce Wolf Recovery Program, told me, the wolves and the elk will work it out.

Wolf recovery has focused mostly on the cost of wolves rather than their benefits, and wolves do bring costs with them. There are places where hunting opportunities are fewer because wolves have played a role in reducing the harvestable surplus of elk. And hunting is not only an important cultural tradition but also equally important economically, giving often-struggling rural communities a much-needed influx of visitors and cash during elk and deer seasons. In 2011 hunters spent $477,548,000 in Idaho, $627,298,000 in Montana, and $288,736,000. It is really a kind of sustainable ecotourism, and harvestable levels of game species are an undeniably valuable natural resource.[25] Through hunting licenses, tags, excise taxes on equipment, and other fees, hunters also support wildlife management and conservation, including protecting and improving wildlife habitat that produces the elk and deer that wolves and other native carnivores need to survive.

But there has been self-inflicted damage as well. Over the years hunters and hunting outfitters have cried loudly that the wolves are destroying elk populations and ruining elk hunting in the northern Rockies, despite being continually told by state wildlife biologists that is not the case. The result of that reverse advertising campaign by outfitters significantly dinged Idaho's and Montana's reputations as prime elk hunting destinations and decreased the number of out-of-state hunters who are willing to pay premium prices for licenses and guide services. In 2012 Idaho spent about forty thousand dollars and Montana eighty thousand in advertising campaigns to undo some of the public relations damage done to their elk hunting cred.[26]

One of the reasons the potential benefits of wolves so seldom rise to the surface is that the prevailing wildlife narrative tends only to recognize the negative aspects of less-favored species like large carnivores, such as wolves, and only the positive aspects of culturally favored animals like deer and elk. But for all their benefits, having enough deer and elk around to hunt involves passing significant costs on to society at large. While elk damage to ranchers and farmers is often mitigated by compensation for that damage, artificial feeding programs to divert elk away from private property, or even special hunts to reduce elk numbers where they are causing problems, it is deer that inflict a tremendous amount of damage to society at large, mostly involving collisions with motor vehicles. There are about a million collisions between deer and motor vehicles each year in the United States, causing around four billion dollars in vehicle damage and killing about two hundred people.[27] State Farm Insurance Company's deer collision statistics for 2011 were 4,352 for Idaho, 7,959 for Montana, and 3,796 for Wyoming. At an average damage claim of $3,305 (double that figure if the cost of collisions in which human fatalities are involved is averaged in[28]), that's more than $14.3 million, $26.3 million, and $12.5 million, respectively, for the three states each year, far outstripping annual property damage by wolves.[29] It also externalizes the costs of having high deer populations to maintain harvestable surpluses and is a significant subsidy to state wildlife agencies and hunters that maintain those high deer numbers but do not have to pay compensation for resulting property damage, as is demanded for wolves.

And while a small number of ranchers suffer financial losses from wolf attacks on their stock, the livestock industry also externalizes many of its business costs onto the public, both directly and indirectly, starting with a publicly funded federal agency, Wildlife Services, that kills publicly owned wildlife to protect livestock that are often grazing on public lands at the discount fee of $1.35 monthly per cow-calf pair when similar nonirrigated rangeland in the private sector leases for an average $11.90.[30] Federal livestock subsidies (including the Livestock Forage Disaster Program, Cattle Feed Program, Livestock Relief, Livestock Indemnity Payments, and more—of which in 2012, Montana, Wyoming, and Idaho were in the top 50 percent of recipients), crop insurance, and corn subsidies that make cattle feed cheaper are just a small sampling of how taxpayers cover many of the livestock industry's business costs.[31]

Damage to the environment is also a substantial cost of grazing livestock on public lands, particularly along streams and rivers where cows have degraded fish habitat in many part of the West and Pacific Northwest, to the detriment of economically important recreational and commercial fishing industries.

Perhaps the real difficulty in quantifying the value of wolves, besides the tremendous bias that exists against them by some, is that their true value to many people may have little to do with how they affect an ecosystem or how much tourist money they generate. The researchers who surveyed visitors to Yellowstone National Park to learn their views on wolves measured something called "existence value"—how much people would pay in order to have something exist, without necessarily bringing them any tangible personal benefit. The existence value for wolves in the Yellowstone region was calculated to be $8.3 million per year.[32] Ultimately, the real value of wolves, at least by those who like and care about them, may simply be in knowing they are out there.

THIRTEEN

Here to Stay

Wolves are here to stay, although it is a statement often made, it seems, by people who hope it is not true. But they are. With wolves well established in the northern Rockies and dispersing into the Pacific Northwest and successfully establishing populations there, it is only a matter of time before they recolonize California, Utah, Colorado, and Nevada. Mexican wolves, which are having a more difficult time becoming reestablished in Arizona and New Mexico, could eventually spread north. In the East, red wolves may one day be returned to the southern Appalachians, and there is considerable potential for Upper Midwest wolves to disperse into and recolonize upstate New York and northern New England.

As has been said so often during the northern Rockies wolf restoration, the most important limiting factor for wolves is human tolerance, and over the long term, public opinion bends in their favor. A 2013 poll commissioned by Defenders of Wildlife found solid support for restoring wolves to appropriate habitats in the West Coast states that transcended political party, gender, and age. In California 69 percent favored wolf restoration in their state, Oregon 66 percent, and Washington 71 percent.[1] A study in the early 2000s found that support for wolves in wilderness areas was also high in the West, at 68 percent in Arizona and Colorado, and 59 percent in New Mexico. A majority of Utah residents are either in favor of or neutral on having wolves back.[2]

By the end of 2013 the gray wolf population in the Northern Rockies Distinct Population Segment, encompassing Idaho, Montana, Wyoming, and eastern Oregon and Washington (and a small part of northern Utah, where there are no wolves yet) was officially tallied at 1,691 wolves in about 320 packs.[3] There were 83 Mexican gray wolves in five packs in Arizona and New Mexico; 3,678 gray wolves in the Great Lakes region consisting of Minnesota, Michigan, and Wisconsin (and about eight in

Isle Royale National Park); and 90 to 110 red wolves in the northeastern North Carolina red wolf recovery area.[4, 5, 6, 7] Between 2011 and January 2014, hunters and trappers had legally killed 2,567 gray wolves in the lower forty-eight states.[8]

And the wolves keep trying to expand their range, as wolves are inclined to do. In 2004 a female gray wolf from Yellowstone, wearing a radio collar, was hit by a car and killed on Interstate 70 near Idaho Springs, Colorado, and in 2009 another radio-collared female, this one a disperser from the Mill Creek pack in Montana, was found in Rio Blanco County, Colorado, dead from ingesting the poison Compound 1080, which is illegal to use in that state.[9] In March 2012 Wildlife Services agents out shooting coyotes from a helicopter in north-central Utah spotted four large canids that looked like wolves. The Utah Division of Wildlife Resources searched the area, finding and following five sets of tracks via helicopter and also spotted the carcass of an unidentified big game animal on which it looked as though the animals had been feeding but didn't find them or confirm that they were wolves. (Utah produced a wolf management plan in 2005.)[10, 11] In March 2013 a hunter shot a wolf in Kentucky, where wolves have been gone since the mid-1800s, mistaking it for a coyote. The animal's origin is unknown, although it had a lot of plaque on its teeth, which is a sign that it may have been held in captivity for some part of its life.[12] In February 2014 the first gray wolf to show up in Iowa in eighty-nine years was also shot by a hunter who mistook it for a coyote. This wolf, a sixty-five-to-seventy-pound female, is believed to have dispersed from the Great Lakes region.[13]

With the success of the wolf restoration in the northern Rockies and their ESA delisting in 2011 (the Great Lakes Distinct Population Segment was delisted in January 2012), in June 2013 the USFWS began the process to remove all gray wolves in the lower forty-eight states from federal protection under the Endangered Species Act except for the Mexican gray wolf subspecies, which would remain endangered. That means any gray wolves found outside the currently delisted Northern Rocky Mountains and Great Lakes DPSs would no longer be an endangered species and would fall under state management authority. In announcing the proposed delisting, the USFWS said that when gray wolves, excepting Mexican gray wolves, were originally listed under the ESA in the 1970s, it "erroneously included large geographical areas outside the species' historical range."[14]

The delisting proposal ran into immediate opposition from environmental groups and some wolf researchers. A major point of contention was the USFWS's interpretation that the wolves' range was where they currently existed, while the Endangered Species Act specifically defines an animal as endangered if it is "in danger of extinction throughout all or a significant portion of its range." The ESA also intended that even if the population of a species was secure in some states, it could still be considered threatened or endangered in most other states and be protected. The "significant portion of its range" statement is particularly important, because currently gray wolves occupy only about 15 percent of their historical range in the conterminous United States. The delisting proposal's contention that wolves have not repopulated other areas because of "a lack of human tolerance to their presence" and therefore makes the habitat unsuitable also drew fire from wolf advocates. Wolves being killed by people who don't like them is a serious threat to wolf recovery and can be a major factor in limiting where wolves are able to expand their range; however, it is not a reason to conclude that wolves can't be recovered in other parts of their historical range. The USFWS regularly protects endangered and threatened species by making it illegal to kill them and keeping states from implementing management policies that allows people to kill too many of them, and it did so during the recovery phase of the northern Rockies gray wolf introduction. It can do the same for wolves in other parts of the United States as well. There is, in fact, plenty of suitable habitat remaining for wolves to reoccupy in the lower forty-eight states. On the West Coast some estimates put the available wolf habitat at more than 145,000 square miles—34,814 in Washington, 56,496 in Oregon, and 53,732 in California. Colorado and the southern Rockies offer still more places that can readily support wolves.[15, 16]

At the same time, the environmental organization Public Employees for Environmental Responsibility, through a Freedom of Information Act lawsuit, obtained documents from a series of closed-door meetings the USFWS conducted with representatives of fish and wildlife agencies from thirteen states beginning in August 2010 to discuss wolf delisting strategies. PEER accused the federal government of deciding the fate of wolves at a "political bazaar."[17] In August 2013 PEER again charged the federal government with playing politics with wolves when the USFWS removed three prominent wolf experts from the delisting proposal peer review committee—Dr. Roland Kays of North Carolina State University, Dr. John Vucetich of Michigan Technological University, and Dr. Robert Wayne of the University of California Los Angeles—because they had previously signed a letter, with thirteen other scientists, criticizing the science behind the proposal.[18]

That letter, sent to Sally Jewell, secretary of the interior, and Dan Ashe, director of the USFWS, in May 2013, expressed concern over removing ESA protections when there was still a substantial amount of good wolf habitat available in the Pacific Northwest, California, the southern Rocky Mountains, and the Northeast.[19] A letter to Secretary Jewell the same month from the American Society of Mammalogists also urged that wolves remain protected, expressing concern over the substantial number of wolves being killed by humans in the northern Rockies and that continued killing could reduce wolf numbers to dangerously low levels. Keeping wolves protected outside the Northern Rocky Mountains DPS, the mammalogists said, would allow wolves to reestablish themselves in other areas, contributing to gene flow among populations, which is needed to keep them healthy and viable. The same thing, they said, held true for wolves dispersing eastward from the Great Lakes DPS.[20]

By the end of 2013 the USFWS had received about one million public comments on the delisting proposal, the vast majority urging the agency to keep wolves outside the already delisted DPSs protected under the ESA.

When the review of the USFWS's proposed rule to delist all gray wolves (except Mexican gray wolves)—conducted by the National Center for Ecological Analysis and Synthesis (NCEAS), a private contractor working with a panel of seven scientists that included Robert Wayne—was published in January 2014, it concluded that the federal government did not use the best available science in coming to its conclusions. The focus was on wolf genetics in particular. One issue is in the Great Lakes region, where the delisting rule asserts that gray wolves were never found in the eastern United States and that the wolf of the Upper Midwest is a separate species rather than a subspecies of the gray wolf—*Canis lycaon* rather than *C. lupus lycaon*, as it is now classified—which the review panel said was not supported by current science and needed more study. The panel also felt that wolves on the Pacific Northwest coast were probably genetically and ecologically distinct from inland wolves, which would make them a Distinct Population Segment and therefore should not be lumped in with wolves from the northern Rocky Mountains DPS.[21]

Presented with those scientific questions and uncertainties, the USFWS reopened the public comment period until March 27, 2014, receiving an additional 460,000 comments opposing delisting.[22] Oregon Congressman Peter DeFazio, a ranking member of the House Committee on Natural Resources, also cosponsored a petition delivered to the US Department of the Interior opposing delisting and signed by 160,000 people. The federal government planned to make a final decision by the end of 2014.[23]

Despite the tremendous media coverage of the northern Rockies wolf reintroduction and recovery, the bulk of news stories have continued to focus on how many elk and cows wolves kill and the complaints of hunters and ranchers—the putative victims of the wolves' return—while wolf advocates are often put on the defensive. What has received much less recognition is how the wolf reintroduction has been a direct challenge to the political status quo that has, for the most part, controlled wildlife management in the West for decades, and its success a serious threat to that continued dominance. It is also a clash between old ways of looking at wild animals, as either a resource to be harvested or a nuisance to be eliminated, and views of wildlife valued as living components of ecologically healthy landscapes that belong there regardless of what inconvenience they might cause human society. For some, the return of the wolf is even a social justice issue, righting terrible wrongs and cruelties done to these animals in past decades—cruelties that some people would return to even today.

In the past, no one questioned killing predators like wolves, mountain lions, bears, and coyotes to protect livestock and big game. With wild carnivores now appreciated for both their ecological and existence values by a majority of Americans—public support mid-twentieth-century predator advocates didn't have—how those animals are managed and treated is coming under increasing scrutiny and being challenged. Conservation writer George Wuerthner has asked if ranchers should have a right to a predator-free landscape, which allows them to avoid adopting animal husbandry methods that reduce predator attacks on livestock and instead pass those costs on to the public by killing, or having the government kill, publicly owned wildlife at public expense.[24] Defending against wolf attacks on livestock on private property is one thing. But why should wolves be killed to protect livestock grazing on public lands? If privately owned livestock on public lands is at high risk of attack by predators, and the rancher isn't willing to accept that risk or employ methods to reduce the incidence of attacks and factor it in to his business costs, then perhaps public lands are not a good place to run his cows or sheep. While some ranchers are adopting nonlethal ways to prevent wolf attacks on their stocks, to their great credit, the old-fashioned method of systematically killing wolves and other carnivores to protect livestock remains in place wherever there are wolves.

A press release issued by the Rocky Mountain Elk Foundation in support of Idaho Fish and Game's wolf control plan in the Frank Church River of No Return Wilderness described wolf advocates as being "a small fraction of people that believe the wolf deserves special rules and designations above and beyond all other wildlife," and reiterated the necessity of human intervention to ensure the "balance of nature."[25] In other words, it was charging environmental groups with wanting an exemption from managing wolves in the wilderness area to maximize elk numbers for hunters to harvest, as they are managed everywhere else. But should wildlife be managed mainly for maximum hunter benefit everywhere? And is it reasonable for hunters to expect maximum possible big game numbers everywhere all the time, especially when it may involve destroying a wildlife resource—wolves—that many people value and don't want killed for frivolous reasons? Wildlife is a public trust, belonging to the citizens of their respective states. Those who aren't interested in harvesting elk or deer for themselves may want "their" share to go to wolves and other native carnivores.

Perhaps there should be exemptions made in places like the River of No Return Wilderness and other wilderness areas, where humans are supposed to stand back and let natural processes take their course, which should rightly include natural interactions and dynamics between wildlife species. These national forests and wilderness areas, where many wolves live, are national public interest lands. While the USDA Forest Service and the Bureau of Land Management usually delegate wildlife management on those lands to the states, under the US Constitution's Property Clause, Congress has complete power over federal lands.[26, 27] The Property Clause authorizes that "Congress may preempt traditional state trustee and police powers over wild animals, giving the federal government authority to regulate and protect wildlife on federal lands." For example, both the USFWS and National Park Service retain authority over wildlife under the Property Clause on lands they manage.[28]

But wildlife management that leans heavily to the needs, wants, and worldview of the political establishment is likely to dominate for some time. In a revealing survey, researchers categorized goals set by states working on mountain lion management plans between 1984 and 2005 and found that utilitarian and dominionistic goals were emphasized 38 to 50 percent of the time, while ecological goals were at 19 to 31 percent and existence value goals at 17 to 31 percent.[29] That hierarchal, utilitarian bent, along with the strong anti-wolf bias that dominates state-level wildlife management, makes it all the more difficult for non-harvest-oriented wildlife conservation groups to argue that wolves have value. Unable to crack the hunter-rancher-wildlife agency complex, wolf advocates often find that lawsuits and voter initiatives are the only practical way to influence wolf and wildlife policy at the state level.

The experience with returning wolves not only to the northern Rockies but also other parts of the lower forty-eight states—the difficulties and ferocity of the opposition—exemplifies the troubles large carnivores are having all over the world. Their large size requires that they hunt large prey; they also need expansive territories that put them into direct conflict with humans over wild game and domestic livestock, which often gets them killed in large numbers with no thought of what value they might have. Of the world's thirty-one largest species of carnivores, seven have been documented as causing trophic cascading effects, including African lions, leopards, mountain lions, gray wolves, dingoes, Eurasian lynx, and sea otters. African lions now occupy only 17 percent of their historical range, leopards 65 percent. Together those two large cats help keep medium-size predator populations from getting out of control and having outsize impacts on their prey species, with cascading effects of their own. With the extinction of the Tasmanian tiger (partially caused by humans because of its unwarranted reputation as a sheep killer), dingoes are now Australia's only large carnivore. It is well established that dingoes control populations of nonnative herbivores and red foxes, an introduced mesopredator. Eurasian lynx, extirpated from much of Western Europe but still distributed through eastern and northern Eurasia, are thought to control roe deer and red fox numbers. Gray wolves and mountain lions are known to regulate deer and elk populations and cause feeding behavior changes that reduce browsing pressure on hardwoods and shrubs, while the effects of sea otters and the kelp–sea urchin community is also well documented.

Loss of habitat; persecution by humans; too many killed for hides, meat, medicinal, and other utilitarian purposes; the decline of prey species—all are contributing to the loss and range contraction of the world's large carnivores.

Current heavy hunting pressure on recovered gray wolf populations in the northern Rockies and the Great Lakes region could eventually lower their numbers enough to reduce their potential positive ecosystem effects.[30] In a 2014 scientific paper, "Status and Ecological Effects of the World's Largest Carnivores," the authors make a pretty blunt assessment of how large carnivores like wolves and mountain lions are managed today: "The classic conception of large-carnivore influences on ecosystems held that predators were responsible for depleting resources such as fish, wildlife, and domestic livestock. This assumption is still used to justify wildlife management practices aiming to limit or eradicate predators in some regions. This conception of carnivore ecology is now outdated and in need of fundamental change."

But the wolves are here to stay, despite the continuing opposition by some people and their willingness to kill them, legally or otherwise, or employ all their political power and influence to stop them. There will be no future eradication campaigns—wolves are too resilient, and too many people support wolf recovery. The Endangered Species Act will keep people from killing them off again—as long as the act is kept strong and defended from politicians and their allies who would like to water it down or repeal it altogether.

Increasingly, scientists are saying that we now live in a new epoch, the Anthropocene, where humanity is so ubiquitous on the planet that we now affect, in some way, nearly everything that happens, including many of the earth's most basic natural processes. If that is the case and we now ultimately call the shots, perhaps it is not so important to justify having wolves because they exert positive impacts on ecosystems or thrill wilderness travelers with their howls in the night. In the Anthropocene perhaps no justification for wolves is necessary, but the fact that so many Americans want "our" wolves back is reason enough to have them.

Wolves are slowly recolonizing their old territories outside the original recovery area and will persevere as long as people aren't allowed to kill them off again. Photo by the Oregon Department of Fish and Wildlife

Notes

CHAPTER 1: B-45

1. Idaho Wolf Recovery Program, Progress Report 1999–2001. Nez Perce Tribe Wildlife Program (January 2002).

2. Niemeyer, Carter. Personal communication.

3. Wertz, Tara. Personal communication.

4. Henjum, Mark. Personal communication.

5. Fattig, Paul. "Teenager wins a closer bond with wolves." *Mail Tribune*. Medford, Oregon (October 14, 1999).

6. *Oregonian*. Portland, Oregon (March 17, 1999).

7. Holyan, Jim. Chronology for B-45-F. Nez Perce Wolf Recovery Program (October 2010).

CHAPTER 2: RETURN TO THE ROCKIES

1. Nowak, Ronald M. "Wolf Evolution and Taxonomy." *Wolves: Behavior, Ecology, and Conservation*. L. David Mech and Luigi Boitani, eds. Chicago: The University of Chicago Press (2003); pp. 239–50.

2. Anderson, Meb W. "Federal Delisting of the Gray Wolf: An Oregon Perspective on the Future of Gray Wolf Recovery Under State Endangered Species Acts," *Vermont Journal of Environmental Law*, vol. 6 (2004); pp. 134–35.

3. International Wolf Center, Ely, Minnesota.

4. Boitani, Luigi. "Wolf Conservation and Recovery." *Wolves: Behavior, Ecology, and Conservation*. L. David Mech and Luigi Boitani, eds. Chicago: The University of Chicago Press (2003); p. 325.

5. Gilchrist, Clint. "Wolves in the Upper Green." *Pinedale Online News*. Pinedale, Wyoming (June 10, 2004).

6. Robinson, Michael J. *Predatory Bureaucracy: The Extermination of Wolves and the Transformation of the West*. Boulder, CO: University of Colorado Press (2005); pp. 65.

7. Dunlap, Thomas R. *Saving America's Wildlife*. Princeton, NJ: Princeton University Press (1988); pp. 50–61.

8. Robinson, Michael J. *Predatory Bureaucracy: The Extermination of Wolves and the Transformation of the West*. Boulder, CO: University of Colorado Press (2005); pp. 115.

9. Young, Stanley P., and Edward A. Goldman. *The Wolves of North America*. Washington, DC: The American Wildlife Institute (1944); pp. 275–85.

10. Lynch, V. E. *Trails to Successful Trapping*. A. R. Harding Publishing Company (1935); p. 74.

11. Dunlap, Thomas R. *Saving America's Wildlife*. Princeton, NJ: Princeton University Press (1988); pp. 50–61.

12. Meine, Curt. *Aldo Leopold, His Life and Work*. The University of Wisconsin Press (1988); p. 468.

13. Sparks, Alan E., and Yaroslav Dovhanych. "The Wolves of Ukraine." *International Wolf* (Winter 2013); p. 17.

14. International Wolf Center, Ely, Minnesota.

15. US Fish and Wildlife Service. "The Reintroduction of Gray Wolves to Yellowstone National Park and Central Idaho Final Environmental Impact Statement" (1994); chapter 3, p. 5; Alternative 1, p. 3.

16. Leopold, Aldo. Review of Young and Goldman, *The Wolves of North America* [1945]. *The River of the Mother of God and Other Essays by Aldo Leopold*. Susan L. Flader and J. Baird Callicott, eds. Madison, WI: The University of Wisconsin Press (1991); p. 322.

17. Dunlap, Thomas R. *Saving America's Wildlife*. Princeton, NJ: Princeton University Press (1988); pp. 170.

18. Fritts, S. H., E. E. Bangs, J. A. Fontaine, M. R. Johnson, M. K. Phillips, E. D. Koch, and J. R. Gunson. "Planning and Implementing a Reintroduction of Wolves to Yellowstone National Park and Central Idaho." *Restoration Ecology* (March 1997).

19. US Fish and Wildlife Service. "The Reintroduction of Gray Wolves to Yellowstone National Park and Central Idaho Final Environmental Impact Statement" (1994); chapter 3, p. 5; Alternative 1, p. 3.

20. US Fish and Wildlife Service. "Northern Rocky Mountain Wolf Recovery Plan" (1987); pp. 3–5.

21. US Fish and Wildlife Service. "The Reintroduction of Gray Wolves to Yellowstone National Park and Central Idaho Final Environmental Impact Statement" (1994); chapter 3, p. 5; Alternative 1, p. 3.

22. US Fish and Wildlife Service. "The Reintroduction of Gray Wolves to Yellowstone National Park and Central Idaho Final Environmental Impact Statement" (1994); chapter 3, p. 5; Alternative 1, p. 3.

23. International Wolf Center, Ely, Minnesota.

24. Fritts, S. H., E. E. Bangs, J. A. Fontaine, M. R. Johnson, M. K. Phillips, E. D. Koch, and J. R. Gunson. "Planning and Implementing a Reintroduction of Wolves to Yellowstone National Park and Central Idaho." *Restoration Ecology* (March 1997).

25. Niemeyer, Carter. Personal communication.

26. Fritts, S. H., E. E. Bangs, J. A. Fontaine, M. R. Johnson, M. K. Phillips, E. D. Koch, and J. R. Gunson. "Planning and Implementing a

Reintroduction of Wolves to Yellowstone National Park and Central Idaho." *Restoration Ecology* (March 1997).

27. Stone, Suzanne. *Idaho StoryCorps:* "Remembering the First Wolves Released in the Gem State." Boise State Public Radio. Boise, ID.

28. Idaho Department of Fish and Game. Wolf Management/Status Timeline.

29. Fritts, S. H., E. E. Bangs, J. A. Fontaine, M. R. Johnson, M. K. Phillips, E. D. Koch, and J. R. Gunson. "Planning and Implementing a Reintroduction of Wolves to Yellowstone National Park and Central Idaho." *Restoration Ecology* (March 1997).

CHAPTER 3: RANCHERS, WOLVES, AND RURAL POWER

1. Anderson, Meb W. "Federal Delisting of the Gray Wolf: An Oregon Perspective on the Future of Gray Wolf Recovery Under State Endangered Species Acts." *Vermont Journal of Environmental Law*, vol. 6 (2004); p. 139.

2. Wilson, Patrick Impero. "Wolves, Politics, and the Nez Perce: Wolf Recovery in Central Idaho and the Role of Native Tribes." *Natural Resources Journal*, vol. 39 (Summer 1999); pp 546–49.

3. Jacobs, Andria. "Wolf Policy in the West." Working Paper 94–95. Conflict Research Consortium, University of Colorado, Boulder (February 1994).

4. Fischer, Hank. *Wolf Wars*. Missoula, MT: Fischer Outdoor Discoveries, LLC (2003); pp. 128.

5. Wilson, Patrick Impero. "Wolves, Politics, and the Nez Perce: Wolf Recovery in Central Idaho and the Role of Native Tribes." *Natural Resources Journal*, vol. 39 (Summer 1999); pp 546–49.

6. US Fish and Wildlife Service. "The Reintroduction of Gray Wolves to Yellowstone National Park and Central Idaho Final Environmental Impact Statement" (1994); appendix 3, pp. 8–10.

7. Dunlap, Thomas R. *Saving America's Wildlife*. Princeton, NJ: Princeton University Press (1988); p. 169.

8. Holyan, Jim, Nez Perce Wolf Recovery Program. Personal communication.

9. Henjum, Mark. Personal communication.

10. Bangs, Ed, US Fish and Wildlife Service. Wolf Presentation. High Desert Museum, Bend, OR (April 11, 2009).

11. US Fish and Wildlife Service. "The Reintroduction of Gray Wolves to Yellowstone National Park and Central Idaho Final Environmental Impact Statement" (1994); appendix 3, pp. 8–10.

12. Bass, Rick. *The Ninemile Wolves*. Mariner Books (1992); p. 29.

13. Hager, Christine A. "Why We Need Wolves in Yellowstone." *Biological Conservation*, Bio 65 (Spring 1997). University of California, Irvine.

14. Barker, Rocky. "Ideological Divide." The Thoreau Institute; www.ti.org.

15. Keefover, Wendy. "The Deadliest Dozen Counties in the American West." WildEarth Guardians, Broomfield, CO (June 2012); p. 5.

16. US Fish and Wildlife Service. "Establishment of a Nonessential Experimental Population of Gray Wolves in Central Idaho and Southwestern Montana." *Federal Register*, vol. 59, no. 224 (November 22, 1994).

17. Fritts, S. H., E. E. Bangs, J. A. Fontaine, M. R. Johnson, M. K. Phillips, E. D. Koch, and J. R. Gunson. "Planning and Implementing a Reintroduction of Wolves to Yellowstone National Park and Central Idaho." *Restoration Ecology* (March 1997).

18. Fischer, Hank. *Wolf Wars*. Missoula, MT: Fischer Outdoor Discoveries, LLC (2003); pp. 157.

19. Fritts, S. H., E. E. Bangs, J. A. Fontaine, M. R. Johnson, M. K. Phillips, E. D. Koch, and J. R. Gunson. "Planning and Implementing a Reintroduction of Wolves to Yellowstone National Park and Central Idaho." *Restoration Ecology* (March 1997).

20. Fritts, S. H., E. E. Bangs, J. A. Fontaine, M. R. Johnson, M. K. Phillips, E. D. Koch, and J. R. Gunson. "Planning and Implementing a Reintroduction of Wolves to Yellowstone National Park and Central Idaho." *Restoration Ecology* (March 1997).

21. Fritts, S. H., E. E. Bangs, J. A. Fontaine, M. R. Johnson, M. K. Phillips, E. D. Koch, and J. R. Gunson. "Planning and Implementing a Reintroduction of Wolves to Yellowstone National Park and Central Idaho." *Restoration Ecology* (March 1997).

22. Cowan Brown, Elizabeth. "The 'Wholly Separate' Truth: Did the Yellowstone Wolf Reintroduction Violate Section 10(J) of the Endangered Species Act?" *Boston College Environmental Affairs Law Review*, vol. 27, issue 3, article 4 (1-1-2000); pp. 441–44.

23. Honnold, Doug. "Lawsuit Seeks to Protect Wolves, Not Return Them to Canada." *Predator Project Newsletter* (Spring 1996).; p. 6.

24. Paquet, Paul C. University of Victoria, British Columbia. Personal communication.

25. Idaho Department of Fish and Game. Wolf Management/Status Timeline.

26. Smith, Douglas W. "Ten Years of Yellowstone Wolves, 1995–2005." *Yellowstone Science*, vol. 13, no. 1 (Winter 2005); p. 11.

CHAPTER 4: IDAHO AND THE NEZ PERCE WOLVES

1. Cowan Brown, Elizabeth. "The 'Wholly Separate' Truth: Did the Yellowstone Wolf Reintroduction Violate Section 10(J) of the Endangered Species Act?" *Boston College Environmental Affairs Law Review*, vol. 27, issue 3, article 4 (1-1-2000); pp. 449–452.

2. Wilson, Patrick Impero. "Wolves, Politics, and the Nez Perce: Wolf Recovery in Central Idaho and the Role of Native Tribes." *Natural Resources Journal*, vol. 39 (Summer 1999); pp. 551–54.

3. National Park Service, Nez Perce National Historical Park.

4. Ruby, Robert A., and John A. Brown. *A Guide to the Indian Tribes of the Pacific Northwest*. Norman, OK: University of Oklahoma Press (1992); pp. 144–47.

5. Nadeau, M. S., C. Mack, J. Holyan, J. Husseman, M. Lucid, and B. Thomas. "Wolf conservation and management in Idaho"; Progress Report 2005 (2006). Idaho Department of Fish and Game, 600 South Walnut, Boise, ID; Nez Perce Tribe, PO Box 365, Lapwai, ID. 61; pp. ii.

6. US Fish and Wildlife Service. Questions and Answers, Wolf 10(j) Final Rule (December 23, 2004).

7. Idaho Department of Fish and Game. Wolf Management/Status Timeline.

8. Cutright, Paul Russell. *Lewis & Clark, Pioneering Naturalists*. Lincoln, NE: University of Nebraska Press (1969); p. 208.

CHAPTER 5: PUSHBACK

1. Stark, Dan. Minnesota Department of Natural Resources. "Moving from Recovery to State Management of Wolves." International Wolf Symposium, Duluth, MN (October 12, 2013).

2. US Fish and Wildlife Service, Montana Fish, Wildlife & Parks, Nez Perce Tribe, National Park Service, Blackfeet Nation, Confederated Salish and Kootenai Tribes, Wind River Tribes, Washington Department of Wildlife, Oregon Department of Wildlife, Utah Department of Natural Resources, and USDA Wildlife Services. *Rocky Mountain Wolf Recovery 2008–2010 Interagency Annual Report*. C. A. Sime and E. E. Bangs, eds. (2011). USFWS, Ecological Services, 585 Shepard Way, Helena, MT 59601.

3. Stahl, Greg. "The B2 Chronicles." *Idaho Mountain Express* (May 5, 2004).

4. Barker, Rocky. "The Long Life of One Idaho Wolf Embodies the Story of Wolf Recovery in Idaho." *Idaho Statesman* (March 4, 2007).

5. Oregon Department of Fish and Wildlife. "Wolves in Oregon."

6. Washington Department of Fish and Wildlife. "Gray Wolf Conservation and Management."

7. Carbyn, Ludwig N., and Paul C. Paquet. "Gray Wolf." *Wild Mammals of North America: Biology, Management and Conservation*. George A. Feldhamer, Bruce Thompson, and Joseph A. Chapman, eds. Baltimore, MD: The John Hopkins University Press (1982, 2003); pp.486, 489–90.

8. "Wolf Disaster Emergency Plan Heading to Governor's Office." Idahoreporter.com (April 6, 2011).

9. Associated Press. "Idaho Group Seeks Anti-Wolf Initiative." *Bend Bulletin* (February 5, 2006).

10. Barker, Rocky. *Idaho Statesman* blog (March 31, 2008).

11. *Idaho Fish and Game News*, vol. 23, no. 2 (February 2011).

12. US Fish and Wildlife Service, Nez Perce Tribe, National Park Service, and USDA Wildlife Services. *Rocky Mountain Wolf Recovery 2003 Annual Report*. T. Meier, ed. (2004). USFWS, Ecological Services, 100 N Park, Suite 320, Helena, MT 59601; p. 65.

13. US Fish and Wildlife Service, Nez Perce Tribe, National Park Service, Montana Fish, Wildlife & Parks, Idaho Fish and Game, and USDA Wildlife Services. *Rocky Mountain Wolf Recovery 2005 Annual Report*. C. A. Sime and E. E. Bangs, eds. (2006). USFWS, Ecological Services, 585 Shepard Way, Helena, MT 59601; p. 130.

14. Kauffman, Jason. "Anti-Wolf Activist Charged with Assault and Battery." *Idaho Mountain Express* (March 28, 2008).

15. Kauffman, Jason. "Gillett Walks for Now." *Idaho Mountain Express* (August 27, 2008).

16. Wilkinson, Todd. "Wolf Pack Train." *Wildlife Art Nature Journal* blog (November 9, 2011).

17. Stone, Lynne, Boulder–White Clouds Council. Personal communication.

18. Ketchum, Christopher. "How to Kill a Wolf." *VICE United States* (March 13, 2014).

19. US Fish and Wildlife Service. *Rocky Mountain Wolf Recovery Interagency Annual Reports (1999–2003)*.

20. Schultz, Rob. "On the Brink of Extinction . . . The Last Wild Red Wolves." *International Wolf* (Spring 2014); p. 3.

21. Ross, Jamie. "Groups Fight Pass Given to Rare Species Killers." Courthouse News Service (May 3, 2013).

22. "Groups Sue US for Failure to Prosecute Under the Endangered Species Act." WildEarth Guardians (May 30, 2013).

23. Cole, Ken. "Wolf Mortality in Idaho, a Final Toll." *The Wildlife News* (May 7, 2012).

24. Calman, Judy. "Comments on the Proposed Revision to the Nonessential Experimental Population of the Mexican Wolf (Docket FWS-R2-ES-2013-0056) and on Removing the Gray Wolf (*Canis lupus*) from the List of Endangered and Threatened Wildlife and Maintaining Protections for the Mexican Wolf (*Canis lupus baileyi*) by Listing it as Endangered (Docket FWS-HQ-ES-2013-0073)." New Mexico Wilderness Alliance (December 5, 2013); p. 8.

25. USDA Forest Service. "Poison Bait Spread in North Fork Area, Salmon-Challis National Forest" (February 1, 2004).

26. "Possible Wolf Poisoning Under Investigation." Wyoming Public Media (June 11, 2004).

27. US Fish and Wildlife Service. "Poisoned Gray Wolf Found in Frank Church Wilderness" (June 1, 2005).

28. "Pesticide Used to Poison Idaho Wolf." *Idaho Mountain Express* (June 3, 2005).

29. Associated Press. "Anti-Wolf Idahoan Charged with Intent to Poison Them." *The Spokesman-Review* (October 21, 2005).

30. Zuckerman, Laura, Reuters Edition: US. "Man Sentenced for Seeking to Poison Wolves." (April 19, 2007).

31. "Anti-Wolf Web Site Proposes Illegal Poisoning of Wolves." Howl Colorado.org (June 7, 2010).

32. "4 Wolves, 6 Eagles Poisoned in Bob Marshall Wilderness." *Billings Gazette* (August 6, 2012).

33. "4 of 5 Gray Wolves Released in Mexico Die of Poisoning." *Arizona Daily Star* (February 24, 2012).

34. Benson, Steve. "Wolf Howls Prompt Wilderness Evacuation." *Idaho Mountain Express* (October 11, 2006).

35. Mech, L. David. *The Wolf.* Garden City, NY: The Natural History Press (1970); pp. 11–12.

36. Duval, Jon. "State Biologist Clarifies Wolf Myths." *Idaho Mountain Express* (April 7, 2010).

37. "Gray Wolf—*Canis lupus.*" *Montana Field Guide*; MT.gov.

38. "Top Yellowstone Expert Takes on the Wolf Critics." *The Montana Pioneer* (January 5, 2014).

39. Fritts, Steven H., Robert O. Stephenson, Robert D. Hayes, and Luigi Boitani. "Wolves and Humans." *Wolves: Behavior, Ecology, and Conservation.* L. David Mech and Luigi Boitani, eds. Chicago: The University of Chicago Press (2003); p. 303

40. Cutright, Paul Russell. *Lewis & Clark, Pioneering Naturalists.* Lincoln, NE: University of Nebraska Press (1969); p. 334.

41. Linnell, John D. C., Erling J. Solberg, Scott Brainerd, Olof Liberg, Håkan Sand, Petter Wabakken, and Ilpo Kojola. "Is the Fear of Wolves Justified? A Fennoscandian Perspective." *Acta Zoologica Lituanica*, vol. 13, no. 1 (2003); pp. 27, 29–31.

42. "The Fear of Wolves: A Review of Wolf Attacks on Humans." Norsk institutt for naturforskning (January 2002).

43. McNay, Mark E. "A Case History of Wolf-Human Encounters in Alaska and Canada." Alaska Department of Fish and Game, Wildlife Technical Bulletin 13 (2002).

44. "Ontario Man Killed in Wolf Attack, Coroner's Jury Finds." Canadian Broadcast Corporation (November 1, 2007).

45. Medred, Craig. "Wolves Killed Alaska Teacher in 2010, State Says." *Alaska Dispatch* (January 26, 2012).

46. Cart, Julie. "Aggressive Wolf at Yellowstone National Park Euthanized." *Los Angeles Times* Greenspace (October 12, 2011).

47. Sweanor, Linda L., and Kenneth A. Logan. *Cougar-Human Interactions, Cougar Ecology & Conservation*. Maurice Hornocker and Sharon Negri, eds. Chicago: The University of Chicago Press (2009); pp. 190–91.

48. Belluck, Pam. "Study of Black Bears Finds It's Not the Mammas That Should Be Feared the Most." *The New York Times* (May 11, 2011).

49. National Park Service, Yellowstone National Park. "Bear Inflicted Human Injuries and Fatalities in Yellowstone" (March 20, 2014); www.nps.gov/yell/naturescience/injuries.htm.

50. Eovaldi, Suzanne. "Wolves Kill Female Hikers, Liberals Cover it Up" (December 2, 2013); www.westernjournalism.com.

51. "Body of Missing Hiker Found at Craters of the Moon." KTVB.COM (October 23, 2013).

52. Bangs, Ed, US Fish and Wildlife Service. Wolf Presentation. High Desert Museum, Bend, OR (April 11, 2009).

CHAPTER 6: SHOOT 'EM ON SIGHT

1. Callens, Judith. Background Brief on Endangered Species. State of Oregon, Legislative Services Committee, vol. 2, issue 1 (May 2004).

2. US Fish and Wildlife Service, Nez Perce Tribe, National Park Service, and USDA Wildlife Services. *Rocky Mountain Wolf Recovery 2003 Annual Report*. T. Meier, ed. (2004). USFWS, Ecological Services, 100 N Park, Suite 320, Helena, MT 59601; p. 1.

3. Greenwald, Noah, Center for Biological Diversity. Personal communication.

4. Montana Fish, Wildlife and Parks. "Gray Wolf Chronology in Montana through 2008" (2008).

5. Dubuc, Rob. "The Northern Rocky Mountain Wolf Delisting: What Would Leopold Think?" *Environs, Environmental Law and Policy Journal*, vol. 32, no. 2 (Spring 2009). University of California, Davis, Law School; pp. 226–52.

6. Dubuc, Rob. "The Northern Rocky Mountain Wolf Delisting: What Would Leopold Think?" *Environs, Environmental Law and Policy Journal*, vol. 32, no. 2 (Spring 2009). University of California, Davis, Law School; pp. 226–52.

7. Mieszkowski, Katherine. "Killing the Wolves Again." Salon.com (May 27, 2008).

8. Dubuc, Rob. "The Northern Rocky Mountain Wolf Delisting: What Would Leopold Think?" *Environs, Environmental Law and Policy Journal*, vol. 32, no. 2 (Spring 2009). University of California, Davis, Law School; pp. 226–52.

9. Dubuc, Rob. "The Northern Rocky Mountain Wolf Delisting: What Would Leopold Think?" *Environs, Environmental Law and Policy Journal*,

vol. 32, no. 2 (Spring 2009). University of California, Davis, Law School; pp. 226–52.

10. Alexander, Kristina. *The Gray Wolf and the Endangered Species Act: A Brief Legal History*. Congressional Research Service (July 27, 2011).

11. Greenwald, Noah, Center for Biological Diversity. Personal communication.

12. Ring, Ray. "Identity Politics, Montana Style." *High Country News* (September 3, 2012); p. 12.

13. Niemeyer, Carter. Wolf Lecture. Eugene, OR (July 10, 2012).

14. "Tester, Simpson Sneak Wolf-killing Rider into Budget Bill." Center for Biological Diversity (April 12, 2011).

15. US Fish and Wildlife Service. "Salazar, Ashe Finalize Agreement with Wyoming on Revised Gray Wolf Management Plan" (August 3, 2011).

16. US Fish and Wildlife Service. "Wyoming and US Department of the Interior Wolf Agreement Fact Sheet."

17. Mills, Ken, Wyoming Game and Fish Department. "Moving from Recovery to State Management of Wolves." International Wolf Symposium, Duluth, MN (October 12, 2013).

18. Mills, Ken, Wyoming Game and Fish Department. "Moving from Recovery to State Management of Wolves." International Wolf Symposium, Duluth, MN (October 12, 2013).

19. Tesky, Julie L. *Canis latrans*. In: "Fire Effects Information System" [online] (1995). USDA Forest Service, Rocky Mountain Research Station, Fire Sciences Laboratory; www.fs.fed.us/database/feis/animals/mammal/cala/all.html http://www.feis-crs.org/beta/

20. Tesky, Julie L. *Canis latrans*. In: "Fire Effects Information System" [online] (1995). USDA Forest Service, Rocky Mountain Research Station, Fire Sciences Laboratory; www.fs.fed.us/database/feis/animals/mammal/cala/all.html http://www.feis-crs.org/beta/

21. Keefover, Wendy. "Northern Rocky Mountain Wolves: A Public Policy Process Failure." WildEarth Guardians, Santa Fe, NM (May 2012); pp. 20–23.

22. Wagner, Eric. "Royal Raptor." *Smithsonian Magazine* (February 2014); p. 21.

23. Dunlap, Thomas R. *Saving America's Wildlife*. Princeton, NJ: Princeton University Press (1988); p. 140.

24. Ring-Keefover, Wendy. "War on Wildlife: The US Department of Agriculture's 'Wildlife Services.'" WildEarth Guardians, Santa Fe, NM (February 2009); pp. 37–47, 51–59.

25. "Ending the War on Wildlife-Denning." WildEarth Guardians; www.wildearthguardians.org

26. "Ending the War on Wildlife-Timeline." WildEarth Guardians; www.wildearthguardians.org

27. Ingles, Lloyd G. *Mammals of the Pacific States*. Stanford, CA: Stanford University Press (1962); p. 424.

28. Andrews, Michael S. "A Grand Animal's Return to the Prairie." *The Zumwalt*. Writings from the Prairie Fishtrap, Inc., Enterprise, OR (2008); pp. 21–39.

29. Andrews, Michael S. "A Grand Animal's Return to the Prairie." *The Zumwalt*. Writings from the Prairie Fishtrap, Inc., Enterprise, OR (2008); pp. 21–39.

30. Hurst, Blake. "Elk Compensation Makes Sense." *St. Joseph News Press* (May 18, 2012).

31. Kimmey, Samantha. *Point Reyes Light* (October 24, 2013).

32. Coggins, Vic, Oregon Department of Fish and Wildlife. Personal communication.

33. Irby, Lynn R., Walter E. Zidack, James B. Johnson, and John Saltiel. "Economic Damage to Forage Crops by Native Ungulates as Perceived by Farmers and Ranchers In Montana." *Journal of Range Management* 49(4) (July 1996); p. 375

34. Kiggins, Steve. "State and Feds Killing Elk to Shrink Skagit Valley Herd." Q13 Fox News (October 31, 2013).

35. Miller, Jason. "The Problem with Elk." *Concrete Herald* (May, 5, 2013).

36. Wilkinson, Eric. "Skagit Farmers Overrun by Marauding Elk." KING5.com (August 21, 2013).

37. Martin, Kate. "Herds of Trouble." goskagit.com (February 24, 2013).

38. Lukens, Jim. "Eleven Years with Wolves—What We've Learned." Idaho Fish and Game Salmon Region News Release, Salmon, Idaho (April 25, 2006).

39. Idaho Department of Fish and Game. "Idaho Elk Management Plan, 2014–2024" (January 2014); table A, p. 28.

40. Smith, Bruce L. *Where Elk Roam*. Guilford, CT: Lyons Press (2012); p. 81.

41. Quatraro, Vito. "Department of Livestock Has No Business Managing Elk." *Bozeman Daily Chronicle* (April 7, 2010).

42. Flatt, Courtney. "Washington Euthanizing Diseased Bighorn Sheep." Oregon Public Broadcasting (April 13, 2013).

43. Torland, Ryan, Oregon Department of Fish and Wildlife. Personal communication.

44. Barker, Rocky. "Simpson Withdraws Payette Bighorn Sheep Rider." *Idaho Statesman* blogs (June 27, 2012).

45. Barker, Rocky. "Federal Judge Upholds Payette Bighorn Sheep Protections." Idahostatesman.com (March 26, 2014).

46. Associated Press. "California Delays Decision on Endangered Species Status for Gray Wolf." *Oregonian* (April 16, 2014).

47. Anti-wolf legislation fact sheet. Defenders of Wildlife, Washington, DC.

48. Associated Press. "N.C. Groups Battle over Bill to Hunt Red Wolves." *Spartanburg Herald-Journal* (June 24, 1994).

49. Keefover, Wendy. "Northern Rocky Mountain Wolves: A Public Policy Process Failure." WildEarth Guardians, Santa Fe, NM (May 2012); pp. 20–23.

50. Keefover, Wendy. "Northern Rocky Mountain Wolves: A Public Policy Process Failure." WildEarth Guardians, Santa Fe, NM (May 2012); pp. 20–23.

51. National Agricultural Statistics Service, US Department of Agriculture (2014).

52. US. Fish and Wildlife Service, Idaho Department of Fish and Game, Montana Fish, Wildlife & Parks, Wyoming Game and Fish Department, Nez Perce Tribe, National Park Service, Blackfeet Nation, Confederated Salish and Kootenai Tribes, Wind River Tribes, Confederated Colville Tribes, Spokane Tribe of Indians, Washington Department of Fish and Wildlife, Oregon Department of Fish and Wildlife, Utah Department of Natural Resources, and USDA Wildlife Services. *Northern Rocky Mountain Wolf Recovery Program 2013 Interagency Annual Report*. M.D. Jimenez and S.A. Becker, eds. USFWS, Ecological Services, 585 Shepard Way, Helena, Montana, 59601 Table 7a: Northern Rocky Mountain Confirmed Wolf Depredation by Recovery Area, 1987-2013 (2014).

53. Associated Press. "Idaho Sheep, Lamb Growers Report Healthy Revenue." *Idaho Press-Tribune* (October 17, 2011).

54. Boitani, Luigi. "Challenges and Opportunities for Wolf Conservation in Europe." International Wolf Symposium, Duluth, MN (October 12, 2013).

55. US.Fish and Wildlife Service, Northern Rocky Mountain Confirmed Wolf Depredation by Recovery Area, 1987–2013.

56. Knudson, Tom. "The Killing Agency: Wildlife Services' Brutal Methods Leave a Trail of Animal Death." *The Sacramento Bee* (April 29, 2012).

57. Ring-Keefover, Wendy. "War on Wildlife: The US Department of Agriculture's 'Wildlife Services.'" WildEarth Guardians, Santa Fe, NM (February 2009); pp. 37–47, 51–59.

58. "Recommendations for the Redirection of Management Operations by Wildlife Services." American Society of Mammalogists letter to USDA Animal and Plant Inspection Services (March 21, 2012).

59. Weaver, Matthew. "WSU to Study Wolf, Cattle Behavior." *Capital Press* (December 5, 2013).

60. Defenders of Wildlife, Wolf Compensation Trust, 1987–2009.

61. "Defenders Shifts Focus to Wolf Coexistence Partnerships." Defenders of Wildlife (August 20, 2010).

62. Moore, Greg. "State Doles Out Funds for Wolf Losses." *Idaho Mountain Express* (September 27, 2013).

63. "US Fish and Wildlife Service Seeks Proposals from States and Tribes for Wolf-Livestock Demonstration Project Grants." US Fish and Wildlife Service (June 3, 2013).

64. *Wolves at a Crossroads: 2011* (2011). Living with Wolves, Sun Valley, ID.

65. Stephenson, John, US Fish and Wildlife Service. Wolf Lecture, High Desert Museum, Bend, OR (May 5, 2010).

66. Morgan, Russ, Oregon Department of Fish and Wildlife. Personal communication.

67. Duara, Nigel, Associated Press. "Federal Biologists Too Quick to Blame Wolves, Panel Says" (January 6, 2012).

CHAPTER 7: A WILD WOLF CHASE

1. Holyan, J., K. Holder, J. Cronce, and C. Mack. Wolf conservation and management in Idaho; progress report 2010 (2011). Nez Perce Tribe Wolf Recovery Project, Lapwai, ID; pp. ii, 23–24.

2. Russell, Betsy Z. "Idaho lays out wolf kill." *The Spokesman-Review* (August 18, 2009).

3. Idaho Department of Fish and Game. "Idaho's First Wolf Hunt Is Over" (April 5, 2010).

4. C. L. "Butch" Otter letter to Ken Salazar regarding Termination of Designated Agent Status (October 18, 2010).

5. Idaho Department of Fish and Game. "Idaho's First Wolf Hunt Is Over" (April 5, 2010).

6. Dubuc, Rob. "The Northern Rocky Mountain Wolf Delisting: What Would Leopold Think?" *Environs, Environmental Law and Policy Journal*, vol. 32, no. 2 (Spring 2009). University of California, Davis, Law School; pp. 226–52.

7. "Enviro Groups Ready to Push Back Against Idaho Wolf Actions." KUOW.org, *EarthFix* (March 24, 2014).

8. Idaho Department of Fish and Game, Boise, ID (April 30, 2014).

9. US Fish and Wildlife Service, Montana Fish, Wildlife & Parks, Nez Perce Tribe, National Park Service, Blackfeet Nation, Confederated Salish and Kootenai Tribes, Wind River Tribes, Washington Department of Wildlife, Oregon Department of Wildlife, Utah Department of Natural Resources, and USDA Wildlife Services. *Rocky Mountain Wolf Recovery 2010 Interagency Annual Report*. C. A. Sime and E. E. Bangs, eds. (2011). USFWS, Ecological Services, 585 Shepard Way, Helena, MT 59601; p. 7.

10. Mack, Curt, Nez Perce Wolf Recovery Program. Personal communication.

11. Oregon Department of Fish and Wildlife. "Identification of Wolf Sign."

12. *"Echinococcus granulosus."* Letter, US Fish and Wildlife Service, Gray Wolves in the Northern Rocky Mountains (March 30, 2010).

13. *The Spokesman-Review*; data.spokesman.com.

14. Idaho Department of Labor. Idaho Census Tables (2010).

15. Rauzi, David. "County's Aging Population Requires New Discussions." *Idaho County Free Press* (April 1, 2014).

16. Bonner, Jessie L., and John Miller, Associated Press. "Idaho County Declares Disaster over Wolves" (September 18, 2010).

17. The Board of County Commissioners, Idaho County, Idaho. "Resolution No. 2010-130, Disaster Declaration" (September 16, 2010).

18. Bonner, Jessie L., and John Miller, Associated Press. "Idaho County Declares Disaster over Wolves" (September 18, 2010).

19. Letter from C. L. "Butch" Otter to Idaho County Commissioners (September 27, 2010).

20. Letter from C. L. "Butch" Otter to Ben Ysursa, Idaho Secretary of State (April 9, 2011).

21. Statesman Editorial Board. "Beware: Legislative 'Scientists' at Work." *Idaho Statesman* (April 5, 2011).

22. Zuckerman, Laura, Reuters. "Idaho Authorizes Sheriff's Deputies to Kill Wolves" (May 18, 2011).

23. Ford, Jason. "Five Wolves Shot in Idaho's Lolo Zone from Helicopter." Talk Radio 950 KOZE-AM (May 13, 2011).

24. Letter to the Editor, *Citizen Review* Online (May 2, 2014).

25. Fritts, S. H., E. E. Bangs, J. A. Fontaine, M. R. Johnson, M. K. Phillips, E. D. Koch, and J. R. Gunson. "Planning and Implementing a Reintroduction of Wolves to Yellowstone National Park and Central Idaho," *Restoration Ecology* (March 1997); p. 5.

26. *The Citizen*. Grangeville, Idaho (Summer 2011)

27. *The Citizen*. Grangeville, Idaho. (May 2010)

28. Chaney, Rob. "Idaho Wolf Hunt Ends, but Hunts Continue on Private Land in Panhandle." *Missoulian* (July 5, 2012).

29. Montana Fish, Wildlife and Parks. *2011 Montana Wolf Hunting Season Report*.

CHAPTER 8: GRAY WOLVES, BLACK HELICOPTERS

1. Fritts, Steven H., Robert O. Stephenson, Robert D. Hayes, and Luigi Boitani. "Wolves and Humans." *Wolves: Behavior, Ecology, and Conservation*. L. David Mech and Luigi Boitani, eds. Chicago: The University of Chicago Press (2003); pp. 289–94.

2. Gorte, Ross W., Carol Hardy Vincent, Laura A. Hanson, and Marc R. Rosenblum. *Federal Land Ownership: Overview and Data*. Congressional Research Service (February 8, 2012).

3. Bridges, Toby. "The Wildlands Project—Forcing You off the Land & into the City." *Montana Mountain Chronicle* (June 8, 2011).

4. Egan, Timothy. "Terror in Oklahoma: In Congress, Trying to Explain Contacts with Paramilitary Groups." *The New York Times* (May 2, 1995).

5. C. L. "Butch" Otter, Governor. Idaho State of the State and Budget Address (January 6, 2014).

6. Beers, Jim. "Why They Love Predators" (November 8, 2011).

7. Bell, Jessica. "Using Critical Discourse Analysis to Identify Implicit and Explicit Stakeholder Perceptions of Wolves." International Wolf Symposium, Duluth, MN (October 11, 2013).

8. Bell, Jessica. "Hierarchy, Intrusion and the Anthropomorphism of Nature: Hunter and Rancher Discourse on North American Wolves." Department of Sociology, Animal Studies, and Environmental Science and Policy, Michigan State University (2013).

9. Nesbitt, Katy. "Couple's Plan to Develop Bed and Breakfast along 'Wolf Highway' Meets Resistance." *The Observer* (October 26, 2011).

10. Nesbitt, Katy. "Proposal to Build B&B Creates Stir." *The Observer* (December 7, 2011).

11. Profita, Cassandra. "Wallowa County Says No to Wolf Highway B&B." *Ecotrope* (January 17, 2012).

12. Report to the Utah Legislature, Number 2013-11: "A Review of Appropriated Wolf Management Funds." Office of the Legislative Auditor General, State of Utah (October 2013).

13. Wharton, Tom. "Wharton: Sportsmen for Fish & Wildlife about Wrong Kind of Bucks." *The Salt Lake Tribune* (March 18, 2013).

14. Olsen, Grant. "6,000 Coyotes Killed in Utah's Bounty Program." KSL.com (May 6, 2013).

15. Van Eyck, Zack. Does Public Understand Prop 5? Backers, Foes Unsure. *Deseret News* (October 7, 1998).

16. Long, Ben, Writers on the Range. "'Sportsmen,' So-called." *The Salt Lake Tribune* (March 28, 2012).

17. Maffly, Brian. "Anti-Wolf Group Likely To Get Second $300,000 Utah Payment." *The Salt Lake Tribune*, March 10, 2013

18. Maffly, Brian. "Anti-Wolf Group Vague On How It Spent Utah Taxpayer Funds." *The Salt lake Tribune* (July 2, 2013).

19. Report to the Utah Legislature, Number 2013-11: "A Review of Appropriated Wolf Management Funds." Office of the Legislative Auditor General, State of Utah (October 2013).

20. www.wolvesingovernmentclothing.com.

21. Gibson, James William. "Sorry, But Wolf Slaughter Is Not American." www.earthisland.org (October 28, 2013).

22. Johnson, Phil. "Hunter: Wolves Mean Less Big Game." *The Western News* (October 25, 2013).

23. Jacoby, Jason. "Wolf Pack Blamed in Elk, Deer Deaths." WesCom News Service, *Bend Bulletin* (February 23, 2014).

24. International Wolf Center. "Animal Planet Cancels Man-Eating Super Wolves Show; Program Nominated for Scat Award by International Wolf Center."

25. Houston, M. J., J. T. Bruskotter, and D. P. Fan. "Attitudes toward Wolves in the United States and Canada: A Content Analysis of the Print News Media, 1999–2008." *Human Dimensions of Wildlife* 15 (5) (2010); pp. 389–403.

26. Bell, Jessica. "Hierarchy, Intrusion and the Anthropomorphism of Nature: Hunter and Rancher Discourse on North American Wolves." Department of Sociology, Animal Studies, and Environmental Science and Policy, Michigan State University (2013).

CHAPTER 9: WOLVES VERSUS ELK

1. US Fish and Wildlife Service, Montana Fish, Wildlife & Parks, Nez Perce Tribe, National Park Service, Blackfeet Nation, Confederated Salish and Kootenai Tribes, Wind River Tribes, Washington Department of Wildlife, Oregon Department of Wildlife, Utah Department of Natural Resources, and USDA Wildlife Services. *Rocky Mountain Wolf Recovery 2010 Interagency Annual Report.* C. A. Sime and E. E. Bangs, eds. (2011). USFWS, Ecological Services, 585 Shepard Way, Helena, MT 59601; p. 5.

2. US Fish and Wildlife Service, Idaho Department of Fish and Game, Montana Fish, Wildlife & Parks, Wyoming Game and Fish Department, Nez Perce Tribe, National Park Service, Blackfeet Nation, Confederated Salish and Kootenai Tribes, Wind River Tribes, Confederated Colville Tribes, Spokane Tribe of Indians, Washington Department of Fish and Wildlife, Oregon Department of Fish and Wildlife, Utah Department of Natural Resources, and USDA Wildlife Services. *Northern Rocky Mountain Wolf Recovery Program 2013 Interagency Annual Report.* M. D. Jimenez and S. A. Becker, eds. (2014). USFWS, Ecological Services, 585 Shepard Way, Helena, MT 59601; p. 1.

3. "Wild Game in Crisis." Big Game Forever; www.biggameforever. org.

4. Montana Sportsmen for Fish and Wildlife; www.mt-sfw.org.

5. Lobo Watch; www.lobowatch.org.

6. Rocky Mountain Elk Foundation. "Elk Facts."

7. *Elk of North America.* Jack Ward Thomas, Dale E. Toweill, eds. Wildlife Management Institute. Harrisburg, PA: Stackpole Books (1982); pp. 24-36.

8. "Elk in Arizona." *Wild Kids*, no. 8. Arizona Game and Fish Department (July 2012).

9. California Department of Fish and Wildlife. "All about Tule Elk, Distribution and Range."

10. Rocky Mountain Elk Foundation. "Elk Facts."

11. *Elk of North America*. Jack Ward Thomas, Dale E. Toweill, eds. Wildlife Management Institute. Harrisburg, PA: Stackpole Books (1982); pp. 24-36.

12. Wright, Gregory J., Rolf O. Peterson, Douglas W. Smith, and Thomas O. Lemke. "Selection of Northern Yellowstone Elk by Gray Wolves and Hunters." *The Journal of Wildlife Management*, vol. 70, no. 4 (August 2006); pp. 1,070–78

13. Lukens, Jim. "Eleven Years With Wolves—What We've Learned." Idaho Fish and Game Salmon Region News Release, Salmon, ID (April 25, 2006).

14. "Study Shows Effect of Predators on Idaho Elk." *Idaho Fish & Game News* (August 2010).

15. Associated Press. "Study: Poachers Kill as Many Deer in Oregon as Hunters" (November 16, 2010).

16. Associated Press. "Poachers Kill More Game Animals Than Wolves, North Idaho Officials Say" (April 18, 2014).

17. Archibold, Randal C. "Poachers in West Hunt Big Antlers to Feed Big Egos." *The New York Times* (December 9, 2006).

18. MacNulty, Daniel R., Douglas W. Smith, L. David Mech, John A. Vucetich, and Craig Packer. "Nonlinear Effects of Group Size on the Success of Wolves Hunting Elk." *Behavioral Ecology* (September 29, 2011).

19. Yellowstone National Park. *Yellowstone Resources and Issues Handbook: 2014* (2014). Yellowstone National Park, Wyoming; p. 201.

20. Pielou, E. C. *After the Ice Age*. Chicago: The University of Chicago Press (1991); pp. 111–12.

21. Mech, L. David, and Rolf O. Peterson. "Wolf-Prey Relations." *Wolves: Behavior, Ecology, and Conservation*. L. David Mech and Luigi Boitani, eds. Chicago: The University of Chicago Press (2003). pp 131–37.

22. "Study Shows Effect of Predators on Idaho Elk." *Idaho Fish & Game News* (August 2010).

23. *Wolves at a Crossroads: 2011* (2011). Living with Wolves, Sun Valley, ID; p.6.

24. Finley, Darby, and Jamin Grigg, *Elk Management Plan for E-2 (Bear's Ears) Data Analysis Unit* (2008). Colorado Division of Wildlife, Meeker Service Center, Meeker, CO; pp. 18–19

25. Oregon Department of Fish and Wildlife. "Elk by Prescription: The 'Management Objective' Process." *Backgrounder* (April 18, 1995).

26. "Study Shows Effect of Predators on Idaho Elk." *Idaho Fish & Game News* (August 2010).

27. Torland, Ryan, Oregon Department of Fish and Wildlife. Personal communication.

28. Mule Deer Working Group. *Mule Deer: Changing Landscapes, Changing Perspectives.* Western Association of Fish and Wildlife Agencies (2003); p. 11.

29. Northern Region, USDA Forest Service. *When Mountains Roared: Stories of the 1910 Fires* (June 2010); pp. 48–49.

30. Pyne, Stephen J. *Year of the Fires.* New York: Penguin Books (2001) p. 102–104.

31. *Idaho Department of Fish and Wildlife Predation Management Plan for the Lolo and Selway Elk Zones,* revised (December 13, 2011).

32. *Idaho Department of Fish and Wildlife Predation Management Plan for the Lolo and Selway Elk Zones,* revised (December 13, 2011).

33. "Study Shows Effect of Predators on Idaho Elk." *Idaho Fish & Game News* (August 2010).

34. Russell, Betsy Z. "Full House for $2 Million Wolf Control Bill Hearing." *The Spokesman-Review,* "Eye on Boise" (February 17, 2014).

35. Associated Press. "Idaho Fish and Game Kills 23 Wolves in Lolo Pass Area." *Missoulian* (March 23, 2014).

36. Barker, Rocky. "Nez Perce Natural Resources Director Calls Lolo Wolf-Killing 'Arrogant.'" Idahostatesman.com (March 4, 2014).

37. Williams, Walt. "Wildlife Bills: How They Fared in the Legislature," *Bozeman Daily Chronicle* (April 30, 2003).

38. Ream, Bob, University of Montana. Personal communication.

39. Sakariassen, Alex. "What's Eating the Elk?" *Missoula Independent* (January 26, 2012).

40. Ream, Bob, University of Montana. Personal communication.

41. Bitterroot Elk Project Progress Reports, Fall 2011, Fall 2012, Spring 2012, Spring 2013, and Fall 2013. Montana Fish, Wildlife and Parks and University of Montana.

42. Backus, Perry. "Numbers Look Good for East Fork Bitterroot Elk Herd; Lions Biggest Threat." *Ravalli Republic* (August 12, 2012.)

43. Backus, Perry. "Survey Shows Elk Numbers Increase in Bitterroot Region." *Independent Record* (May 17, 2013).

44. Backus, Perry. "In Bitterroot Wolf Numbers Remain Steady." *The Montana Standard* (March 27, 2014).

45. Absaroka Elk Ecology Project. Kauffman Lab, Wyoming Cooperative Fish and Wildlife Research Unit; www.wyocoopunit.org.

46. Nolan, John. "Patrick Durkin: Research Shows Wolves Not Linked to Fawn Deaths In Northern Forest." Madison.com (June 13, 2014).

47. Yellowstone National Park. *Yellowstone Resources and Issues.* Mammoth, WY/Division of Interpretation (2010); p. 117.

48. Christofferson, April. "Bighorn Sheep Population Studied." *Yellowstone Discovery,* vol. 27, no. 1 (Spring 2012); p. 7.

49. "Researchers Begin First Moose Count on Northern Range." Yellowstone Association e-newsletter (April 2014).

50. Kramer, Becky, Associated Press. "Hunting for Elk Proves More Challenging." *Bend Bulletin* (December 25, 2013).

51. Moore, Greg. "Elk Plan Addresses Crop Damage." *Idaho Mountain Express* (January 29, 2014).

52. Wyoming Game and Fish Department. "Wyoming Hunters Enjoy Near Record Elk Harvest" (March 24, 2014).

CHAPTER 10: INTO THE PACIFIC NORTHWEST

1. Ely, Craig, Oregon Department of Fish and Wildlife. Personal communication.

2. Stephenson, John, US Fish and Wildlife Service. Personal communication.

3. Morgan, Russ, Oregon Department of Fish and Wildlife. Personal communication.

4. Henjum, Mark, USDA Forest Service. Personal communication.

5. Holyan, Jim, Nez Perce Wolf Recovery Program. Personal communication.

6. Oregon Department of Fish and Wildlife. "Gray Wolf Found Dead in Union County, Oregon" (July 12, 2007).

7. Oregon Department of Fish and Wildlife. "Wolf Pack with Pups Confirmed in Northeastern Oregon" (July 21, 2008).

8. Oregon Department of Fish and Wildlife. "Gray Wolf Found Dead in Union County, Oregon" (July 12, 2007).

9. Oregon Department of Fish and Wildlife. "Radio-collared Wolf Verified in Northeast Oregon" (January 24, 2008).

10. Oregon Department of Fish and Wildlife. "Imnaha Pack Timeline of Events, 2008–2014."

11. Oregon Department of Fish and Wildlife. "Oregon Wolf Population 2011–2013."

12. Wiles, Gary J., Harriet L. Allen, and Gerald E. Hayes. *Wolf Conservation and Management Plan, State of Washington* (December 2011); pp. 9, 16–25.

13. Wiles, Gary J., Harriet L. Allen, and Gerald E. Hayes. *Wolf Conservation and Management Plan, State of Washington* (December 2011); pp. 9, 16–25.

14. Oregon Department of Fish and Wildlife. *Oregon Wolf Management Plan* (December 2005 and 2010); pp. 6.

15. "Public Opinion on Hunting and Wildlife Management in Washington." Responsive Management, Harrisonburg, VA (2008) p. vi.

16. Rod Sando presentation, Wolf Workshop, Oregon Department of Fish and Wildlife, Portland, OR (April 11, 2002).

17. Mack Birkmaier presentation, Wolf Workshop, Oregon Department of Fish and Wildlife, Portland, OR (June 6, 2002).

18. Wiles, Gary J., Harriet L. Allen, and Gerald E. Hayes. *Wolf Conservation and Management Plan, State of Washington* (December 2011); pp. 9, 16–25.

19. Oregon Department of Fish and Wildlife. *Oregon Wolf Management Plan* (December 2005 and 2010); pp. 26-31.

20. Stone, Lynne, Boulder–White Clouds Council. Personal communication.

21. Strong, Zack. "Re: Proposed Amendments of A.R.M.12.9.1301-12.9.1305 Regarding Gray Wolf Management." Natural Resources Defense Council, Bozeman, MT (December 20, 2013).

22. Chaney, Rob. "Proposed Legislation Would Strip Feds of Wolf Authority In Montana." *The Montana Standard* (November 8, 2010).

23. House Bill 3562. Oregon State Legislature, 2011 Session.

24. Friedman, Mitch. "Finding the Middle Way." *Conservation Northwest* (June 28, 2013).

25. Coggins, Vic, Oregon Department of Fish and Wildlife. Personal communication.

26. Barnard, Jeff, Associated Press. "Caught Red-Handed: Wolves Kill Lambs Near Baker City" (April 16, 2009).

27. Barnard, Jeff, Associated Press. "Wolves That Attacked Livestock Ordered Killed" (September 2, 2009).

28. Oregon Department of Fish and Wildlife. "Two Problem Wolves Involved in Chronic Livestock Losses Killed" (September 5, 2009).

29. Young, Stanley Paul. *The Wolf in North American History*. Caldwell, ID: The Caxton Printers, Ltd. (1946); pp. 138–40.

30. Andrews, Michael S. "A Grand Animal's Return to the Prairie." *The Zumwalt*, Writings from the Prairie Fishtrap, Inc., Enterprise, OR (2008) pp. 22–23.

31. Oregon Department of Fish and Wildlife. *Living with Wildlife, Black Bears*.

32. Defenders of Wildlife. *Livestock and Wolves, A Guide to Nonlethal Tools and Methods to Reduce Conflicts* (2008); pp. 5–15

33. Kramer, Becky. "Ranchers Track Wolves Using Digital Means." *The Spokesman-Review* (November 10, 2013).

34. Stone, Suzanne. "The Idaho Wood River Project; Resolving Wolf and Livestock Conflicts with Nonlethal Methods Using a Community Stakeholder Model." International Wolf Symposium, Duluth, MN (October 11, 2013).

35. Morgan, Russ, Oregon Department of Fish and Wildlife. Personal communication.

36. Oregon Department of Fish and Wildlife. "Imnaha Pack Timeline of Events, 2008–2014."

37. Oregon Department of Fish and Wildlife. "Settlement of Oregon Court of Appeals Case" (May 28, 2013).

38. Oregon Department of Fish and Wildlife. "Areas of Depredating Wolves, Specific Wolf or Pack Information" (May 30, 2014).

39. Holyan, Jim, Nez Perce Wolf Recovery Program. Personal communication.

40. Kramer, Becky. "Ranchers Track Wolves Using Digital Means." *The Spokesman-Review* (November 10, 2013).

41. Washington Department of Fish and Wildlife. "WDFW Plans to Eliminate Wolf Pack to End Attacks on Livestock and 'Reset' State for Recovery in the Wedge" (September 21, 2012).

42. Washington Department of Fish and Wildlife. "WDFW Concludes Action to Remove Northeast Washington Wolf Pack" (September 27, 2012).

43. Associated Press. "Conservation Groups Ask Washington to Limit Killing of Wolves" (June 9, 2014).

44. Kramer, Becky. "Killing Washington Wolf Pack Cost $77,000." "The Today File," *The Seattle Times* (November 14, 2012).

45. Barnard, Jeff, Associated Press. "Wandering Wolf That Made Headlines Likely Photographed" (January 4, 2012).

46. "Wolf OR7 Enters California." *California Department of Fish and Wildlife News* (December 29, 2011).

47. Oregon Wild. "Advisory: Oregon Wild Announces Finalists in OR-7 Naming Contest" (December 21, 2011).

48. "Gray Wolf OR7"; www.californiagraywolf.wordpress.com.

49. Fimrite, Peter. "Gray Wolf Wins Endangered Status in California." *San Francisco Chronicle*; www.sfgate (June 4, 2014).

50. Cone, Tracy, Associated Press. "Notable Wolf's Presence Sparks Protection Effort" (February 28, 2012).

51. "Gray Wolf Status Evaluation Report." California Department of Fish and Wildlife memorandum (February 5, 2012).

52. Associated Press. "Border County Passes on Wolf Ban" (May 11, 2012).

53. Oregon Department of Fish and Wildlife. "Area of Known Wolf Activity—OR7" (February 4, 2014).

54. Cockle, Richard. "Male Wolf OR-9 from Imnaha Pack Killed by Idaho Hunter with Expired Tag." *Oregonian* (February 10, 2012).

55. Cockle, Richard. "Idaho Gov. Butch Otter Offers 150 Wolves to Oregon to Make Up for One Idaho Hunter Shot." *Oregonian* (February 13, 2012).

56. Morgan, Russ, Oregon Department of Fish and Wildlife. Personal communication.

57. "Reward Offered in Wolf Death." US Fish and Wildlife Service Pacific region news release (October 8, 2010).

58. Dennehy, Michelle, Oregon Department of Fish and Wildlife. Personal communication.

59. Connelly, Joel. "Wolf Poachers Get More Than Slap on Wrist." *Seattle PI* (July 11, 2012).

60. Le, Phuong, Associated Press. "Gray Wolf Killed during Big Game Hunt in Okanogan County" (September 30, 2013).

61. Associated Press. "California State Game Commission Won't Intervene in Controversial Coyote Hunting Contest" (February 6, 2013).

62. Kramer, Becky. "Ranchers Track Wolves Using Digital Means." *The Spokesman-Review* (November 10, 2013).

63. Gray Wolf Conservation and Management. *Wolf Packs in Washington, Annual Report—Pack Statistics* (December 31, 2013).

64. Oregon Department of Fish and Wildlife. "2014 Genetic results on OR7's mate and pups (September 5, 2014)

65. US Fish and Wildlife Service, Oregon Fish & Wildlife Office. "Pups for Wolf OR7" (June 4, 2014).

66. Dennehy, Michelle, Oregon Department of Fish and Wildlife. Personal communication.

CHAPTER 11: A-WOLF HUNTING WE WILL GO

1. US Fish and Wildlife Service, Idaho Department of Fish and Game, Montana Fish, Wildlife & Parks, Nez Perce Tribe, National Park Service, Blackfeet Nation, Confederated Salish and Kootenai Tribes, Wind River Tribes, Washington Department of Fish and Wildlife, Oregon Department of Fish and Wildlife, Utah Department of Natural Resources, and USDA Wildlife Services. *Northern Rocky Mountain Wolf Recovery Program 2011 Interagency Annual Report.* M. D. Jimenez and S.A. Becker, eds. (2012). USFWS, Ecological Services, 585 Shepard Way, Helena, MT 59601; pp 1, 2.

2. Montana Fish Wildlife and Parks. *2011 Montana Wolf Hunting Season Report.*

3. Montana Fish Wildlife and Parks. *2012 Montana Wolf Hunting Season Report.*

4. Bradley, L., J. Gude, N. Lance, K. Laudon, A. Messer, A. Nelson, G. Pauley, K. Podruzny, M. Ross, T. Smucker, and J. Steuber. Montana Gray Wolf Conservation and Management. *2013 Annual Report.* Montana Fish, Wildlife & Parks, Helena, MT (2014). pp 1, 54.

5. Idaho Fish and Game. *Status of Elk and Wolves* (July 2013).

6. Rachael, Jon. "Idaho Department of Fish and Game. Moving from Recovery to State Management of Wolves." International Wolf Symposium, Duluth, MN (October 12, 2013).

7. Rachael, Jon. "Idaho Department of Fish and Game. Moving from Recovery to State Management of Wolves." International Wolf Symposium, Duluth, MN (October 12, 2013).

8. Wyoming Game and Fish Department, US Fish and Wildlife Service, National Park Service, USDA-APHIS Wildlife Services, and Eastern Shoshone and Northern Arapahoe Tribal Fish and Game Department. *2012 Wyoming Gray Wolf Population Monitoring and Management Annual Report.* K. J. Mills and R. F. Trebelock, eds. (2013). Wyoming Game and Fish Department, 5400 Bishop Blvd., Cheyenne, WY 82006; p. 1.

9. Mills, Ken. "Wyoming Game and Fish Department. Moving from Recovery to State Management of Wolves." International Wolf Symposium, Duluth, MN (October 12, 2013).

10. Lance, Nathan. "Montana Fish, Wildlife and Parks. Moving from Recovery to State Management of Wolves." International Wolf Symposium, Duluth, MN (October 12, 2013).

11. Associated Press. "$2M Aimed to Kill More Than 500 Idaho Wolves." *EarthFix*, Oregon Public Broadcasting (January 28, 2014).

12. Moore, Greg. "Local Legislators Oppose Wolf-Control Bill." *Idaho Mountain Express* (February 10, 2014).

13. Geranios, Nicholas, Associated Press. "Governor Signs Wolf-Control Bill." *Seattle Post Intelligencer* (March 27, 2014).

14. www.defenders.org/the-war-on-wolves/idahos-war-wolves.

15. Berry, Harrison. "Wildlife Group Blasts Idaho's Wolf Policy in New Ad Campaign." *Boise Weekly* (June 2, 2014).

16. "Idaho Wolf Population Declining, but State Wants It Lower." KTVB, KTVB.com, Boise, ID (April 8, 2014).

17. Rappaport Clark, Jamie. "Wolves and Humans at the Crossroads: Wolf Management Practices, Loss of Habitat and Wolf Human Conflicts." International Wolf Center keynote speech (October 11, 2013).

18. Adams, L. G., R. O. Stephenson, B. W. Dale, R. T. Ahgook, and D. J. Demma. "Population Dynamics and Harvest Characteristics of Wolves in the Central Brooks Range, Alaska." *Wildlife Monographs* 170:1–25 (2008).

19. Idaho Department of Fish and Wildlife. *Predation Management Plan for the Lolo and Selway Elk Zones*, revised (December 13, 2011).

20. Gude, Justin A., M. S. Mitchell, R. E. Russell, C. A. Sime, E. A. Bangs, L. D. Mech, and R. Ream. "Wolf Population Dynamics in the U.S. Northern Rocky Mountains Are Affected by Recruitment and Human-Caused Mortality." *The Journal of Wildlife Management* 9999:1–11 (2011).

21. Associated Press. "Northern Rockies See Sharp Decline in Gray Wolves." OregonLive.com (April 12, 2013).

22. Phillips, Rachel. *The Hunt for the Gray Wolf: A Case Study in Recovering Top-Predator Management Policy in Washington State.* MAPS Capstone, University of Washington Bothell (June 2013); pp. 20–27.

23. Pacific Wolf Coalition. "Wolf News Update 7.3.14."

24. Borg, Bridget L., S. M. Brainerd, T. J. Meier, and L. R. Prugh. "Impacts of Breeder Loss on Social Structure, Reproduction and Population Growth in a Social Canid." *Journal of Animal Ecology* (2014).

25. Cause No. DV-2013-1, Findings of fact, Conclusions of Law and Order Issuing Preliminary Injunction, Montana Sixth Judicial District Court, Park County (January 18, 2013).

26. National Park Service. Information on the 2012–13 Wolf Hunt near Yellowstone National Park; www.nps.gov/yell/naturescience/wolf-hunt.htm.

27. Banks, Marnee. "MT Governor Signs Wolf Management Bill." www.ktvg.com (February 13, 2013).

28. National Park Service. "Legal Wolf Harvests near Yellowstone National Park (YNP) as of 3/1/2013."

29. Associated Press. "Collared Wolves from Yellowstone National Park Killed by Hunters, officials say." www.oregonlive.com (November 15, 2012).

30. Lynch, Kathie. "Yellowstone Wolf Update." www.thewildlifenews.com (July 14, 2014).

31. Associated Press. "Peter DeFazio Requests Curb on Gray Wolf Hunting around Yellowstone National Park." www.oregonlive.com (July 8, 2014).

32. Idaho Department of Fish and Game. *Predation Management Plan for the Middle Fork Elk Zone* (February 2014); pp. 1–2, 7.

33. Duval, John. "Will Helicopters Land in the Church Wilderness?" *Idaho Mountain Express* (December 18, 2009.)

34. Declaration of Roy Heberger, Case No. 09-cv-686-BLW (February 2, 2010).

35. "Idaho Fish and Game Only Manages to Collar 4 Wolves in Frank Church." www.thewildlifenews.com (March 15, 2010)

36. Frank Church-River of No Return Wilderness; www.wilderness.net.

37. Barker, Rocky. "Wolf-killing Plan Complicates Balancing Act." Idahostatesman.com (January 14, 2014).

38. Zuckerman, Laura, Reuters. "Judge Refuses to Halt Wolf Trapping in Idaho Wilderness" (January 17, 2014).

39. Idaho Department of Fish and Game. *Predation Management Plan for the Middle Fork Elk Zone* (February 2014); p. 10.

40. Preso, Tim J., Earthjustice. Personal communication.

41. Cole, Ken. "Idaho Suspends Wilderness Wolf-Killing Plan in Face of Court Challenge." *The Wildlife News* (July 29, 2014).

42. Declaration of Jeff Gould, Appeal No. 14-35043, D.CT No. 4:14-cv-00007-EJL, District of Idaho, Pocatello (July 24, 2014).

43. Third Declaration of Keith Lannom, Case No. 4:14-CV-0007-EJL (July 24, 2014).

44. Kruesi, Kimberlee. Untamed Idaho Blog: Wildlife Activists Oppose Wolf Killing Competition. *Magic Valley Times-News* (December 16, 2013).

45. "Salmon Residents Receive Death Threats over Wolf-Hunting Contest." Local News 8, Idaho Falls, ID (December 22, 2013).

46. Associated Press. "Wolf Hunting Derby Allowed by Idaho Judge." *The Oregonian* (December 27, 2013).

47. Associated Press. "Hunting Derby Kills 21 Coyotes, No Wolves." *The Oregonian* (December 30, 2013).

48. Pynn, Larry. "Contest Offers Cash Prizes for Wolf Kills in Northeastern B.C." *Vancouver Sun* (November 19, 2012).

49. Montgomery, Marc. "Alberta Conservation Groups Concerned over Private Wolf Bounties." Radio Canada (March 28, 2013).

50. Carbyn, Lu, Canadian Representative, IUCN Wolf Specialist Group. Personal communication.

51. Niemeyer, Carter. Wolf Lecture, Eugene, OR (July 10, 2012).

52. Stalling, Dave. "A Once-Proud Conservation Group Has Lost Its Way." *High Country News* (August 31, 2012).

53. Darling, Dylan J. "Predator, Protector: As Costs Mount, Some Researchers Point Out Benefits." *The Bulletin* (January 7, 2012).

54. Landers, Rich. "Elk Group Gives Idaho $50,000 for Wolf Management." *The Spokesman-Review* (September 3, 2013).

55. Rocky Mountain Elk Foundation. "RMEF Donates for Wolf Management in Montana" (April 17, 2012).

56. Associated Press. "Rocky Mountain Elk Foundation Donates $25,000 to FWP for Wolf Management." *Great Falls Tribune* (May 30, 2014).

57. Landers, Rich. "Elk Group Gives Idaho $50,000 for Wolf Management." *The Spokesman-Review* (September 3, 2013).

58. Chaney, Rob. "Rocky Mountain Elk Foundation Offers to Finance More Aggressive Wolf Killing." *Missoulian* (March 20, 2012).

59. Black, Jerry. "Wolves: RMEF Buying Wildlife Management." Letter to the Editor, *Missoulian* (April 25, 2012).

60. Murie, Adolph. *The Wolves of Mount McKinley*. Fauna of the National Parks of the United States, Fauna Series No. 5, US Fish and Wildlife Service (1944).

61. Letter to David Allen, Rocky Mountain Elk Foundation from Donald Murie (July 11, 2012).

62. "Creator of the Olaus J. Murie Award Bemoans the Degeneration of the Rocky Mountain Elk Foundation." Statement of David Stalling. *The Wildlife News* (July 25, 2012).

63. Vucetich, John A., J. Bruskotter, M. Nelson, R. Peterson, M. Gore, and J. Bump. "The Principles of Wildlife Management and Wolf Harvesting in Michigan," draft document (July 18, 2013).

64. Vucetich, John A. "Wolf Hunting in Michigan and the North American Model." 2013 International Wolf Symposium, Duluth, MN (October 12, 2013).

65. Nelson, Michael P., J. Vucetich, P. Paquet, and J. Bump. "An Inadequate Construct?" *The Wildlife Professional* (Summer 2011); pp. 58–60.

CHAPTER 12: WHAT GOOD ARE WOLVES?

1. National Park Service Yellowstone. *Wolf Project Annual Report 2010*, YCR-2011-06; p. 7.

2. Eisenberg, Cristina. *The Wolf's Tooth*. Washington, DC: Island Press (2010); pp. 30–32, 58–63.

3. Best, Michael. "Salamanders Found to Impact Forest Carbon Cycle." *EcoNews*, vol. 42, no. 5 (October/November 2012). The Northwest Environmental Center.

4. Ripple, William. Yellowstone National Park Aspen-Wolf Research Lecture, Bend, OR (June 21, 2011).

5. Ripple, W. J., and R. L. Beschta. "Trophic Cascades in Yellowstone: The First 15 Years after Wolf Reintroduction." *Biological Conservation* (2011); doi:10.1016/j.biocon.2011.11.005.

6. Eisenberg, Cristina. *The Wolf's Tooth*. Washington, DC: Island Press (2010); pp. 94-101.

7. Ripple, W. J., and R. L. Beschta. "Trophic Cascades in Yellowstone: The First 15 Years after Wolf Reintroduction." *Biological Conservation* (2011); doi:10.1016/j.biocon.2011.11.005.

8. TEEBcase by J. Duffield. "Local Value of Wolves beyond a Protected Area USA" (2010). Available at: TEEBweb.org.

9. Duffield, John W., C. J. Neher, and D. A. Patterson. "Wolf Recovery in Yellowstone, Park Visitor Attitudes, Expenditures and Economic Impacts." *Yellowstone Science*, vol. 16, no. 1 (2008).

10. Stark, Mike. "UM Economist: Wolves a Big Moneymaker." *Billings Gazette* (April 7, 2006).

11. Templeton, Amelia. "Researchers Say Wolves Help Plants by Eating Deer, Elk." *EarthFix*, Oregon Public Broadcasting (April 11, 2012).

12. Wilkinson, Todd. "Do Wolves, Cougars Help Curb Diseases?" *Jackson Hole News and Guide* (April 2, 2014).

13. Krumm, C. E., M. M. Conner, N. Thompson Hobbs, D. O. Hunter, and M. W. Miller. "Mountain Lions Prey Selectively on Prion-Infected Mule Deer." *Biology Letters*, doi: 10.1098/rsbl.2009.0742 (published online October 28, 2009).

14. Oregon State University. "Animal Trapping Record Reveals Strong Wolf Effect across North America." *News & Research Communications* (June 16, 2014).

15. "Are Wolves the Pronghorn's Best Friend?" *Science Daily* (March 4, 2008).

16. Ripple, William. Yellowstone National Park Aspen-Wolf Research Lecture, Bend, OR (June 21, 2011).

17. Stahler, D., B. Heinrich, and D. Smith. "Common Ravens, *Corvus corax*, Preferentially Associate with Grey Wolves, *Canis lupus*, as a Foraging Strategy in Winter." *Animal Behaviour* (2002); pp. 64, 283–290.

18. Oregon State University. "Wolves May Aid Recovery of Canada Lynx, A Threatened Species." *News & Research Communications* (August 30, 2011).

19. Zuckerman, Laura, Reuters. "Wolves Help Preserve Berries for Imperiled Yellowstone Bears." www.nbcnews.com (July 29, 2013).

20. Yellowstone National Park. *Yellowstone Resources and Issues Handbook: 2014.* Yellowstone National Park, WY.

21. Yellowstone National Park. *Yellowstone Resources and Issues Handbook: 2014.* Yellowstone National Park, WY.

22. Wright, G. J., R. O. Peterson, D. W. Smith, and T. O. Lemke. "Selection of Northern Yellowstone Elk by Gray Wolves and Hunters." *The Journal of Wildlife Management*, vol. 70, no. 4 (August 2006); pp. 1,070–78.

23. Vucetich, J. A., D. W. Smith, and D. R. Stahler. *Influence of Harvest, Climate and Wolf Predation on Yellowstone Elk, 1961–2004.* Oikos 111: 259–270 (2005).

24. Yellowstone National Park. *Yellowstone Resources and Issues Handbook: 2014.* Yellowstone National Park, WY.

25. US Department of the Interior, US Fish and Wildlife Service, and US Department of Commerce, US Census Bureau. *2011 National Survey of Fishing, Hunting and Wildlife-Associated Recreation*; p. 105.

26. Kramer, Becky, Associated Press. "Hunting for Elk Proves More Challenging." *Bend Bulletin* (December 25, 2013).

27. "Car and Deer Collisions Cause 200 Deaths, Cost $4 Billion a Year." *Insurance Journal* (October 24, 2012).

28. US Department of Transportation, Federal Highway Administration. *Wildlife-Vehicle Collision Reduction Study.* Report to Congress (August 2008).

29. State Farm Mutual Automobile Insurance Company. "Likelihood of Collision with Deer" (2011).

30. Center for Biological Diversity; www.biologicaldiversity.org/pro grams/public_lands/grazing/index.html.

31. "United States Livestock Subsidies." Environmental Working Group Farm Subsidy Database; farm.ewg.org.

32. TEEBcase by J. Duffield. "Local Value of Wolves beyond a Protected Area USA" (2010). Available at: TEEBweb.org.

CHAPTER 13: HERE TO STAY

1. "New Poll Finds Strong Support for Wolf Protection in Western States." *Tulchin Research* (September 12, 2013).

2. Switalski, T. A., T. Simmons, S. L. Duncan, A. S. Chavez, and R. H. Schmidt. "Current Public Attitudes toward Wolves in Utah." *Natural Resources and Environmental Issues*, vol. 10, issue 1, article 4 (January 2002).

3. US Fish and Wildlife Service, Idaho Department of Fish and Game, Montana Fish, Wildlife & Parks, Wyoming Game and Fish Department, Nez Perce Tribe, National Park Service, Blackfeet Nation, Confederated Salish and Kootenai Tribes, Wind River Tribes, Confederated Colville Tribes, Spokane Tribe of Indians, Washington Department of Fish and Wildlife, Oregon Department of Fish and Wildlife, Utah Department of Natural Resources, and USDA Wildlife Services. *Northern Rocky Mountain Wolf Recovery Program 2013 Interagency Annual Report*. M. D. Jimenez and S. A. Becker, eds. (2014). USFWS, Ecological Services, 585 Shepard Way, Helena, MT 59601; p. 1.

4. US Fish and Wildlife Service. *Mexican Wolf Recovery Program: Progress Report #16* (Reporting Period: January 1–December 31, 2013); p. 22.

5. US Fish and Wildlife Service. *Gray Wolf Population in Minnesota, Wisconsin, and Michigan (excluding Isle Royale) 1976 to 2013*.

6. Meador, Ron. "Howling Pups Show Isle Royale Wolves Are Reproducing, but Not out of Danger." www.minnpost (August 16, 2013).

7. US Fish and Wildlife Service. Red Wolf Recovery Program.

8. Hance, Jeremy. "Grey Wolf Appears in Iowa for First Time in 89 Years—And Is Shot Dead." Guardian Environmental Network, *The Guardian* (May 12, 2014).

9. Tsai, Catherine, Associated Press. "Wildlife Investigators: Poison Killed Colo. Wolf." *The Denver Post* (January 1, 2011).

10. Associated Press. "Air Search Turns up Tracks, but No Wolves in Utah." *Las Vegas Sun* (March 11, 2012).

11. Utah Division of Wildlife Resources. *Wolves in Utah*.

12. Bruggers, James. "Yes, It Was a Wolf in Kentucky." Watchdog Earth, *The Courier-Journal* (August 15, 2013).

13. Hance, Jeremy. "Grey Wolf Appears in Iowa for First Time in 89 Years—And Is Shot Dead." Guardian Environmental Network, *The Guardian* (May 12, 2014).

14. US Fish and Wildlife Service. "Service Proposes to Return Management and Protection of Gray Wolves to State Wildlife Professional Following Successful Recovery Efforts" (June 7, 2013).

15. Bruskotter, J. T., J. A. Vucetich, S. Enzler, A. Treves, and M. P. Nelson. "Removing Protections for Wolves and the Future of the US Endangered Species Act" (1973).

16. Weiss, Amaroq, Center for Biological Diversity. "West Coast Wolves: Can Things be Different Here?" International Wolf Symposium, Duluth, MN (October 13, 2013).

17. Public Employees for Environmental Responsibility. "Politics Dominated Wolf De-Listing Meetings" (June 27, 2013).

18. Public Employees for Environmental Responsibility. "Gray Wolf Peer Review Panel Purged By Agency" (August 8, 2013).

19. Letter to Sally Jewell, secretary of the interior, from sixteen scientists regarding gray wolf delisting (May 21, 2013).

20. Letter to Sally Jewell, secretary of the interior, from the American Society of Mammalogists regarding gray wolf delisting (May 22, 2013).

21. "Review of Proposed Rule Regarding Status of the Wolf under the Endangered Species Act." National Center for Ecological Analysis and Synthesis, Santa Barbara, CA (January 2014).

22. "Nearly 500,000 More Americans Speak Out Against Federal Plan to Strip Wolves of Protections." *Oregon Wild* (March 31, 2014).

23. Fessenden, Helen. "Gray Wolf: Endangered-List Decision Looms as Lawmakers Debate." *The Oregonian* (May 12, 2014).

24. Wuerthner, George. "Do Ranchers Have a Right to Predator-Free Landscape?" *New West* (November 22, 2010).

25. NOWA Field Notes, Northwest Outdoor Writers Association. *NOWA News* (February 2014); p. 11.

26. Bureau of Land Management fact sheet. "Special Recreation Permit for Predator Hunting Derbies." BLM Salmon Field Office, Salmon, ID.

27. *Kleppe v. New Mexico*, 426 US 529, 535 1976.

28. Negri, S., and H. Quigley. *Cougar Conservation: The Growing Role of Citizens and Government, Cougar Ecology & Conservation*. Maurice Hornocker and Sharon Negri, eds. Chicago: The University of Chicago Press (2009); pp. 223–24.

29. Mattson, David J., and S. G. Clark. *People, Politics, and Cougar Management, Cougar Ecology & Conservation*. Maurice Hornocker and Sharon Negri, eds. Chicago: The University of Chicago Press (2009) p. 214.

30. W.J. Ripple, et al. "Status and Ecological Effects of the World's Largest Carnivores." *Science* 343, 1241484 (2014); DOI: 10.1126/science .1241484.

Index